THE LUCAN
CONSPIRACY

THE LUCAN CONSPIRACY

HOW THE ESTABLISHMENT CONNED THE WORLD
INTO BELIEVING LORD LUCAN WAS BARRY HALPIN

DUNCAN MACLAUGHLIN
WITH WILLIAM HALL

JOHN BLAKE

Published by John Blake Publishing Ltd,
3, Bramber Court, 2 Bramber Road,
London W14 9PB, England

www.blake.co.uk

First published in paperback in 2004

ISBN 1 84454 065 0

British Library Cataloguing-in-Publication Data:

A catalogue record for this book is available from the British Library.

Design by www.envydesign.co.uk

Printed in Great Britain by Bookmarque Ltd, Croydon, Surrey

1 3 5 7 9 10 8 6 4 2

Papers used by John Blake Publishing are natural, recyclable products made
from wood grown in sustainable forests. The manufacturing processes conform
to the environmental regulations of the country of origin.

Pictures reproduced by kind permission of UPP, Rex Features,
Mark Winch, Jean Pestell and William Hall

Dedicated to the memory
of Sandra Rivett

Contents

Acknowledgements ix
Introduction xi
Foreword xiii

PART ONE
Chapter 1 – THE KILLING 3
Chapter 2 – HUE AND CRY 13
Chapter 3 – FAMILY TREE 21
Chapter 4 – GAMBLING MAN 29
Chapter 5 – VANISHED 39
Chapter 6 – DRAGNET! 49
Chapter 7 – DOWNHILL SLIDE 55
Chapter 8 – THE DARK CONTINENT 67
Chapter 9 – INQUEST 77

PART TWO

Chapter 10 – THE HUNTER 89

Chapter 11 – FIRST HINT 99

Chapter 12 – PICTURE POWER 105

Chapter 13 – MARK'S STORY 109

Chapter 14 – ON THE RUN 119

Chapter 15 – ENTER 'JUNGLE BARRY' 125

Chapter 16 – TRUE OR FALSE? 135

Chapter 17 – IF THE FACE FITS… 145

Chapter 18 – PASSAGE TO INDIA 153

Chapter 19 – ON THE SCENT 165

Chapter 20 – CONNIE 181

Chapter 21 – 'OH, CECILIA..' 191

Chapter 22 – BOB'S INN 201

Chapter 23 – THE PLOT THICKENS 213

Chapter 24 – CRIME BUSTER 225

Chapter 25 – ASHES TO ASHES 235

Chapter 26 – GOODBYE, OLD COCK! 245

Chapter 27 – WATERFALL 255

Conclusion 263

Aftermath 285

ACKNOWLEDGEMENTS

I would like to thank the following for their invaluable assistance in making this book possible: Professor Sue Black, OBE, BSc, PhD, DSc; Mrs Emin Po, Administrator, Panjim General Hospital; Mr Vinayak Pai Bir, Circulation Manager, the *Herald* newspaper, Panjim; Superintendent Octaviano B. Dias, Panjim Municipal Council; Mr Raju Ashwekar; Inspector Gundu Naik and Deputy Inspector Rajesh Kumar, Calangute Police Area Division; Detective Chief Inspector Karnah Singh, Panjim Police Headquarters; Hilda McGauley, Public Records, Ireland; Will Hall; Rebekah Wade; Chester Stern; Jeff Walden, BBC Written Archive Centre, Caversham; and to Don Cleary, Statesman Travel.

I particularly wish to express my appreciation to William Hall, who accompanied me to Goa and has been instrumental in writing this book with me, and to Dr Mike Maloney, Hon. FRPS, the award-winning photographer who provided visual proof of the witnesses I interviewed there during the investigation.

Finally, I would like to thank Mark Winch, my partner in crime in one of the most challenging investigations of my career.

Duncan MacLaughlin
Shepperton, Surrey
October, 2004

INTRODUCTION

They called it the manhunt of the century. Following a sensational murder in the heart of Belgravia that shocked high society and gripped the world, a new name was written into criminal folklore.

Lord Lucan.

Where is he? And what happened to him?

On that 'night of madness' in November 1974 when his children's nanny Sandra Rivett was bludgeoned to death in the basement kitchen of his family's home, and his wife was attacked, the aristocrat they called 'Lucky' Lucan at Mayfair's gaming tables disappeared off the face of the earth. Wanted for murder, he went on the run – and was never seen again.

In the 30 years since he vanished, numerous books and TV documentaries have theorised on his possible fate. But all they have done is churn over facts that are common knowledge, and conclude with a stab in the dark as to what really happened to the runaway earl in the hours, days and weeks after that infamous and terrible night.

The one thing that the books, TV and newspaper articles have in common is their need to rely on dated photographs of the distinguished-looking aristocrat – photographs taken in the sixties and early seventies.

Until now…

Now at last former detective Duncan MacLaughlin, dubbed Scotland Yard's top undercover cop, has reached an astounding conclusion, with amazing photographs to confirm his coup.

He has unearthed the audacious charade which enabled the earl to elude the long arm of the law and escape justice, aided and abetted by his powerful friends back home, the 'club within a club' that lived by its own rules and, as one put it, 'to hell with the law'.

The masquerade might never have been discovered except, by a freak chance, Lucan was photographed by a small-time dope dealer named Mark Winch, himself a wanted man.

Suddenly everything makes sense, as MacLaughlin resolves all the unanswered questions. *The Lucan Conspiracy* reveals where Lucan fled, the astounding disguise he adopted to fool the world… and his ultimate fate.

Just as identical twins can fool even those closest to them, so Lucan and his lookalike, a globetrotting hobo named Barry Halpin, created a smokescreen that fooled the world.

As Sherlock Holmes famously remarked to Dr Watson: 'How many times, my dear Watson, have I told you that when you have eliminated the impossible, whatever remains – however improbable – must be the truth?'

I'll go along with that.

William Hall
Highgate Village, London
October 2004

FOREWORD

The first piece of the jigsaw fell into place in the summer of 2002. I had been publicising volume one of my autobiography, *The Filth*, on local radio stations around the country. The title comes from the street vernacular for the CID, known to cops and villains alike, and worn by the plainclothes guys like a badge of honour. Someone had heard me on BBC Radio Derby and wanted to get in touch.

He had called the publishers, and the publishers called me. 'He says it's important.'

For some reason, call it a moment of weakness, I said: 'OK, you can give him my mobile number.' This can be a big mistake, especially if you've spent the best part of your life mingling with the criminal fraternity and making a lot of enemies along the way. But too late for recriminations. Maybe he wouldn't ring anyway.

But he did. I was relaxing by the fireside in my cottage at Shepperton in Surrey, idly thumbing through the TV listings for the night, when the phone rang. A voice on the other end said: 'The name's Mark Winch. Do you remember me?'

I didn't, but politeness doesn't cost anything. 'The name rings a bell,' I said, adding cautiously: 'A faint one.'

The voice said: 'Ten years ago I was living in Slough and I was tipped off by the local Old Bill that Scotland Yard's finest were after me. I heard your name mentioned. You were with the Drugs Squad at the time. I was dealing dope, knocking out keys of cannabis to Oxford undergrads. The tip-off said you were going to come calling, so I did a runner. I went abroad.'

The bell sounded louder. There had indeed been a dealer based in the Thames Valley around the winter of 1991, a very busy boy whose remit extended all the way to the hallowed portals of Oxford University. We had a name, and an address.

As part of the drugs wing of the Regional Crime Squad, I was putting a team together to pay this young man an early-morning call. The wing was descended from the Central Drugs Squad, set up to counter the sharp increase in drug-related crimes. Broadly speaking, a call meant kicking his door in at 5am, wishing him a happy Christmas and turning his place over. We call it 'spinning the drum'.

Winch ... yes, that was him. But before we could reach him he had simply vanished into thin air. The word came back that our target had heard a whisper – and been gone in 60 seconds, or something close to it.

'What can I do for you?' I kept my voice level, but not unfriendly.

Mark answered with a question of his own: 'Are you still after me?'

'No, I'm not. I'm no longer a police officer, and there's no warrant out for your arrest. You'd gone. What's the problem?'

'Listen. I've got some photographs I took ten years ago. They've been in the back of a drawer the whole time. I forgot all about them until I saw a TV documentary recently, and realised it's *him*. I've been scared to do anything about them, because I thought if I put my head above the parapet I'd get lifted.'

'What photos? Who are you talking about?'

'Don't laugh,' said Mark. 'I think they're Lord Lucan.'

Lord Lucan!

Christ! I thought. Another nutter! And I put the phone down. A few minutes later it rang again, and Mark said more urgently: 'I'm not wasting your time. If you're not going to nick me, can I at least show them to you?'

'No,' I said shortly, and put the phone down again abruptly. Why had I agreed to let them give this oddball my number?

In under a minute it rang again. Give him his due: Mark was nothing if not persistent.

This time I listened to him. It was a good story. He had fled to Goa, in India. Ended up in a hippie commune. Met a strange Englishman there, a tall, bearded man living like a hermit, but with a cultured accent, who played backgammon with him every day for beer money. A first tremor stirred inside me, that frisson of excitement every cop knows when his instincts are trying to tell him something.

Maybe, just maybe, there was something in it after all.

'All right,' I said. 'I'll meet you.'

'My place,' he said. 'I'm not risking these photos out of the house.'

It was the first hint I had of the paranoia which understandably would grip anyone suddenly finding he has stumbled on the solution to one of the great mysteries of the last century.

Mark's home was a modest terraced cottage in a village not far from Chesterfield in Derbyshire. Now a 'reformed character', as they say on parole boards, he had set up home with a girl named Sarah, who was the mother of his two small boys.

Chesterfield is 150 miles from London. As I turned into the slip road leading off Junction 29 of the M1, I wondered if it was a waste of both a day and a lot of petrol.

Mark opened the door, a tall young man in T-shirt and jeans, and extended a hand in one of those no-hard-feelings handshakes. In the living room he laid out a bunch of colour photographs like a hand of cards in a poker game.

I looked down at a man in a rocking chair – and went cold!

The similarities leaped out of the photographs. The broad, aristocratic forehead. The thick hair sweeping up from its natural parting on the left. The distinctive dark eyebrows, and the crease that stood out between them. Then the hands: they weren't the hands of a labourer, more those of an artist. I could see a scar on the knuckle of his right hand.

Above all, in the other photographs, the unmistakable 'Lucan look' – arrogant, almost baleful, the eyes staring into the distance with an aloof, remote gaze.

Christ, that's him! I thought.

Game on.

They say that truth is stranger than fiction.

Read on, and believe it.

PART ONE

CHAPTER 1

THE KILLING

The date is Thursday 7 November 1974. The time: 8.45pm. The place: 46 Lower Belgrave Street, London SW1. Outside, a fitful drizzle of rain sweeps across the terraced Regency houses, shrouding the streets, blurring the elegant buildings of Belgravia, where traditionally the wealthiest, most powerful and aristocratic names in British society make their London home. The night air is laced with tendrils of autumn fog, and passers-by scurry on with heads down against the stinging droplets.

In the darkened basement kitchen a figure waits, with a nine-inch length of lead pipe bound in surgical tape poised in one black-gloved hand. The 100-watt bulb he has removed from the ceiling socket lies on the stairs beside him, so that only a faint glow filters in through the venetian blind from a street lamp outside.

The door at the top of the stairs leading up to the main hall opens. A young, slender woman in a flowered dress carrying a tray of crockery flicks the switch, and pauses when the light fails to come on. Then she continues uncertainly down the eight stairs towards the kitchen.

The lurking figure pounces. Against the pale wash from the street lamp his arm rises and falls again and again, savagely beating the young woman into unconsciousness and then death, her head lolling among broken cups and saucers.

Six vicious blows from the lead pipe to her skull and three to her face leave indentations the pathologist would later confirm came from a blunt instrument, and send blood coursing down her body. More heavy bruising to her shoulders and right arm attest to the frenzied ferocity of the attack. The skull is not fractured, but her brain is severely bruised by the blows.

The murderer works quickly. Grabbing a heavy mail bag from the floor, he picks up the slender girl and stuffs the blood-soaked body inside the bag, doubled up but with one pale arm dangling outside.

Poor Sandra Rivett, aged 29 and nanny to the three children of the Earl and Countess of Lucan since August, died within two minutes from brain damage after choking on blood that had seeped into her throat and clogged her windpipe. Put simply, she was an innocent who found herself in the wrong place at the wrong time in what would later prove to be a tragic case of mistaken identity.

The nanny usually had her night off on a Thursday, but this week she had changed it to Wednesday so that she could meet a friend. Sandra Rivett should not have been in the house that evening. She was exactly the same height – five feet two inches – as her mistress. They weighed the same: less than eight stone.

It was the Countess of Lucan that the earl meant to kill.

Much has been written about the murder that shocked Belgravia's high society to its blue-blooded roots and evolved into the manhunt of the century in the search for Richard John Bingham, 7th Earl of Lucan. It would become a case dominated by doubt, rumour, red herrings and false trails. Seven books would be published, along with enough newsprint to denude a small forest. None came up with a satisfactory solution.

So we have to start with the facts.

The Plumbers Arms is a quiet public house 100 metres from the Lucans' home on the same side of Lower Belgrave Street, in the direction of Victoria Station which lies at the far end. Striped awnings draped over the two windows outside partially keep the rain away. At 9.50pm on that murky November night there were only ten customers in the warmth of the saloon, clustered at the long bar. A murmur of voices talked over the gossip of the day, news that was dominated by the Watergate scandal in the USA, where the White House tapes were about to be aired.

All conversation stopped abruptly as the door crashed open and a woman staggered in out of the night. She was barefoot and slightly built, with fair hair matted with blood and a brown jumper and green pinafore dress soaked scarlet. Her face was contorted, panic-stricken.

'*Help me! Help me!*' she cried. '*He's murdered my nanny... he's in the house... He tried to strangle me... I've just escaped from a murderer!*'

In the stunned silence the head barman, Derrick Whitehouse, reacted quickly. He grabbed the woman before she collapsed, helped her to one of the red plush banquettes by the wall and laid her gently on her back. Then he tried to staunch the ugly wounds that were pulsing blood from her scalp and forehead. Other customers ran up with bar towels, while someone dialled 999.

The woman was almost delirious, and gasping for breath.

Derrick, striving to stem the blood, could dimly make out her words. *'My children... I think my neck has been broken... I'm dying...'*

Then he recognised her. It was Veronica Bingham, the 37-year-old Countess of Lucan, estranged wife of the aristocratic gambler known to his friends as 'Lucky' – and the man who would shortly become the quarry in the most sensational manhunt since Dr Crippen was apprehended at sea in 1910.

That same night four people sat down to dinner in the elegant restaurant of the Clermont Club, an exclusive gambling casino in Berkeley Square in the heart of Mayfair, the gilt and marble décor reflecting the class, wealth and privilege of its membership. Below was the basement discotheque Annabel's, haunt of the celebrity A-list crowd, visiting movie stars and social high flyers, and a prime target for paparazzi photographers and gossip writers. The quartet were old friends, for whom gambling was a mutual pastime or talking point: Clermont regular Greville Howard, socialite Sarah Smith-Ryland, merchant banker James Tuke and his wife Caroline.

Their host had booked the table, but his seat remained empty. Eventually, with midnight approaching, they got on with their meal, raising a glass of champagne to an absent friend and agreeing how unusual it was for Lord Lucan not to at least phone in with an explanation.

The 999 call from the Plumbers Arms had been logged at 9.57pm. A telex from New Scotland Yard reached Gerald Road police station, half a mile from the pub, stating simply: 'Person assaulted. Ambulance called. Distressed female.' An ambulance was dispatched from the London Ambulance Service headquarters in Waterloo Road.

At that point nobody had the slightest inkling that this was the curtain-raiser to a mystery that could have come straight from the pages of an Agatha Christie crime thriller – only with enough complexities to baffle even Hercule Poirot or Miss Marple.

Two uniformed police officers arrived in a Panda car at the same time as the ambulance. Sergeant Donald Baker and PC Christopher Baddick checked briefly on Lady Lucan's condition, then left her in the capable hands of two paramedics, who dressed her wounds before taking her into Casualty at St George's Hospital at Hyde Park Corner, two minutes away.

Outside the pub the officers spotted flecks of blood that formed a trail on the pavement leading to the Lucans' house, and were visible despite the rain. They followed it to number 46, and stared up at the building, evaluating the scene. The front door, beneath its ornate semicircular fanlight, was closed.

Behind the spiked railings the house was apparently in darkness, and there was no movement that they could detect. But then, upstairs on the fifth floor, they noticed a lighted window.

Like so many other houses in Belgravia, number 46 was redolent of the grandeur of past decades. Many of the neighbouring properties were now converted into spacious flats, the outside walls painted white in contrast to the shining black wrought-iron railings that surrounded their first-floor balconies. Even if the atmosphere was one of faded elegance, Lower Belgrave Street was still one of the most sought-after addresses in London.

But at this particular house there were dark patches of blood on the steps. Losing no time, Sergeant Baker forced the door to gain entry, and shone his torch into the shadowy hallway. What the officers saw inside would lead to the place being dubbed the 'House of Horror' by the tabloid newspapers.

The entrance hall was more spacious than one would have suspected from outside. To the left, behind open double doors, was a dining room. The sergeant glimpsed a staircase ahead, and a cloakroom at the end of the landing. Oil paintings of uniformed soldiers who would later be revealed as Lucan ancestors stared haughtily down from the shadows – framed by smears of blood on the wallpaper close by.

But what focused the officer's attention and caused him to draw a sharp intake of breath was the thick pool of blood that his torch picked out at the foot of the main staircase.

Close by, a door under the stairs led to the basement. Working his way cautiously down the eight steps, Baker saw that they led to a kitchen at the front of the house, and then on to a breakfast room with french windows that gave access to the rear garden.

There was something else. His torch had flashed over more dark pools on the floor here and caught a large canvas kitbag, standing upright with the top folded over, with the words 'US Mail' stencilled on it. The cords around the rim were loose. He swung the torch back – to see a woman's arm dangling out of the sack.

Detective Chief Inspector David Gerring, one of the first CID detectives to reach the murder house, described the grisly scene in detail. 'The mail bag was surrounded by a large pool of blood that had soaked through the sack and spread along the parquet floor. Somebody had walked in the dark puddle and left a trail of footprints. A pair of black high-heeled shoes lay beside the bag. There was something eerie about the blood-stained sack with the white arm sticking grotesquely out of it…'

Upstairs on the top floor, where the light was on, the officers found the three young Lucan children in their bedrooms: Frances, ten, George, seven, and Camilla, four. They were unharmed and blissfully unaware that a terrifying tragedy had been played out below them. On the same floor was the bedroom of their nanny, Sandra Rivett, within earshot in case one of them cried out during the night.

But what had happened down below in the previous hour was worse than a bad dream. It was the stuff of nightmare.

Details of the assault on Lady Lucan would emerge later as she described in harrowing detail how she had herself been attacked when she went in search of the nanny. Sandra had gone down to the basement to wash up the cups and saucers after the family had taken tea upstairs. According to Veronica, she reached the door on the ground floor that led to the basement stairs, which were in darkness.

Without warning a figure came at her out of the cloakroom behind her and smashed her over the head with a blunt weapon. Once ... twice ... in all, seven times the attacker struck as they struggled by the stairs. When she screamed in terror, gloved fingers were shoved into her mouth, and a voice she recognised as her husband's snarled: '*Shut up!*'

His hands went for her throat, and she sank her teeth into his finger. As he tried to strangle her, she managed to grab and twist his testicles – which temporarily 'calmed him enough' to persuade him to sit down with her on the stairs. After that, they went up to the bedroom and eventually Lucan made his way into the bathroom to soak towels for her wounds.

When she heard the tap running, Veronica ran for her life – down the stairs and out of the front door, turning blindly into the rain and fleeing barefoot along the slippery pavement until she reached the sanctuary of the Plumbers Arms.

Now the investigation went into overdrive.

They had a body in a bag, a titled woman accusing her husband of attempting to kill her – but no sign of the aristocrat himself, who might be a murder suspect or, if the assailant had been an outside intruder, might not. Yet the hunt for Lord Lucan did not begin immediately.

The reason is that the earl made two telephone calls that same night to his mother, the 75-year-old Dowager Lady

Kaitilin Lucan, known to her friends as 'Kait'. The calls came through to her home in St John's Wood, close to Lord's cricket ground. A police constable had already been dispatched to be with her, just in case Lucan appeared.

Instead he phoned. Lady Kaitilin had taken the first call at 10.45pm, and listened in horror as her son told her in a choked voice: 'There has been a terrible catastrophe at number 46. Veronica is hurt. I want you to collect the children as quickly as possible.' He asked her to ring his old friend Bill Shand Kydd, who was also his brother-in-law through marriage to Veronica's sister Christina, and tell him what had happened.

More significantly, Lucan gave his mother another version of the night's drama. He had been driving past the house, he said, when he saw a fight going on in the basement between Veronica and a man. He had rushed in to help, and driven the man off. His wife had been screaming and was covered in blood. Quite how he could have seen anything in the basement from a car in the road on that murky night, with the room in darkness, was unclear.

Lady Kaitilin assured her son she would go straight to the house and collect the children, then asked him: 'Where are you going?'

Lucan replied: 'I don't know,' and rang off.

He called again at 12.30am, by which time his mother had collected the children and tucked them up in bed in her own flat. This time a police constable was standing beside her when she answered the phone. In the brief conversation that followed she assured their father that the children were safely asleep, and asked him if he wanted to speak to the officer. Lucan declined. 'No, not now. I'll ring them in the morning.' The line went dead.

Both calls had been made from private phones. There was no indication of a pay phone or a long-distance line. At that point, although Lucan was the person they were seeking for 'help in their enquiries', the Murder Squad detectives on the case felt the earl would be true to his word and appear in person the next morning at a local police station with a solicitor in tow. There was never any question of tracing the calls.

For some reason it never occurred to any of them that the noble lord might not fulfil his obligations. After all, a gentleman's word is his bond, isn't it?

A Murder Squad team had been set up in a room at Gerald Road, which happened to be one of the more attractive police stations in London, with colourful hanging baskets and geranium-filled window boxes to keep up with the appearance of the area. Inside the detectives took bets on the time his lordship would walk through the door. With the usual dark humour of cops who have seen it all, the odds were on 'midday' since the titled gentry like to sleep in late. In fact, Lucan was a known insomniac who would stay up into the early hours until he felt ready for sleep, and seldom got up before noon.

Meanwhile, they left the body in the bag for the rest of the night, until forensic experts could be called to examine the crime scene by daylight. Why a US Mail bag? It was the kind frequently used by sailors to stow their nautical gear, so one cannot help but surmise that Lucan, a man with a passion for power boats, planned to use it to stow something else – the body of his wife.

This, for me, researching the case in meticulous detail, is when the time bomb starts to tick.

Up to now it had been a fairly routine murder enquiry. If it had not been for the individuals involved it would be just another sad, rather squalid crime of passion, the kind I would investigate myself a decade later many times over as a CID detective. From this moment the players raised the game to celebrity status, with the added dividend of intrigue in high places.

And now, unbeknown to any of the parties involved, Lord Lucan was on the run … and he wasn't coming back.

CHAPTER 2

Hue and Cry

The first hint the waiting detectives had that their prime suspect was not a man of his word was perceived the next day, as the investigation started to come to the boil. The press had got hold of the story, and were camped out on the pavement around 46 Lower Belgrave Street. The first headline appeared in Friday's *Evening Standard*, and it was front-page news: 'BELGRAVIA MURDER AT EARL'S HOME', and below it: 'Body in Sack'. That must have sold a few papers. The famous photograph of Lucan that we all came to know was alongside, the one that always reminded me of a Hollywood star of the fifties with its raffish good looks, dark hair and full Edwardian moustache.

The *Standard* story stated that police were anxious to interview the 39-year-old earl in case he could provide information about a nanny found battered to death at his Belgravia home. Ever cautious, a Scotland Yard spokesman issued a statement to the hungry newshounds: 'We are trying to trace Lord Lucan to tell him of the incident.' Message received and understood. The public would already be making up its own mind.

With the knowledge of hindsight, I often wonder just where Lucan was when the scandal was breaking like a tidal wave across the canapés and cocktail parties of elegant London society. Did he first hear it on the radio? Or perhaps catch a reflection of his picture flashed up on the lunchtime TV news bulletins in a shop window? In those tense hours it would only have added impetus to the concern that was dominating his thoughts. Saving his own skin.

For the hunters, facts were emerging that were starting to rock the boat. What had looked like a straightforward investigation, however sensational, was proving to be anything but cut and dried. The plot thickened by the hour, and – like clotted cream left in the sun – was starting to turn sour.

With Detective Chief Superintendent Roy Ranson and Detective Chief Inspector David Gerring in charge, the team played it by the book. The Murder Squad office at Gerald Road was converted into a control centre, with special phone lines installed, blackboards with coloured chalks propped against the walls and a board with Lucan's photographs pinned to it so that his face would constantly be staring out as a reminder. While the detectives at base camp tapped their fingers waiting for Lucan to make his appearance, others were busy doing what always has to be done in a major crime situation.

The divisional police surgeon, Dr Michael Smith, had been called in straight away. He arrived before midnight, certified the victim dead and was careful not to disturb the corpse. The next morning photographs were taken of the sack, after which the body was taken to Westminster mortuary, still in the mail bag, for Home Office pathologist Professor Keith Simpson to carry out the *post mortem*. He confirmed death had come from severe injuries from a blunt instrument – once described as 'the classic offensive weapon of the enthusiastic amateur'. There were no signs of a sexual attack. Sandra's estranged husband, Roger Rivett, had the unhappy task of identifying her.

Sandra had not been your archetypal Mary Poppins, the prim matron who used to push prams around in crisp uniforms and smart hats for wealthy employers. A vivacious redhead, Sandra came to the Lucans on 26 August via an agency. She was a former hairdresser with working-class roots and no nursing qualifications. But she was a willing worker, got on well with the children, and had become a trusted companion to Veronica.

They say that nothing is quite as it seems, and it was never more true than in this case. At 2am on the night of the murder, Ranson and Gerring were at Lady Lucan's bedside in her private room at St George's Hospital, having a discreet but essential chat with her to try to get to the vital facts. According to Gerring, 'a great wedge of her scalp was missing … she looked small and frail, like an injured bird'.

Veronica Lucan was drowsy from the sedation she had been given to alleviate the pain, but she managed some answers as the two detectives gently probed for the truth. She confirmed that her husband had admitted he had killed Sandra, but her main concern was for the children. Ranson assured her they were safe with their grandmother, the dowager countess. They left her to sleep.

Gerring himself would have no rest for 40 hours. As the night wore on, and then the next day, rumours started filtering back to the Murder Squad. The earl and his wife were living separate lives after a bitter court case filled with vicious antagonism. He had walked out nearly two years ago, in January 1973.

Their children had been made wards of court, with Veronica awarded custody. But she had been seeing psychiatrists, who had diagnosed her as a manic depressive and prescribed drugs for depression and anxiety after she refused treatment in a psychiatric clinic.

Lucan, who was known to have a short fuse, was said to be beside himself with rage over the court order. There was also talk of gambling debts running into thousands – the earl was an avid backgammon player, with a passion that bordered on addiction.

The water was getting murkier by the minute.

The investigation team ascertained that Lord Lucan had moved out of the family home into a £300-a-month flat at 72a Elizabeth Street, five minutes' walk away. That same night Gerring went straight from the hospital to pay a 3am visit to the flat on the off chance that its occupant might return.

Two constables had already been stationed there. The inspector found it was a large basement flat, sparsely furnished and with no pictures on the walls. Only a few books – an odd collection of Hitler's speeches, a pile of detective novels and a study of mental illness. More important in the short term were piles of unpaid bills on the sideboard – and, tucked away in a drawer, Lucan's passport.

A watch was ordered on all airports and harbours, while Interpol in Paris was asked to place the name of Richard John Bingham, Earl of Lucan, on its Red Alert list. Priority, wanted for questioning. To be arrested on sight.

As the investigation progressed, a statement taken after the murder from the Lucans' ten-year-old daughter, Lady Frances, brought a vivid insight into the events of that night. It shows how remarkably cool and collected this young girl was after an experience that would have been traumatic to most children – and adults.

Her statement was taken by a woman police officer, Detective Constable Sally Bower. Some of it gives a chilling dimension to the drama that had been enacted in Lower Belgrave Street that night:

'On Thursday evening we all had our tea together, Mummy, George, Camilla and Sandra and I. At about 7.30pm I watched *Top of the Pops* on television in the nursery. I had a bath before I started watching, and was wearing my pyjamas after my bath.

'I went downstairs to Mummy's room, and at about 8.40pm I asked her where Sandra was, and she said she was downstairs making some tea. After a while Mummy said she wondered why Sandra was so long. I don't know what time this was, but it was before the news came on the television at 9pm. I said I would go downstairs to see what was keeping Sandra but Mummy said no, she would go. I said I would go with her, but she said no, it was OK, she would go.

'Mummy left the room and I stayed watching the television. She left the bedroom door open, but there was no light in the hall because the light bulb is worn out and it doesn't work.

'Just after Mummy left the room I heard a scream. It sounded as though it came from a long way away. I thought maybe the cat had scratched Mummy and she had screamed. I wasn't frightened by the scream, and I just stayed in the room watching television. I went to the door of the room and called out "Mummy!" But there was no answer, so I just left it.

'At about 9.05pm, when the news was on television, Daddy and Mummy both walked into the room. Mummy had blood all over her face, and she was crying. Mummy told me to go upstairs. Daddy didn't say anything to me, and I didn't say anything to either of them. I don't know how much blood was on Mummy's face, as I only caught a glimpse of her.

'Daddy was wearing a pair of dark trousers and a fawn-coloured overcoat. I was sitting on the bed as they came in the door, and I couldn't see them very well. There were two lights on above Mummy's bed, and one other side light on. I couldn't see if Daddy's clothes had any blood on them. I wondered what had happened, but I didn't ask.

'I went upstairs to my bedroom, got into bed and read my book. After a little while I heard Daddy calling out for Mummy. He was calling out: "Veronica, where are you?" I got up and went to the banisters, and looked down and I saw Daddy coming out of the nursery on the floor below me. He then went into the bathroom on the same floor. He came straight out and then he went downstairs.

'That was the last I saw of him. He never came up to the top floor of the house that night, either to look for Mummy or to say goodnight to me.'

What interested me as I dusted off the files and searched for clues that might have been overlooked was not just Lucan's apparently blatant guilt, but how he had made his getaway in the greatest escape act since Houdini. This meant probing into his background, to try to get under the skin and into the head of the fugitive. The police had Lucan's passport. They also had his car, a two-year-old blue Mercedes, which had been spotted near his flat and removed for examination. The forensic boffins would go over it with a fine-tooth comb. The keys had been found in his bedroom, so no escape route there, and no intention to use the car.

So, how had our Houdini vanished so effectively?

The first part of the answer came from a retired company director named Michael Stoop, an old Clermont Club gambling chum of Lucan who shared his friend's passion for backgammon. When he heard the news on the radio he contacted the Yard, and told them he had lent the missing earl his old Ford Corsair car two months previously.

In the bar at the Portland Club, another gambling haunt, Lucan had asked him if he could borrow it 'as the Merc's battery is flat'. Stoop offered his own Mercedes, but his friend said he preferred 'the old banger'. Within minutes of Stoop's call, a description went out across the country and to Interpol: dark-blue Ford Corsair, licence number KYN 135D.

The hue and cry was on with a vengeance.

CHAPTER 3

FAMILY TREE

Who exactly are we talking about? Who is this man, this scion of a noble dynasty, who with one insane act stepped from the pages of Debrett and Burke's Peerage into the murky archives of crime? This professional 'aristo-gambler' who would become a household name for millions for all the wrong reasons, and keep the world guessing for 30 years?

Lord Lucan came from military stock. Ramrod straight, he belonged to another, more romantic age and would have been in his element as a Regency buck. Standing an impressive six feet two inches tall, he was every inch the English aristocrat, preferring the gaming tables, fast cars and power boats to a life of hard work, and exhibiting a remarkably offhand attitude to women.

As someone remarked about the young Lord Bingham: 'His love of sport and gambling to the exclusion of all else, his lack of aptitude for any career and his reactionary political views made him dangerously near a caricature.' Reactionary views?

Unlike his father, who was a prominent socialist, Lucan was a confirmed right-winger, deeply worried about the 'decline of Britain' and fearful of communism, though he never did get around to making his maiden speech in the House of Lords in the ten years after he inherited the title in 1964.

He did manage a modest 17 appearances there, but stayed silent, indicating to his friends that if he ever rose to his feet amid the ermine and the oratory he would warn his fellow lordships, and the entire country, about 'the perils of immigration'. Indeed, at one time, following his marriage, Lucan would insist that his wife listen to recordings of the Nazi Nuremberg rallies. Intriguingly, the German element would figure strongly in the years after his disappearance.

Caricature or not, Lord Lucan's credentials were on the one hand impeccable, and yet, on the other, tarnished beyond belief. By credentials, we are talking about tradition, honour and the family bloodline. But if you had a relative who had ordered the fatal Charge of the Light Brigade at Balaclava, would you sleep easy at nights?

This is grossly unfair, of course, to the modern progeny. But the sins of the fathers do tend to get visited on their sons, and when one digs closely into the Lucan dynasty more intriguing factors are thrown up. The family tree has its rotten branches, dating back to the Crimea and beyond. The Lucan crest shows two chained wolves on their hind legs guarding a shield and a coronet, with the motto *Spes Mea Christus* – 'In Christ lies my hope'. Whoever chose the emblem acted with uncanny foresight: the wolves are snarling, jaws open, tongues hanging out, unconsciously reflecting the vicious temper of some of the distinguished holders of the title.

The young Richard John Bingham knew nothing of this until he grew old enough to delve into his personal family history. Born on 18 December 1934, son of the 6th Earl of

Lucan, the boy was evacuated from London to America at the age of six, when the clouds of war darkened the skies over Britain. Along with his younger brother Hugh and their two sisters, Frances and Sarah, his parents sent him to stay with a wealthy property tycoon with homes in both New York State and Florida, where they sat out the war in enviable luxury in the grounds of magnificent country mansions.

After the war the youngsters came home. Lord Bingham – or 'Johnny', as his friends called him – went to preparatory school in Oxford, then took the gilt-edged route to Eton, where he was house captain in his final year. The first signs of Johnny's gambling addiction were there to see when he risked expulsion by indulging in nightly sessions of poker with his upper-class chums, as well as 'skiving off' on illicit trips to Ascot to lay bets on the horses for fellow students.

In 1953 the dreaded brown envelope containing his call-up papers for National Service dropped through the letterbox of the family home in Eaton Square, Belgravia. But the adventure-loving teenager had an edge on his fellow conscripts, the squaddies who were reluctantly being drafted into two years of boredom in some Middle Eastern desert or far-flung tropical jungle.

Johnny headed for the élite Coldstream Guards, courtesy of his father, George Charles Patrick Bingham, who had commanded the regiment's 1st Battalion in World War II and won the Military Cross for distinguished services to King and Country.

The future Lord Lucan saw out his two years in Germany, stationed at Krefeld as a second lieutenant. With the Swiss Alps nearby, the athletic young soldier was able to make sorties to the slopes to try his hand and hold his nerve at bobsleighing. But it was back in the officers' mess that Johnny felt most at home, sharpening his gambling skills every night at the poker table – for money, not matchsticks. His addiction to the green baize cloth was confirmed, and he would be acknowledged as the best poker player in the regiment as well as a leading light in the bridge evenings.

One lasting friend he made during those two years was Bill Shand Kydd, also from upper-class stock and the heir to a wallpaper fortune, who would remain a pivotal figure in the life of Lucan and his children and later play an integral part in the murder inquiry.

National Service over, Lucan found a post with the merchant bank Brandt's in the City, at a salary of £500 a year. That was the day job. After dark he would earn more than his annual wage packet on the throw of a dice playing backgammon at the gaming tables of Mayfair clubs, or dealing from a deck of cards at *chemin de fer* and poker.

On the personal side, Johnny's life was a bachelor's dream. Adoring debutantes jostled for his arm at parties, and his social diary was as full as the amount of ink he wanted to expend on it. He was as handsome as a matinee idol, boasted a title and exuded the style to go with it. He drove a soft-top Aston Martin. But friends would recall how this natural born charmer was a 'man's man', an unashamed male chauvinist intent on living the high life and more interested in sporting adventures of the outdoor kind than bedding every doe-eyed deb who fluttered her lashes at him.

Johnny went water-skiing, played golf (handicap: a respectable 14) and took the wheel of a powerful speedboat called *White Migrant*, which he would race in the Solent, and which once sank ignominiously in an offshore race at Cowes. He battled his way into the British bobsleigh team and was the driver of a four-man bob at St Moritz when it came ninth at an international meeting in 1957. His friend Bill Shand Kydd was brakeman.

Lucan's daredevil approach meant risking life and limb against the forces of nature on the open sea and the bobsleigh course – or pitting his finances against Lady Luck in the casinos. His ancestors would have been proud of him.

The Lucan family has connections with Ireland dating back to the sixteenth century, when three enterprising Bingham brothers bought land in County Mayo on the west coast, invested their money in large estates and became leading pillars of the community. But they ruled their fiefdom by fear, not good stewardship, establishing a reputation of the 'take no prisoners' kind.

One of this doughty trio, Sir Richard Bingham, governor of the province of Connaught, ordered the massacre of the crews of two galleons from the Spanish Armada that had been driven ashore by a gale in 1588. Today you can find the graves of the victims at Spanish Point on the Loop Head peninsula. It was in 1776 that the Lucan name first came into play, when George II conferred the title Baron Lucan of Castlebar on Charles Bingham. In 1795 Charles became the Earl of Lucan by royal favour.

But the darkest shadow over the Lucan family tree is that of George Charles, the 3rd Earl and Johnny's great-great-grandfather, who was held responsible for one of the most appalling blunders in military history: the ill-fated yet ultimately heroic Charge of the Light Brigade at Balaclava in 1854. As commander of the Cavalry Division, the earl gave the order to charge head-on into the Russian guns, apparently fully aware of the consequences. His command 'Forward, the Light Brigade!' would echo down through history, and become a byword for battlefield valour and high-level bloody-mindedness.

In possible mitigation, the written orders that came down from the Commander-in-Chief, Lord Raglan, were badly scrawled and confusing about which valley the 3rd Earl should use for the attack, and this has always added to the controversy that rages to this day. But still Lucan went ahead.

What intrigued me when I first heard of this skeleton rattling noisily in the Lucan family cupboard was to learn that the 3rd Earl, variously described as 'humourless', 'pedantic' and 'eccentric', also had a violent temper. Could those same genes have lingered down the generations until another reckless act of violence was perpetrated 120 years later? I tucked the thought away for later evaluation.

Furthermore, before that day of disaster in the hills of the Crimea, this arrogant individual was already one of the most hated men in his native Ireland. During the Irish famine he had earned himself the nickname of 'the Exterminator' for the way he treated his tenant farmers as he ruthlessly evicted them from their homes on his land, leaving them to starve to death in ditches. In Victorian England that arrogance and aggression carried the stamp of authority. Today his personality might be defined as close to that of a paranoid psychotic.

But the 3rd Earl would live on to become the oldest soldier in the British Army, finally passing on to that great parade ground in the sky in 1888 at the age of 93. He had become a respected member of the House of Lords. At the funeral his body was carried on a gun carriage with full military escort.

Scrutinising the Lucan lineage, it is uncanny how the same facial characteristics can be detected through the generations: flat, rather heavy features, thick dark eyebrows, hair always parted on the left and the inevitable moustache. Take note of the man in the rocking chair…

An eighteenth-century print of the 1st Earl of Lucan shows a typical nobleman of the period, portly and complacent. The 3rd Earl, George Charles, possessed a huge beard, as did the 4th Earl, who at the age of 60 also had a fine head of hair – parted on the left.

Lucan's father, George Charles Patrick Bingham, had been born in 1898 and was an Eton and Sandhurst man.

Commissioned into the Coldstream Guards in World War I, he was awarded the Military Cross in 1917 for his bravery in the field of battle. In World War II he commanded the 1st Battalion of the Coldstream Guards from 1940 to 1942 before being appointed to the important role of Deputy Director of Ground Defence at the Air Ministry.

After the war politics became the focal point of 'Pat' Bingham's life. He established himself as a committed socialist, as did his wife Kaitilin, a keen party worker. When he succeeded to the title as 6th Earl in 1949 and entered the House of Lords, he took the Labour Whip and later held the position of Chief Opposition Whip until his death in 1964, when his son became the 7th Earl of Lucan, with the baronies of Melcombe Bingham in Dorset and Castlebar in Ireland as a bonus.

So much for history, and the physical clues that emerged from dusty files and old prints. Now to the present. It was time to check out the gambling man.

CHAPTER 4

GAMBLING MAN

I f it's in the bloodstream, what can you do? Lord Lucan had been bitten by the gambling bug from an early age. By the time he was 20 he was already a class act, displaying the style and demeanour ingrained into him by the playing fields of Eton and two years with the Coldstream Guards. Finally the lure of the gaming tables took over his life.

For 'Johnny', now read 'Lucky'. Lucan earned the nickname that would stick with him as a high roller on one spectacular session of *chemin de fer* at the White Elephant in Mayfair in 1960. It lasted over two nights and ended with him walking away with a cheque for £26,000 burning a hole in his wallet. That was the moment he gave up his post at Brandt's after six years, telling a friend: 'Why toil in the City when I can make ten times my salary in one week?'

Lucky Lucan had found his mission in life. He was now a professional gambler.

His parents didn't like it, and his friends urged caution. But the reckless streak in him brooked no denial, and as the sixties dawned with all the heady excitement of 'the greatest decade of the century', Lucan set about becoming a leading figure in the action. Where it counted: at the tables.

The Betting and Gaming Bill went through in July 1960, replacing the 1854 Gaming Act to legalise betting shops, bingo halls – and casinos. In 1962 John Aspinall opened the Clermont Club at 44 Berkeley Square, a beautiful building which would become a second home to Lucan. It was a retreat from the outside world, symbolised by the fact that it had no clock on any wall or mantelpiece, and therefore time had no meaning. Inside this hushed and elegant citadel, its newest conscript could devote all his skills and instincts to the drama of the gaming tables.

As Aspinall would reveal later: 'Lucky began as a wild and reckless gambler. But he was advised that if he wanted to go on with it he would have to learn to survive. He became a shrewd player, intending to stay around as long as possible.'

John Aspinall himself, then aged 33, was a one-off, a flamboyant extrovert whose attitude appealed to the rebel in Lucan and made them natural social bedfellows. 'Aspers' played by his own rules. He had been born in Delhi to a well-off family who sent him to England to be educated at the prestigious Rugby School. As an undergraduate at Oxford, his own version of the early inclinations for gambling he shared with Lucan surfaced when he bet an entire term's allowance on the nose of a horse at Ascot – and won.

Aspinall would become world famous for his unorthodox style of wildlife conservation, with his private zoos where he could 'bond' with elephants, tigers, lions and gorillas. In the mid-fifties he had found a chink in the law that enabled him to run 'floating' *chemin de fer* sessions, after discovering that the 1854 Gaming Act actually allowed private gambling provided it did not occur more than twice at the same venue. It was the cue for rich landowners who enjoyed a flutter to throw open the doors of their country estates to other like-minded – and loaded – individuals for all-night gambling sessions fortified by champagne, cigars and a five-star buffet.

The clique that welcomed Lucky Lucan into its midst with open arms consisted of a heady mixture of the titled, the ultra-rich, big business and celebrities. These were the élite of the social scene, their faces regularly appearing in glossy magazines and gossip columns. Most of them enjoyed the oxygen of publicity, even if they would never admit it.

Names like Dominic Elwes – known as the 'court jester' of this jovial crowd – Mark Birley, owner of Annabel's (named after his wife), stockbroker Stephen Raphael, banker Greville Howard, Ian Maxwell-Scott, old Etonian Daniel Meinertzhagen, racing tipster George Benson, the Duke of Devonshire, the Earl of Derby and international power broker James 'Jimmy' Goldsmith all rubbed shoulders with Lucan over the cards or the canapés.

Some of them would become known as the 'escape committee'. In fact on the Friday following the murder John Aspinall hurriedly arranged a luncheon meeting at his Lyall Street home, with friends rounded up to answer the call. A handful who gathered – Shand Kydd, Elwes, Benson, Raphael and Meinertzhagen – were dubbed 'the Five Just Men' after a famous Edgar Wallace thriller, but apparently there were others present, though Goldsmith was away in Dublin on business. Elwes revealed later: 'We discussed ways and means of helping Lucky and his family if it became necessary.' Much later, those words would take on a special significance.

In fact, Lucky was one of the select guests invited to join Goldsmith's famous house party to celebrate the tycoon's fortieth birthday – in Acapulco. The billionaire businessman, 'rich beyond the dreams of avarice', was once memorably reported as declaiming 'luxury is the most addictive substance in the world'. The chairman of Cavenham Foods and co-founder of Mothercare had put his money where his mouth was, as the owner of an incredible 18,000-acre estate carved out of the jungle near the Mexican coast, with more than 300 staff to look after the house, grounds and the privileged guests invited to savour them. Henry Kissinger and Richard Nixon were among the great and the sometimes less than good who had partaken of his largesse.

This palatial corner of paradise was called Cuixmala, more informally known as 'Xanadu' to Jimmy's rich and famous chums, who now included Lord Lucan. The pair had much in common: Goldsmith, 18 months Lucky's senior, was also educated at Eton and likewise spent more of his spare time gambling than studying. One bet he put on became a talking point around the college for months afterwards: a £10 wager on a horse that won Jimmy £8,000 – when he was only 16. His father took him away soon afterwards to a 'cramming' school to get his wayward son through his examinations and later into the army.

So Lucky and Jimmy had a lot to talk about. Now the earl was part of the inner circle, and relishing every minute of it. Eventually that circle would form part of an exclusive clique known in the drawing rooms of Belgravia and the gaming rooms of Mayfair as the 'Lucan Set'.

Backgammon and *chemin de fer*, or 'chemmy', were Lucan's favourite kind of gaming. For the uninitiated, chemmy is a form of baccarat, basically a game like pontoon with the court cards counting as zero and aces counting as one. One player, who deals from the 'shoe', is put up by the casino. The other players bet against him. The winner is the player holding two or three cards totalling closest to nine. You could find the dealer facing anything up to half a dozen punters, or maybe just a single gambler sitting opposite, depending on the time of day or night. Sometimes a casino can be virtually empty. Other times it can be buzzing like a beehive on fire.

Those who have never been saluted through the portals of a truly exclusive casino by a top-hatted doorman, whether it be in Mayfair or Monte Carlo, can have no idea of the cathedral-like atmosphere of the high-stakes areas as the worshippers gather in obeisance to the god Mammon.

Forget the holiday gaming spots, where you can lay 50p on a spinning roulette wheel – though even in coach-party Las Vegas, today's minimum on the Strip is an exorbitant $10 a throw. For genuine high rollers, the *salons privés* behind the traditional tasselled gold rope are havens of calm broken only by the whisper of the cards and the murmur of the croupiers as their clients play for stakes that can cost them a king's ransom – or their life savings.

What would you call a high roller? Photographer Mike Maloney, who would be with me throughout the final stages of the investigation, was once the personal photographer of the notorious tycoon Robert Maxwell. In his own book *Flash! Splash! Crash!* Mike details an extraordinary night out with 'the Boss' at Maxim's in Kensington, where he was deputed to take along a suitcase stuffed with bundles of £50 notes, amounting in all to £750,000. Maxwell played roulette, betting on his 'lucky number 17'. It never came up. In 90 minutes he lost the lot.

Unfazed, Maxwell walked away – and as they left, a croupier confided to Mike that the previous month 'the Boss' had won £1.5 million in one night, playing the same system. Easy come, easy go.

Now that's what you call a high roller.

Alas for the gossip columns and for gambling folklore, Lord Lucan and Robert Maxwell never met over the tables, though I suspect they might have been made for each other. But roulette wasn't Lucky's game.

Eventually Lucan would become a 'house player' of *chemin de fer* at the Clermont, which meant facing the dealer and encouraging other punters to join him. His personal favourite game of backgammon turned him into the class of expert who, if it had been Wimbledon, would have been one of the seeded players. At one point he was rated among the top ten backgammon players in the world.

But, with the adroitness of the experienced gambler, Lucan kept his true face hidden, along with the violent streak that even those who had borne witness to his famous flashes of temper could never have suspected. Like every gambler worth his salt, he had taught himself to remain impassive and show no emotion however the dice fell or whatever cards he was dealt.

The complex sides of his character ranged from the reckless and feckless to total affection for his children – 'he was completely dotty about them,' confided one friend. Irrational outbursts were the only clue to the dark side of the moon hidden behind the veneer of old-world charm symbolised by the neatly trimmed hair, the ready smile and the blue pinstripe suits – he had 12 hanging in his wardrobe, all of them exactly the same.

Looking in the mirror and seeing a rakish devil staring back at him must have persuaded Lucan to put himself up for a screen test for the part of James Bond after Sean Connery temporarily handed in his 007 licence to kill in 1971 after *Diamonds Are Forever*. Certainly Lucky would have been a natural for the gambling sequences that are an integral part of every Bond film, added to which he had the looks and bearing to hold down the role. But producer Cubby Broccoli saw the results, decided the blue-blooded wannabe was 'too wooden', and the test came to nothing.

Lucan was clearly not one to give up easily, for several years earlier he had flown to Paris at the invitation of Vittorio De Sica to test for a part in the film *Woman Times*

Seven, a satirical comedy with a sprinkling of household names that included Peter Sellers, Michael Caine and Robert Morley. The eminent Italian director had spotted the earl at the casino in Deauville, and thought him 'just the man for the job'. Lucan jumped at the offer, and indeed the part could have been written for him: a British diplomat at the UN who vies with an Italian delegate (played by Vittorio Gassman) for the favours of the star, Shirley MacLaine.

Lucan's role was somewhat unusual for a peer. It called for him to sit side by side on a bed with his fellow suitor while MacLaine knelt at their feet practising yoga and lecturing them on choosing a woman for her brains rather than her beauty. Eventually the two rivals came to blows. As written, the scene was enlivened by the fact that Ms MacLaine was supposed to be nude.

It would have been a small but noticeable cameo. Alas, the would-be thespian 'froze' in front of the cameras, perhaps not surprisingly in the circumstances even though another actress stood in for Ms MacLaine for the test. Lucky offered his apologies, and caught the next plane home to excel at what he knew best, and tell his friends at the Clermont: 'Actually, I rated my chances at 50/1!'

Back on the gambling scene, Lucan found himself facing another problem. The truth is that inside that close-knit circle gambling and women were as discordant as a rusty hubcap on a Rolls-Royce. After his marriage to Veronica Duncan in 1963, Lucan had made initial efforts to educate her into the complexities of the gaming world, instructing his new bride in the subtleties of backgammon, *chemin de fer* and blackjack.

She was at first genuinely intrigued by the charismatic aristocrat she had married, an impressive figure resplendent at the tables in a white dinner jacket with a blood-red carnation in its buttonhole. She caught the fascination of the green baize and the turn of a card that could make or break a player.

Lucan's mistake in those days was introducing her to the Clermont Club.

Members of the top Mayfair gambling clubs tend to regard their hallowed precincts as a male preserve, a refuge from the female gender. Women were barred, for instance, from Lucan's other clubs, White's and St James's. At least on this score Aspinall was more relaxed, though the boundaries were still there, albeit invisible and unspoken.

At the Clermont there was a booth known as the 'widows' bench', where wives or girlfriends prepared to risk hours of boredom could see the night out in the tense hush of the gaming rooms and the smoke-filled silence beneath the ornate chandeliers.

Away from the action there was a large-screen television set in the lounge, where Veronica would sit for hours either watching the TV or eyeing her husband from the sidelines, with an occasional sip from a glass of wine to sustain her. The only break in this mind-numbing routine was when she shared a brief dinner of smoked salmon and lamb cutlets with Lucan, always timed for 9pm, after which he returned to the tables. Invariably the wine would be a white Sancerre. Lucky had a penchant for fish, and to finish his meal he would choose a ripe Camembert, accompanied by a glass of Croft '60 vintage port or a mirabelle, a plum-flavoured French liqueur.

Aspinall remarked later: 'Veronica would sit down on the banquette night after night and hardly speak to anyone. She had a rotten life in that sense. But then she had no business to be there.' Sure enough, as their relationship foundered, Lucan came to see his wife as his bad luck, his albatross.

The tension behind the scenes became evident one dramatic night in 1972 when a sudden argument broke out in the lounge between Lady Lucan and another 'widow'. It seems the other woman was talking too loudly while Veronica was trying to watch TV. A noisy row developed and a glass of wine was thrown. Lucan was horrified and deeply embarrassed.

The incident violated all the social niceties that were expected to be observed and had happened in the worst possible place – shaming him in front of his friends. It was one of the first nails in the coffin of their doomed marriage.

CHAPTER 5

VANISHED

By noon on the day after the attack on his wife and nanny, Lord Lucan had still not surfaced. All bets were off at Gerald Road that Friday morning as the police finally came to terms with the fact that their prime suspect was not going to appear after a good night's sleep to help with their enquiries. Instead Ranson and Gerring realised they had the makings of a first-class scandal on their hands, one that would shake the complacent society of Belgravia and the closed world of the Mayfair gambling salons to their very foundations.

And so it proved.

Newspaper headlines screamed murder. The name of Lord Lucan was plastered over the front pages, and the face that would become familiar to millions stared out with its steady, implacable gaze, yet without any expression that you could readily penetrate. The face of a gambler, certainly. But of a murderer? That had yet to be proved, even if Fleet Street had rushed to its own judgement.

Lucan's face also appeared in regular news bulletins on TV, so the detectives were confident that only a hermit or a monk would be unlikely to recognise the fugitive if they bumped into him somewhere in the country.

In the first three days following the killing, nothing of significance was turned up. The problem for Ranson and his Murder Squad was that this time the underworld was no help. There were no informers to 'grass', no criminals to lean on, no favours to be called in. On the contrary: the team scouring every lead found themselves up frustrating blind alleys. It seemed that the earl's chums had circled the wagons and closed ranks to protect their embattled comrade from the tiresome questions that were being asked.

The officers at Gerald Road complained, with some justification, of the patronising attitudes of the upper-crust 'snobs' they were forced to question, a group who became known as the 'Lucan Lobby' of influential people united in a belief that their man was innocent. An early example was the attitude of Lady Kaitilin after that second call from her Johnny. She had put the phone down and said calmly to the waiting policeman beside her: 'That was my son. He won't speak to you now. He'll phone you in the morning.' It wasn't meant with any malice, but the tone of the words, and the dowager countess's belief that she had the clear right to utter them, speaks volumes.

More significantly, as Aspinall himself put it: 'If a close friend of yours came in covered in blood, having done some frightful deed, the last thing that would occur to you is to turn him in. It goes against every last instinct of human loyalties, and to hell with the law or the common norms of civic behaviour...'

The common norms! If the Lucan Lobby saw themselves outside the law and above the common herd, it wrapped a tourniquet of perceived privilege around the arteries of the police enquiries. The team at Gerald Road found themselves saddled with the nickname of the 'Nob Squad', which didn't help.

At least Aspinall allowed a notice to be pinned up at the Clermont which read: 'If Lord Lucan comes in, will he please ring 999 as someone wants to interview him.' Wonderful!

One false alarm that had reporters rushing off to a stately home in Kent ended when they rang the bell and asked the lady of the house point blank: 'Is Lord Lucan here?'

The reply enlivened drawing-room conversation for months afterwards. 'I'm not too certain,' the lady responded, one eyebrow arched in amused disdain. 'We do have 60 rooms, and I haven't set foot in some of them since he disappeared. But I'm fairly confident he isn't here. Nobody has sent down for food yet.'

Another elderly soul, questioned by police on her doorstep in Belgravia and informed gently of the reason for the enquiry, responded: 'Oh, dear. Nannies are so hard to get nowadays.'

As one footsore officer would remark later, trying to get someone to talk in this tight-knit circle was 'like finding a traitor in Colditz'.

A social commentator of the scene summed up the situation nicely: 'A very public display of undisguised snobbery laid bare what quickly seemed an absurd and antiquated way of looking at life. With Britain gritting its teeth in the face of social unrest, bellicose trade union meetings and rocketing oil prices, it was a pivotal moment in our social history. It did a great deal of damage, because Lucan was allowed to get away with it, whereas a poor man would not have been able to do so.' The realities of 'us and them' were highlighted in stark relief once again.

The first breakthrough came on Sunday afternoon. An alert detective in southern England, Detective Sergeant David

DeLima of the Sussex Police, had spotted Michael Stoop's blue Ford Corsair abandoned in a backstreet in Newhaven. Roy Ranson and three other detectives took off down the A23 at high speed – in other words, like bats out of hell. This was the first tangible clue since the night of the murder three days before.

The quiet backstreet in the port town was cordoned off. They forced the boot – and inside, lying on top of a pile of old clothing, was a piece of lead pipe bound in medical tape. It could have been the twin of the weapon found at the murder scene – and Michael Stoop would later confirm to a coroner's jury that there had been no piece of lead pipe in the Corsair when he had lent it to Lord Lucan.

The interior of the car was photographed. Then the vehicle was loaded on to a trailer and taken back to London for forensic tests. Blood found on the floor of the car by the foot pedals was similar to that of both Sandra and Veronica. The net of evidence was closing ever tighter.

Back at base camp the detectives pored over their notes, and took legal advice. Two days later Roy Ranson applied to Bow Street Magistrates Court for an arrest warrant for Lucan. It was granted on the spot after a brief hearing. In fact, there were two warrants, one for the murder of Sandra Rivett, the other for the attempted murder of Lady Lucan.

The Detective Chief Superintendent told the press: 'I am now in a position to have Lord Lucan arrested abroad. He may be anywhere. I don't know if he is abroad or in this country.' Note the order in which he said that: abroad first, this country second. Ranson had his suspicions the bird had flown the nest – and the tree as well. But where could the runaway earl have fled?

The description went out: 'Richard John Bingham, Earl of Lucan. Born: London, December 18 1934. Height: 6ft 2ins.

Hair: dark brown. Thick moustache. Eyes: blue. No ear lobes. Complexion: ruddy. Right-handed. Teeth: some may be gold crowns or gold fillings. Cigarette smoker. Speaks German and some Portuguese.'

The gloves were off. Now the hunt was on with a vengeance. Veronica always insisted that her husband had committed suicide 'within 48 hours' of the attacks. But how well did she know him – *really* know him?

You won't find Lady Lucan's family tree in the pages of Debrett. She was plain Veronica Duncan, a trainee commercial artist, when she arrived in London in 1957 at the age of 18 with a suitcase in each hand, and moved into a cheap bedsitter in the Baker Street area. The only thing she had in common with her future husband was that her father, too, had been a military man – an army major who died in a car accident two years after she was born. Her stepfather was the manager of a hotel near Basingstoke in Hampshire.

Like so many other girls who headed for the bright lights of London in the late fifties, Veronica's ambition was to be a model. Blonde and petite, with a mass of fair hair and the kind of face that people like to call gamine, she was intelligent and sharp-witted, and for a time it looked as if she would succeed in her quest. A three-week course led to modelling teenage clothes, followed by a full-time post with a fashion house.

But the money wasn't enough, and the job bored her. So Veronica started her own business duplicating film and stage scripts, then took a major step up the social ladder by moving out of her lodgings and into a flat she shared with her younger sister, Christina. The pair, independent, lively and attractive, became popular with the 'smart' set, and invitations to parties and country-house weekends soon filled the sideboard.

It was when Christina married millionaire wallpaper heir and amateur jockey Bill Shand Kydd in January 1963 that the keys to high society fell at Veronica's feet. She was a bridesmaid on the day, and drew murmurs of approval from the male guests with the eye-catching red dress she wore for the wedding at fashionable Holy Trinity Church, Brompton, in Sloane Street.

Soon afterwards an invitation arrived from her sister and brother-in-law to join them for a weekend at Horton Hall, the Shand Kydds' country mansion at Leighton Buzzard in Bedfordshire. It was there, at a cocktail party after a golf match – 'the women were hauled along for some light relief,' she recalled – that she was introduced to a tall, dark, handsome stranger with an Edwardian moustache and a formal, reserved manner. He took her hand, and bowed. 'Call me Johnny,' he said.

Lord Bingham was not yet the Earl of Lucan. That would come a year later – and with it a £250,000 bequest from his father. For Veronica Duncan, the golden years were about to dawn.

They met again at the same country house two months later. To the surprise of friends on both sides, it was the start of a whirlwind romance, with the dashing peer sweeping the impressionable young girl off her feet and into a new life. From middle-class to the aristocracy in one mighty bound!

Now Johnny introduced her into the champagne and caviar set. He made his lifestyle and extreme sporting pursuits seem glamorous and dangerous – which, to an extent, they were.

The engagement ring came from Cartier. The high-society wedding took place at the same Holy Trinity Church on 28 November 1963, just ten months after her sister's, and was followed by a lavish reception at the Carlton Tower Hotel in Knightsbridge. For the honeymoon, Johnny booked the Orient Express to Istanbul.

Two months later, on 21 January 1964, his father died at the family home in Belgravia at the age of 65, and Lord Bingham became the 7th Earl of Lucan.

The glittering decade of the sixties was reflected for Veronica in her new lifestyle. Some of Lucan's friends held private reservations about the marriage – 'It will never last, they're just not from the same class' was the opinion, but it was only voiced quietly behind the couple's backs, never to their face. The same friends even referred to her stepfather's hotel as 'that pub on the way back from Ascot'. But the early years were still a heady roller-coaster of parties and social functions. Veronica had an account at the top Knightsbridge stores, with the food hall at Harrods her favourite shopping counter. Meanwhile, the earl himself had a string of thoroughbred racehorses stabled at Newmarket.

Six months into the marriage the couple bought the lease of 46 Lower Belgrave Street for £19,000, and embarked on an impressive spending and travel spree. The world became their oyster. They mixed with top society figures from Paris to New York, Monte Carlo to Acapulco, with the group heading for the nearest casino at the end of the day. They cruised the Mediterranean and the Caribbean in private yachts such as the 70-foot *Crin Bleu*, and were served champagne by white-jacketed stewards.

A month after he inherited the title, the new 7th Earl could be found with friends at the ringside in Miami Beach watching Cassius Clay, later Muhammad Ali, challenge the apparently invincible Sonny Liston for the world heavyweight crown and win, after the fearsome champion, complaining of an injured shoulder, refused to come out for the seventh round.

To all intents and purposes the Lucans were an ideal pair. 'I was looking for a god, and I found a dream figure,' the waif-like countess happily told a friend. Her Johnny epitomised the ultimate aristocrat, rich and running, the darling of high society, holding all the aces. She was happy to be the devoted and caring wife, and to relish the perks that came with the job.

Together they shared a cheery, vibrant circle of like-minded friends, and the world was theirs to enjoy. For a time they had a Dobermann pinscher guard dog named Otto, but eventually he had to be put down after attacking other dogs in the street.

On the domestic scene, Lucky was generous with his gifts, if not his emotions, buying Veronica diamond bracelets and necklaces 'worth thousands'. On the more intimate side, it appeared that the word 'stud' probably only applied to horses and five-card poker. 'He didn't really like women, or sex,' confided a friend to Lucan analyst James Fox. 'I would say he would prefer to perform the occasional boff *de politesse*.' Boffing being genteel slang for sex. In fact, it could be said that Lady Luck was the only mistress Lucan knew who could truly gratify his needs.

Lucan now allowed his talent for music – hitherto kept virtually hidden from all but his immediate family – to flourish. An upright piano stood against one wall of the basement where Sandra Rivett would meet her savage death, and Lucan would sit at the keyboard to lead his family in choruses of 'Onward, Christian Soldiers' and other rousing songs. He took classical piano lessons from a friend and music teacher, Caroline Hill, at her home in Kensington. In fact, on the Wednesday, less than 36 hours before the night of horror, Lucan had his weekly lesson as usual.

His demeanour that day did nothing to rouse Caroline's suspicions – 'his hands were steady, and he wasn't shaking,' she told police. Indeed Lucan's 'natural musical ability' would prove a factor in my eventual hunt to track down the truth about his fate.

Back in happier times, three children were added to the family, and it seemed the Lucans had everything to live for. On the night Veronica produced a son and heir, 21 September 1967, three years after their daughter Frances, it was the icing on the cake. To celebrate little George Bingham's entry into the world Lucan treated himself to an expensive dinner at the Mirabelle restaurant in Curzon Street, and then walked up the road to the White Elephant to gamble into the early hours. Reportedly he lost several thousand pounds but dismissed it with his customary panache.

During those early years the pair took regular family summer holidays in Portugal. Lucan fell in love with the country, learned enough of the language to get by and spent many happy months with his wife and young children in rented holiday villas. He even persuaded his friend, two-times Formula One motor-racing world champion Graham Hill, to fly him down there in his Piper Aztec, which Hill piloted himself.

How could anyone guess that this would provide a vital clue in the drama to come, and ultimately a potential escape route from murder?

CHAPTER 6

DRAGNET!

The tentacles of justice reached out across the world in search of the fugitive earl. Eventually he would be 'spotted' as far afield as Australia, South America, Guam, Mauritius, South Africa and all points of the compass. Closer to home, house-to-house enquiries were going on in Belgravia and Chelsea. Shopkeepers were questioned. Sightings came thick and fast, and with them a host of hoax calls that made the task of the Nob Squad ever more difficult. Roy Ranson tersely dismissed most of these as 'horseplay of the upper classes'.

But not all members of the Lucan Set or its periphery were willing to turn a blind eye to the fugitive earl's crime. Some major players came on the scene to aid police investigators. Three of Lucan's intimate circle provided vital information to the case within 48 hours of the murder. Early on the Saturday morning Bill Shand Kydd rang to tell Ranson that he had received two letters from his errant brother-in-law. He brought them in personally to Gerald Road, and the Detective Chief Superintendent immediately noticed smears of blood on the envelopes.

The first began: 'Dear Bill, the most ghastly circumstances arose tonight...' The writer went on to claim that he had interrupted a fight in the basement, that the circumstantial evidence against him was too strong, that his wife hated him and that he would now 'lie doggo for a bit'.

It ended with the words: 'For my children to go through life knowing their father had stood in the dock for attempted murder would be too much. When they are old enough to understand, explain to them the dream of paranoia, and look after them. Yours ever, John.' The second letter was concerned with Lucan's finances.

The postmarks were from Uckfield in East Sussex, only 15 miles from Newhaven. Shand Kydd confirmed that two of Lucan's oldest friends lived there – fellow gambler Ian Maxwell-Scott, who had helped Aspinall establish the Clermont Club, and his wife Susan, who had qualified as a barrister.

Sure enough, interviewed separately by Ranson and Gerring, Mrs Maxwell-Scott gave a dramatic account of the murder night. Lucan had turned up on the doorstep of their country home, Grants Hill House, at 11.30pm, telling her he had driven straight down from Belgravia. He was, she said, looking dishevelled in a blue polo-necked shirt, sleeveless pullover and grey flannels that had a dark patch on the right hip. The detectives surmised later it could have been caused by damp from sponging off blood stains before knocking at the door.

Her husband was spending the night in town. Susan invited Lucan in and gave him a whisky while he unburdened himself of the night's events. 'I've been through a nightmarish experience that is so incredible that no one will believe it,' he told her.

According to Susan, her unexpected visitor went on to reiterate the story he had concocted for his mother and Bill Shand Kydd: how he had witnessed a struggle in the basement of number 46, and fled in panic when his wife started screaming blue murder. 'She accused me of hiring a man to kill her,' he told the startled barrister.

Lucan phoned his mother from the drawing room, and tried unsuccessfully to reach Bill Shand Kydd. He then wrote two letters to Bill that were posted next morning by the Maxwell-Scotts' daughter Catherine on her way to school. Lucan drove off shortly after 1am, leaving Susan with the impression he was returning to London.

The story fitted the facts as the police knew them. But they had no idea what was really in Lord Lucan's mind as he drove away into the night. Had he already finalised his plans to vanish into thin air? If so, what were they? Who else would he have needed to call?

A third letter in Lucan's distinctive spidery scrawl arrived for Michael Stoop on the Monday. It began: 'Dear Michael, I have had a traumatic night of unbelievable coincidences...' and ended with the words: 'I no longer care, except that my children should be protected. Yours ever, John.'

As Detective Chief Inspector Gerring would affirm later: 'What the letters did *not* look like were suicide notes. People about to kill themselves do not sit down and calmly write cleverly phrased letters like these.'

The funeral of Sandra Eleanor Rivett took place at Croydon crematorium on 18 December – ironically the same date as her killer's birthday. It was a low-key affair. Plainclothes detectives mingling with the mourners and a wreath from Lady Lucan containing the message 'To Sandra, with love' were the only indications of the tragedy that had caused it. The inquest was opened five days later, and adjourned indefinitely. When it finally took place, six months later in June 1975, the jury was out for only 31 minutes and their verdict was 'Murder by Lord Lucan'. It was the last time that an inquest jury exercised its right to name a murderer. As a direct result of this case, the right was abolished by the Criminal Law Act of 1977.

The search spread out from Newhaven. Police with tracker dogs peered under every bush and tramped over every blade of grass on the South Downs in a wide radius, while frogmen plumbed the River Ouse as well as a network of water holes on the cliff top. Below, they walked the desolate shore line at low tide, looking for a clue among the seaweed-covered rocks. Other divers investigated the local marina, and a close watch was kept on the beaches for days afterwards. More than 1,000 small boats were checked at moorings from Brighton to Eastbourne, while several country houses and two stately homes were searched.

One immediate target for the detectives was John Aspinall's celebrated 55-acre zoo park at Bekesbourne in Kent. But there was no scent of the fugitive. The police issued a stern public warning: 'Any of Lord Lucan's friends who harbour or aid him will be arrested.' In all more than 1,000 people were interviewed by the police in the quest for their elusive quarry.

The newly renamed Sussex Police came up with an imaginative idea, after discussion with the Home Office. James Bond fans will remember a spectacular aerial battle in the 1967 thriller *You Only Live Twice*. Set in Japan with Sean Connery yet again facing his old arch enemy Blofeld (this time played by Donald Pleasence), the battle takes place above a volcano. It was a dramatic dogfight with Bond at the controls of a mini-helicopter, dodging rockets and zapping the bad guys out of the sky.

The machine was a one-man autogyro. Seven years later the police called on this little gem to scour the East Sussex coastline, with an aerial camera shooting infrared film mounted underneath for a 'spectral survey' of the Seven Sisters cliffs and the thick gorse land west of Newhaven. From a height of 2,000 feet they were looking for decomposing flesh, which infrared pictures would show as a discoloration on the negative, but in the end all they came up with was the remains of dead birds and rats.

It was a brave attempt, and the press had a field day. The bizarre postscript was the discovery of the body of a man hanging from a tree. Later they established it had been there for three years and was too old to register on the infrared scans.

The hunt dredged up other bizarre moments. One letter that arrived at Gerald Road was particularly intriguing, since it was written on notepaper headed '10 Downing Street' and delivered in an official envelope from Prime Minister Harold Wilson's residence. The writer seemed strangely well informed of the background to the inquiry, and part of the letter stated prophetically: 'With continuing support from his cronies at the Clermont, he will stay abroad and never return.'

Was someone playing games? And what kind of people played games to lead the police on a wild goose chase? People who *liked* games – in casinos, perhaps? In the realm of conjecture, the wildest theories can abound, and take root. A £50 premium bond came up with Lord Lucan's name on the number – but the elusive earl was not tempted to come forward and claim his prize.

Meanwhile the police dragnet hauled in a number of Lucan 'doubles'. Any man close to 40, over six feet tall and sporting a heavy moustache was up for grabs. One blameless stockbroker found himself surrounded by squad cars while out strolling through the West End and was closely questioned as to his identity. For two decades the bookmakers Ladbroke's offered 1,000/1 against Lucan being found. The odds were withdrawn without explanation in the nineties.

Other 'sightings' had Lucan buying roses from a Chelsea flower stall, climbing aboard a train in Edinburgh and, most risible of all, directing traffic in Whitehall in a policeman's uniform. With the Channel ports closely watched, it was inevitable that the fugitive gambler would be spotted trying to get to the Continent. Sure enough, he was fingered in Cherbourg, and a car load of detectives raced from London to interview 'a tall Englishman with a moustache dressed in tweedy clothes'. The suspect turned out to be a farmer from Jersey named David Dixon, aged 42 – who happened to be six feet six inches in height.

Somehow, in the heat of the chase the public 'sighters' just did not get it into their heads that the one way Lord Lucan surely would *not* look would be like himself. The moustache might come off. Or, more likely, he would simply grow a beard to hide those distinctive aristocratic features.

Most ironic of all, police in Melbourne spotted a 'tall, well-educated Englishman who had arrived in Australia mysteriously around the time of the murder'. He was detained as an illegal immigrant – and turned out to be none other than another fugitive, Labour MP John Stonehouse, who had done a similar vanishing act from the world. The former Postmaster General, suspected of an international bank fraud, had left a pile of clothing on a Miami beach in an amateurish attempt to put his pursuers off the track. He would be extradited to England from down under and in 1976 sentenced to seven years in jail.

They sought him here, they sought him there. Meanwhile the elusive Lord Lucan, if he was still alive, remained at large. The question was: where?

CHAPTER 7

DOWNHILL SLIDE

What made him snap? Lucan's world was falling apart, and it all happened with overwhelming speed once the slow-burning fuse finally touched off the explosion on that night of shocking violence in November 1974.

In hindsight, you could say that the touchpaper was lit with the birth of the couple's third child, Lady Camilla, in 1970. It was a difficult pregnancy for Veronica. One observer had already termed her 'a highly strung filly', and the fact that she had suffered from post-natal depression after the birth of Lord George aggravated the tension in the marriage. Under the growing strain, Lucan's own behaviour became increasingly erratic, and he started drinking more heavily than any seasoned gambler should allow himself. His favourite tipple was now neat chilled vodka, accompanied by Peter Stuyvesant cigarettes.

Lucan gradually became convinced that his wife had become unbalanced by the depression that followed George's birth. In 1967 he took her to a private psychiatric hospital in

Roehampton, south-west London. Veronica refused point-blank to be admitted. Four years later, after Camilla's birth, he tried again, driving her to a nursing home in Hampstead. This time she ran out of the building and flagged down a taxi to take her home. Lucan was heard to confide to his friends: 'She's mad!'

Matters went from bad to worse. Lucan persuaded himself that his wife was unfit to take care of the children. He bought a miniature tape recorder and taped arguments with her. Finally, in January 1973, he walked out of the family home and moved into the furnished basement flat in nearby Elizabeth Street.

With the break-up came a bitter dispute over the children. Lucan, who doted on them, wanted custody. He even hired a team of private detectives to follow his wife, searching for proof of her instability. On 23 March 1973 he won the first round, when the High Court granted him temporary custody until a full hearing could be held. But then the reckless side of his nature took over: for no apparent reason, since he had legal backing, Lucan jumped the gun, and with two men in a car unceremoniously took George and Camilla from their nanny in the street in broad daylight, then picked up Frances from school that same afternoon. The youngsters stayed with him in Elizabeth Street while the lawyers burned the midnight oil and the phone lines to resolve the drama.

Taking the law into his own hands – shades of Aspinall's defiant words later – was not the best move to impress the judges. Three months later the High Court reversed the earlier ruling, and Veronica had the children under her roof once again.

Lucan was shattered by the verdict. And by the legal bill he faced: £40,000. This is the moment, it has been suggested, that he started making plans.

Along with the emotional strain came something worse. Lady Luck started looking the other way over the green baize cloth, and her once-favoured son found himself further and further out on a financial limb. Some onlookers suggested Lucan's gambling nerve was starting to fail him. His losses could no longer be shrugged off as temporary aberrations.

Like a creeping cancer, his bad luck at the tables advanced on him remorselessly. At this time he was reputedly earning £12,000 a year as a basic income from his inheritance, not nearly enough to fund his addiction with the cards or the dice. So now he was chancing his arm with that riskiest of all dice games, the American invention called craps.

According to Hollywood movies like *Guys and Dolls*, the action seems to be all about shaking and shouting – one man standing by a long table with low side walls shaking two dice that bounce along the surface and rebound off the far end, and excited punters doing all the shouting as a seven or 11 appears. In truth the game has a complex system of odds and is heavily slanted in favour of the casino. A first throw of seven or 11 wins the bet. A first throw of two, three or 12 loses. A first throw of any other number must be repeated a second time.

In other words, it's a dangerous game to play. Especially if you're on a losing streak. Backgammon, Lucan could handle. Craps was in another league. He would borrow from wealthy friends, lose and borrow again. The debts mounted and his luck went from bad to worse. By now Lucky was a drowning man, with no lifebelt to cling to. He even put the family silver up for auction as collateral, and had overdrafts at four banks amounting to more than £14,000. The gravy train had hit the buffers. After his disappearance, the auditors would find the 7th Earl had run through his £250,000 inheritance and owed a massive £74,000 – with no hope of repaying it.

The golden years at the Clermont had come to an end in 1972, when Aspinall sold the club to the Playboy empire. At least Lucky's old friend bestowed a gift upon him when the £500,000 deal was closed – an envelope stuffed with his own bounced cheques. It didn't put any cash in his account, but it got him off a very costly hook.

Now the chips were finally down, and Lucan knew there was no escape. Trapped in a spiral of debt, he had lost his family and his fortune. The only things he had left to sustain him were his honour, such as it was, and the loyalty of his friends.

He had to do something drastic.

In the Murder Squad office at Gerald Road, they played 'the mind game'. Getting inside the mind of a criminal, whether it be a killer, a drug smuggler or a bank robber, is part of the challenge to any policeman out to prove himself a modern-day Sherlock Holmes. When I joined the force some years later, it was a game I came to relish playing myself.

With Lucan, they had a field day. The most likely theory in the days before his financial woes were fully realised went like this:

MOTIVE: Lucan was embarrassed and demoralised by the unfavourable custody decision and wanted his children with him more than anything in the world. Since it was his estranged wife who stood in the way of this, the easiest way to solve the problem was to make her disappear – but it must not look like foul play. Given her questionable mental state, if she was listed as a missing person questions would be asked but surely none too probing.

METHOD: Lucan would get hold of a car with a large boot. He had decided to use his own front-door key to enter the house on the nanny's night off, taking along a mail bag and the wrapped length of lead pipe. The ease of obtaining, wielding and disposing of the blunt instrument had convinced him it was the best weapon to use. He was a foot taller, heavier and stronger than his frail wife, so overcoming her with the heavy weapon would be a simple matter. After the deed was accomplished he would stuff her body into the sack, along with the murder weapon, and bundle them up in the boot of the car. He could then take the time for a leisurely late dinner with his set at the Clermont Club to establish an alibi, before driving down to the coast to dispose of the body at sea in the weighted bag from a speedboat he had moored and ready in a quiet marina for the purpose. He could be home before dawn, long before his wife's absence was noticed by the children or the nanny.

Fascinating … and plausible, too. But it all went horribly wrong. There was no way the beleaguered peer could know the nanny had changed her night off. The devil, as they say, is in the detail – and this was vividly illustrated in the botched series of events that surrounded the murder and attempted murder masterminded and carried out by the Earl of Lucan.

So where did he go that November night after all his plans fell apart in the worst and most dramatic possible way? That was the $64,000 question, to be repeated again and again as the days dragged on into weeks, the weeks into months and the months into years.

Meanwhile the detectives at Gerald Road created their own special Nob Squad tie. It is not generally known outside the Metropolitan Police that various Scotland Yard squads sport their own ties, not unlike regimental neckwear.

The Flying Squad have a dark-blue tie with a golden eagle, claws extended. The Central Drugs Squad – now disbanded – boasted a Chinese dragon as its emblem, representing the smoke from burning heroin that addicts sniff to get their high, a practice commonly known as 'chasing the dragon', since the forms the smoke takes no doubt appear more and more dragon-like the longer it has been burning. The Fraud Squad has a quill pen, while members of the 'Bomb Squad' (the Anti-Terrorist Branch, to give the department its correct title) sport a Bible, a bell and a candle, a combination based on their mission to 'exorcise terror'.

In addition to squad ties, a tradition within the CID is that individual ties are frequently created after a high-profile investigation and occasionally – if the investigation is a particularly long one – during it. If they have served on a major case, officers are entitled to wear one with a suitable logo following the design's approval by a committee at the Yard.

The memento for the Lucan Nob Squad was a blue tie with a small gold coronet over the initial 'L'. The members of this select group must have worn it with a mixture of pride and frustration: pride because it would be a talking point at any pub or party, frustration because their man was still tantalisingly out of sight – if never out of mind.

But where was he hiding? Like a cat chasing its tail, the investigation was going round in circles – and ever-decreasing ones at that. Like falling leaves in autumn, sightings were now coming in thick and fast from all over the world, leaving the thwarted team at Gerald Road to sort through them and decide which needed following up and which could safely be thrown in the rubbish bin.

Some were plausible, others merely preposterous. Postcards from exotic sunspots came in the post signed 'L.L.' and taunting the hunters with rib-tickling wit like: 'Having a lovely time, glad you're not here' or simply: 'Lucky'. The name 'Lord Lucan' would appear on the forms holidaymakers were required to fill in at third-rate casinos from the Costa Brava to Dubrovnik.

The files grew thicker by the day, and with them the theories. These were divided into two camps: dead or alive?

The suicide hypothesis brought its own fanciful ideas. Lucan had thrown himself off a cross-Channel ferry in the early hours of the morning after fleeing from London. He went to a remote spot in some forest where he had already dug a grave in preparation for his wife's body, clambered into it and shot himself. His body would be eaten by wild animals. In fact a skeleton believed to be Lucan's *was* discovered in the gorse behind Beachy Head, only to turn out to be a female art student who had been missing for nine years. Another flight of fancy that went the rounds was that he had been murdered himself by a hit man hired by the Guards Division to prevent the disgrace of a fellow officer facing a murder trial.

More fun and games. If he was alive, Lucan could be hiding out in Algeria after enlisting with the French Foreign Legion – that moustache would look good under a kepi.

Capitalising on a lifetime's ease in the saddle, he was sporting a Stetson and herding cattle on a remote South American ranch owned by James Goldsmith. Or, using his knowledge of German, he settled in a German enclave somewhere in southern Africa – and had even married a German woman to keep up the façade. According to some reports, Lucan underwent plastic surgery abroad to alter his jawline and wore lenses that changed the colour of his eyes. He was seen backpacking on Mount Etna, working as a waiter in San Francisco, relaxing in a hotel in Madagascar, playing cards at a casino in Botswana and fishing in the Seychelles. Altogether, a much-travelled wanderer. It was no easy task for Roy Ranson's team to determine which of the whispers were worth following up.

The most far-fetched was a suggestion that his lordship was being employed as one of Saddam Hussein's doubles. But then, as more than one person remarked, there was a certain likeness…

Two major figures in the mystery supported the suicide theory. Lady Lucan herself was quoted as saying: 'My husband was a nobleman. Having failed to do what he set out to do, he would have taken his own life. I'm sure he would have thought it the only honourable thing to do. If he could find a gun, he might well have used it on himself.' John Aspinall told a Sunday broadsheet in 1990: 'Of course he's dead. He's at the bottom of the English Channel.' And a member of the so-called 'Silent Knights of Lucan's Round Table' added his twopenn'orth: 'He is the kind of man who, having done the dastardly deed, would retire with a bottle and a pistol.'

But the suicide theory has been discounted by some powerful figures, experts in their own field. Detective Superintendent Alec Edwards has been variously described as a 'veteran investigator' and a 'crusader against crime'. He created his own personal file on Lucan after taking over the case from Roy Ranson following the Chief Super's retirement from the Yard to become Chief Investigator for the BBC.

'Lucan is alive and out there somewhere,' Edwards assured one enquirer. 'There is not a shred of evidence on the file to suggest that he is dead. He was not the type of man to commit suicide and, if he had, he would have ensured his body was found – and left a note. So … he escaped. We have to keep an open mind that he might have changed in appearance in one way or another. I also believe he wouldn't have stayed free without assistance.'

As for Lucan toppling overboard off the midnight ferry, tug skipper and 'nautical undertaker' Bob Domin specialised in carrying out the requests of people who wish to be buried at sea, and knew the tidal vagaries of the Channel better than most. 'In 99 cases out of 100 the body will be washed up on a beach somewhere,' he insisted.

'Top psychic' Robert Cracknell was even brought into the equation, maintaining in a tabloid interview in 1981: 'Lord Lucan is being protected by the same highly placed people who helped him escape. No way is that man dead. I don't believe for one moment that he committed suicide, he is far too stubborn and bloody-minded to take that way out.' Mr Cracknell's earlier brush with crime was to accurately predict the date of the last murder committed by Peter Sutcliffe, the infamous Yorkshire Ripper, along with the timing of his arrest.

On the lighter side, T-shirts with 'I AM NOT LORD LUCAN' emblazoned on them were selling well. Designs of the missing earl's face were sewn on pillows and cushions, and west London boutique owner Anna Gibbons claimed: 'His face is folk-hero stuff, sort of like Bonnie and Clyde. He's selling better than Andy Warhol!' My predecessors at New Scotland Yard were not amused. 'The whole business is in bad taste,' commented a spokesman stiffly.

Newspaper artists also had a field day guessing how the fugitive might have changed his appearance. Computer-generated images showed Lucky bald, bearded and/or bespectacled. For the British press, finding Lord Lucan became a cat-and-mouse game, with the Holy Grail waiting at the end of the trail for the journalist who cracked it.

Or rather, *not* finding Lord Lucan ... because after thousands of pounds in air travel and hotel fees had been spent by Fleet Street's finest, 'Not Getting Lucky' was the only tale to tell at the end of the chase.

Indeed, the week after the 7th Earl was officially declared dead by the High Court in October 1999, this was the headline that appeared above an article penned by the stalwart Lucan hunter Garth Gibbs, who himself had once set off on a wild goose chase all the way to Cape Town to follow up a 'definite' sighting for the *Daily Mirror*. He found a restaurant with an empty table where a waitress swore, hand on heart, that the world's most wanted man had dined the week before.

In a tongue-in-cheek feature for the trade paper *Press Gazette*, Garth wrote: 'For a quarter of a century Fleet Street scribes have spent countless thousands of pounds searching for Lord Lucan. Deep down, they've heaved a great sigh of relief every time they haven't found him. It's not that they haven't been searching for him as vigorously as they would search for a blank taxi receipt – it's just that the game would be spoiled if he turned up.' How true.

And he recalled a comment from legendary *Sunday Express* editor John Junor: 'You don't ever want to shoot the fox. Once the fox is dead there is nothing left to chase.' True again.

Garth relates how he spent 'three glorious weeks' in Cape Town not finding Lucky, another 'wonderful' week in the Seychelles not finding him and a further week scouring the Black Mountains in Wales and not finding him there either. Most CID trackers only got as far as Cherbourg, while Fleet Street reporters and photographers travelled the world.

The opening paragraph to the 'Lucan story' that appeals to me most was filed from Botswana, and began like this: 'Lord Lucan is lying on his verandah, betting with himself which fly will reach the rim of his whisky glass first. In this corner of Africa which is for ever England, there's not much else to do…'

It's said that one of the classic stories they tell in the Press Club bar is about the foreign correspondent who was tipped off that Lord Lucan was hiding away on a small island in the Pacific. The doughty scribe flew out to the spot, a journey involving flights via Montreal, Vancouver, Los Angeles and then the long haul to Guam, finally taking a two-seater Chipmunk to the tiny island. He spotted his man downing a vodka at a bar, but the quarry, sensing trouble, disappeared into the night before he could get to him.

The reporter hastened to the glass, carefully picked it up in a cloth, packed it in his suitcase and returned to London after informing his office he had the earl's fingerprints, if not the body. Back home, he informed the Yard he had the wanted man's prints – only to find his mother had unpacked his case for him, and washed the glass! Thinking quickly, he gave his father the glass to hold, then took it to the Yard. Much later, after making his excuses to his editor, the ingenious scribe was able to say: 'At least I found my father didn't have a criminal record!'

It's the stuff of Fleet Street, though no more bizarre than countless other stories that followed Lucan's trail like a pack of faithful bloodhounds.

The Nob Squad found themselves in hot water at one point when a magazine story lampooning their coverage of the Lucan investigation reported tongue-in-cheek that Sir Robert Mark, the lantern-jawed Scotland Yard Commissioner, was asking questions about the expenses being claimed by officers on the case.

'It appears that the Nob Squad have felt impelled to pursue their enquiries into Lord Lucan's disappearance by "in-depth" research and interrogation at various upper-class establishments once frequented by the errant earl,' ran the piece. 'They have claimed expenses for many a meal at the Mirabelle, London's most expensive restaurant. One member of the force became so emotional while pursuing his enquiries at Annabel's night club that he had to be forcibly ejected.

'Worst of all, they have run up a formidable bill at the Clermont Club ... reviving their sleuthish wits with liberal potions of Château Lafite 1947, costing a delicate £30 per bottle.' This scurrilous item came from the satirical magazine *Private Eye* – under the heading 'On the Beat – by "Hobnail"'. A facetious piece, certainly, but where there's smoke...

But now, for those sifting through the mountain of paperwork, a pattern was at last starting to emerge.

CHAPTER 8

THE DARK CONTINENT

It was becoming increasingly clear that the trail led to Africa. In his illuminating book *Looking for Lucan*, published in 1994, ex-Detective Chief Superintendent Roy Ranson outlined his conviction that his quarry had headed south, all the way to the Dark Continent. He learned of 'positive' sightings in southern Africa, more specifically in Botswana and the capital Gaborone, where a man fitting Lucan's description had been seen at the casino playing craps. Botswana is larger than France, but with a population of just over a million. Another glimpse of the earl came from Johannesburg, where a man on the run could easily get lost. Ranson headed out to South Africa.

He was also aware that Lucan's younger brother, the Honourable Hugh Bingham, had chosen South Africa as the place in which to start a new life after the scandal broke. Ranson had interviewed him in London as part of his murder enquiries and found him 'a decent and honest man'. In Johannesburg, after a brief phone conversation and to the detective's surprise and considerable disappointment, Hugh refused point-blank to meet him – 'and I could elicit no reason why'.

The brothers had both enjoyed a privileged upbringing, but that was where the similarities between their lives ended. Johnny was educated at Eton. Hugh went to Charterhouse before becoming an undergraduate at Hertford College, Oxford. Extrovert Johnny responded to the beckoning finger of the gambling casinos. Hugh, younger by six years, living a bachelor existence in South Kensington, was the quiet one and was soon eliminated from police enquiries.

Nine months after the murder, Hugh suddenly left Britain to live in his adopted South Africa. 'I was well aware that people were suspicious. But I was pursuing a job opportunity and it was as simple as that,' he asserted. The Hon. Hugh settled in Johannesburg, moving between rented flats before settling into a modest bungalow with a small garden in the northern suburbs of the city.

He specialised in banking and computer programming for the Rand Merchant Bank, before leaving after 20 years to work from home. Hugh added fuel to the flames of controversy in the mid-nineties when he finally broke his silence to tell a reporter from the *Sunday Express* who had tracked him down: 'A secret is only a secret if it is kept to one person. As soon as another person knows, it is no longer a secret and there is a risk of other people finding out.'

This, of course, was in response to the question the whole world, or so it seemed, had been asking for more than a score of years by then: 'Where is Lord Lucan?' But when the reporter, Oonagh Blackman, persisted, Hugh clammed up. She found him 'noticeably uncomfortable' when talking about his brother, and reluctant to elaborate.

But what could Hugh possibly mean – or have to gain from stating the obvious so publicly? Defensively, he insisted: 'There are still so many theories and supposed sightings, but nothing has proved conclusive. I realise the police think my brother's children visit Africa to see him, but as far as I know they only come here to see friends.

'Is he alive or dead? I just don't know. It is very strange, but after 21 years there has been no conclusive proof either way. I have not seen my brother nor have I heard from him since it all happened.'

Thirty years on, searching for the final truth, I believe him. Johnny had never been that close to Hugh anyway. And, after researching Lucan's missing decades, I find no reason whatever for the fugitive earl to risk everything by calling up his younger brother. It would have served no purpose. Perhaps Hugh's enigmatic statement to the reporter was only meant to explain why others who were in his brother's confidence had never broken their silence.

It was known that Lucan had often holidayed in Portugal, and his links with that country were to prove more and more significant. Among the legal manoeuvres that shadowed this extraordinary case, Lucan's personal correspondence was examined when bankruptcy proceedings began in 1975 to clear his estate. Hidden among the letters and accounts were several bills for Portuguese holiday homes. The police knew he had taken the family there many times in happier days, but this was the first real clue to where his attachments lay in the land of sunshine, pink wine and grilled sardines. Suddenly the bloodhounds had a new scent to follow ... in Estoril.

Eventually, with every new lead hitting the buffers, the police would delve deeper into the possibilities of Portugal being the bolt hole for the Invisible Man. They dug up some interesting background that might mean something – or nothing. In the end, for me, it would take on huge significance.

Estoril is a small town situated on the coast 30 minutes out of Lisbon, a prime spot for the denizens of the capital to get away for a spot of rest and relaxation at weekends. The travel brochures also wave a colourful flag to tempt holidaymakers into its palm-fringed bosom: 'A cosmopolitan resort with superb cuisine, and some of the finest five-star hotels to be found in the region. Palm-lined avenues, elegant buildings and an air of grandeur reflect its link with the rich and famous.' So the earl, with his knowledge of Portuguese, would certainly have felt at home, renting a holiday villa on the edge of town for the family, with trips to the attractive fishing harbour of Cascais down the road as a diversion from the sunny beaches during the daytime.

However, one suspects it may well have been the nightlife possibilities and the kind of action they promised that Lucan was bearing in mind when he settled on the area as a regular family destination. Besides the sun and sand, Estoril's other great draw is that it boasts the biggest casino in Europe. This enticing carrot to an inveterate gambler is located across the road from the Hotel Palacio, itself a monument to a bygone age with its glittering chandeliers and a bar 'furnished in the style of a gentleman's club' – just the sort of refined atmosphere Lucky preferred as the setting in which to indulge his compulsion.

Small wonder that he chose Estoril for his family holidays – it embraced everything he wanted and had the best of both worlds. Picture-perfect family pursuits in the daylight hours – and the excitement of the gambling tables once the children were safely tucked up in bed and in the care of the nanny.

Lucan's last known visit to Estoril was a summer holiday in July 1974, barely four months before the murder. He and Veronica had already separated and had been living apart for a year and a half, and even the hotly contentious custody dispute had been resolved for more than a year. So for the first time

Veronica remained in London while he took their three children to a spacious villa in the hills behind the town. With them came a nanny – not Sandra Rivett, who would be hired at the end of August, but a Cambridge University student named Yvonne Drewry, taken on as a temporary childminder by Lucan.

Intriguingly, when putting the puzzle pieces together all these years later, I noticed Yvonne had told detectives that at one point Lucan drove off to spend a day with a German family 50 miles away who apparently were good friends. His lifelong fascination with things German continued to make itself known.

As a regular and respected 'face' among the high rollers, Lucan would have mingled easily with many of his own kind. It is not beyond the realm of possibility that, when he needed it, he could have been helped with a new passport and an air ticket. To where? One place stood out above all others: the African country of Mozambique. And Portugal was the key.

Another familiar name surfaced in some of the possible equations. One of Lucan's close friends for almost three years before the tragic and infamous events of 7 November 1974 was Graham Hill. As previously mentioned, the former motor-racing world champion also happened to hold a pilot's licence. While he was living life to the full, Lucan regularly chartered light aircraft to swan around Europe with parties of friends to attend social and sporting events, mainly major horse races.

Hill was doing the same with members of his newly formed Formula One motor-racing team; flying them to European racetracks in his twin-engined Piper Aztec, which he had bought from his winnings in the 1967 Indianapolis 500 Race. He had the fuel tanks converted to take the plane deep into the Continent. He would be at the controls to fly his wife Bette and their family on holidays abroad and used the aircraft for business purposes as frequently as most people use their cars.

Sadly, Hill, together with members of his racing team, was killed in 1975 when the aircraft crashed into trees and exploded on to Arkley golf course, in Hertfordshire, while he was attempting to land in thick fog at Elstree aerodrome after returning from a test at the Paul Ricard circuit in the South of France. At the inquest, a report by the accident investigation section of the Department of Trade and Industry showed that certain formalities had been overlooked on the flight: the pilot had the aviation equivalent of no licence, no insurance and no tax disc. Had he not died, Hill faced prosecution for flouting aviation laws.

Graham Hill was only 46 when he was killed. Apart from being a national sporting hero, he led the kind of buccaneering lifestyle that appealed to Lucan, and had the attitude to go with it. Like the earl, Hill lived life to the full, and was also ready to take chances. As he said once: 'It keeps a man balanced if he experiences danger every now and again. It titillates him, and makes him more aware of being alive.'

It later emerged that in 1973 the earl had asked his chum for help in getting his Mercedes from London to Portugal so that he and his family could use the big car for their summer holiday. No problem. Hill was happy to ask one of his drivers to oblige, and the car was duly delivered to the villa in Estoril, with Lucan presumably picking up the tab.

But after the murder the whispers started, and wouldn't go away. Could Graham have spirited his old friend out of the country to help him on the first leg of his escape route, before depositing him at a remote airfield near Lisbon?

The definition of coincidence is: 'An accidental sequence of events that appear to have a causal relationship.' One other fact emerged that set my personal alarm bells ringing: on the night before the killing, Lucan and Hill had dined together at the Clermont Club. Coincidence? The two always had a lot in common, with living on the edge a prime topic of conversation.

No one is remotely suggesting that Hill would have been a party to a planned murder. But if a frantic phone call had come through after the event, mere hours after he had spent the evening in the company of his old friend, who knows what he might have done to help?

With the nose of the true bloodhound, Roy Ranson delved deeper. In the years that followed the murder he picked up more clues from increasingly diverse sources. One was an address book that came into his possession in 1980 following a car crash in Essex in which a former Grenadier Guards officer named David Hardy was killed.

In it was a curious entry that read: 'Lord Lucan, c/o Hotel Les Ambassadeurs, Beiras, Mozambique.' Ranson established that Hardy was a man who liked a drink, and enjoyed a flutter – at the Clermont, no less. His enquiries led him to believe the entry had been made in 1975, when the hunt for the peer was at its height. Curiouser and curiouser.

One particularly tenacious reporter, the *Mail on Sunday*'s crime correspondent Chester Stern, flew down in the eighties to investigate further – and came up with gold dust. Staff at Les Ambassadeurs made a positive identification when he showed them pictures of Lucan, recalling that the fugitive had stayed there 'many years ago'.

Mozambique was Portuguese, and had been since 1505, when it was first colonised. The call for independence began after World War II, turning the place into a cauldron of unrest in 1964 with the formation of the Frelimo, otherwise known as the Mozambique Liberation Front, led by Samora Machel. The terrorists (or freedom fighters, depending which side of the fence you were on) brought chaos and carnage to the country before Samora succeeded in setting up a one-party Marxist state in 1975 – during the very time Lucan would have been trying to smuggle himself into the country.

In those volatile days Mozambique still had close links with its mother country, and in particular strong commercial ties with Lisbon. Lourenço Marques, the country's capital and main port, situated close to the border with South Africa, was virtually an open city. Vital for anyone on the run from the UK was the knowledge that in this festering and dangerous spot there were no diplomatic relations with Britain – and therefore no chance of anyone wasting time or red tape on extradition. Perfect for a runaway earl!

Even more significant, at the height of the investigation in 1975 Ranson had located a British doctor who was on remand in Cardiff Prison on charges relating to a mortgage fraud. Credible or otherwise, Dr Brian Hill had recently returned from Mozambique, and had a strange story to relate.

He told the detective how he had been sitting in an open-air café in the centre of Lourenço Marques when he fell into conversation with a fellow Englishman who gave his name simply as 'James'.

The pair got on well – so well that they embarked on a drinking spree that evening. As the night wore on and they trawled the backstreet bars with increasing unsteadiness and bonhomie, 'James' grew more talkative. Finally, as happens to strangers who become intimate buddies on a boozing binge, he broke down and apparently revealed some startling information about himself.

He could never return to England to see his three youngsters, he said. He had tried to kill his wife and he was wanted for murdering the children's nanny. Adding dramatically: 'I can never go back. I'm Lord Lucan!'

Fact or fantasy? The last the good doctor reported hearing

from 'James' was that he had taken refuge in a farm 'somewhere in the interior'. Back in Cardiff, about to go down for a spell as Her Majesty's guest and despite close questioning, Dr Hill declined to tell the Yard man any more about Lucan's intended final destination.

With what I would learn later, I personally am convinced that Mozambique was indeed the penultimate watering hole for Lord Lucan.

Back home, like petrol being poured on smouldering ashes in a grate, public interest in the Lucan case suddenly flared again. Six months after the night of horror, a date for the full inquest on Sandra Rivett was finally set: Monday, 16 June 1975.

CHAPTER 9

INQUEST

The inquest began at 10.30am at Westminster Coroner's Court in Horseferry Road, with Dr Gavin Thurston presiding. The moment of truth was approached with mixed feelings by everyone involved. Only the ranks of the press, bunched together inside with their notebooks, and the assembled media outside with their cameras and microphones, looked forward to the day. With public interest kindled to fever pitch, sales and audience figures were guaranteed to go through the roof.

Ostensibly it was a coroner's inquest, intended to decide the cause of death and the truth behind it rather than point the finger of blame. In fact, it would be nothing less than a murder trial, and a sensational one at that, with a peer of the realm expected to be named as a killer for the first time in two centuries of British justice. It was obvious that a load of dirty linen was going to be washed in public, and it seemed that everyone involved had something to lose and precious little to gain. The police hadn't caught their prime suspect. Lady Veronica's mental state would be on public show. In turn she would be expected to excoriate her missing husband, and at the very least accuse him of attempted murder. The cupboard was about to be opened to let a heap of family skeletons fall out.

Inquests are normally sombre affairs, with the participants dressed appropriately as a mark of respect for the dead, and an atmosphere of gloom reflecting the solemnity of the proceedings. This one was different in nearly every respect, partially because it rather unfortunately coincided with Royal Ascot week.

The result was that the waiting cameras were treated to a veritable fashion parade of outfits more suitable to a garden party, as the Lucan Set showed their true feelings about the whole sorry business. Lucky didn't do it, and you'd better believe it – that was the defiant message to the world from some of the upper-crust witnesses who would be summoned to give evidence, and from their friends on the public benches who were there to demonstrate their support.

Bill Shand Kydd actually excused himself on the second day by saying he had important business to attend to. He was later spotted in the Royal Enclosure in top hat and brown morning suit, his glamorous wife on his arm wearing a striking blue and white flowered costume and the kind of picture hat, complete with blue ostrich feather, that is *de rigueur* at Ascot. Other members of the clan sported bright smiles and a positive attitude.

Inside the court the highly charged atmosphere was the type that would more normally be expected in a Perry Mason TV thriller. One observer wrote how the place bristled with the hostility of Veronica's relatives towards her, and indeed the feelings were almost palpable. She was described as 'an outsider banished from the family she had been proud to belong to, but had never really been accepted into with open arms'.

As for the real victim in all this, it was noted that not a single person among the Lucan Set went to console the grieving family of Sandra Rivett. Her stepfather, Albert Hensby, together with her aunt and sister, sat quietly at the back of the court. Her mother stayed at home, unable to endure the ordeal. As Mr Hensby commented afterwards: 'My daughter's name has hardly been mentioned, yet she is the reason we are all here.' Her aunt, Mrs Vera Ward, added: 'They make Sandra seem that she didn't matter. But she's in the middle of what seems to be a battle between the two sides of the Lucan family.'

Amid this maelstrom of swirling emotions, there was in-fighting brewing among the Lucan Set as well. Dominic Elwes, 44, a flamboyant playboy and sometime artist who once made his own sensational headlines by eloping with Princess Marina's god-daughter, Tessa Kennedy, was regarded as always ready with a laugh and a quip. But he would incur the wrath of the Lucan Set with a painting that was published alongside an article that appeared in a Sunday supplement under the headline 'The Luck of the Lucans'.

The story provided a sympathetic picture of Veronica as the wronged wife and showed Lucan up in a bad light. As for the painting, it was an extraordinarily evocative work set in the Clermont Club restaurant, with all the leading characters assembled: Goldsmith, Aspinall, along with upper-crust worthies like the Earl of Suffolk, Stephen Raphael and Nicholas Soames. But they didn't like it.

Elwes was ostracised overnight. He was banned from Annabel's and other clubs run by the clan. Perhaps to make amends, he urged his fugitive friend in a dramatic entreaty published in the *Daily Express* to make contact. 'I am sure he is still alive somewhere and hiding in the most desperate circumstances. Why, oh why, doesn't he get in touch with us?' His final words to an associate showed the depths of his feelings: 'I know Lucky is alive. He has got a lot to answer for.'

It was a fruitless gesture, and Elwes stayed out in the cold, an outcast blackballed by the 'clan' and rapidly declining into severe depression. If Lucan read the plea, it was too late. Elwes committed suicide in November 1977. He was found dead in his Chelsea flat after swallowing an overdose of barbiturates washed down with alcohol.

The inquest into Sandra Rivett's death began. Dr Thurston was 62, a coroner with vast experience and widely respected by everyone in the legal field. He had qualified as a doctor in his early twenties, later studying law to add to his medical skills. In his time he had dealt with thousands of cases, but never one like this – for there had never been one like this. Dr Thurston had adjourned the hearing twice before bringing it to a close, and in those months of recess he studied the pitfalls that loomed ahead like a legal minefield waiting to explode in his face.

The major potential problem was the chief witness: Lady Lucan. In a criminal trial a wife was not permitted in law to give evidence against her husband. Even if she had seen him commit a murder or robbery, her evidence could never be heard by a jury – unless the attack had been on herself. Then she was allowed to speak out. Which meant that Veronica could tell the coroner's jury how her husband had attacked her, but say nothing about the death of Sandra Rivett. If she did, none of the details would be permissible to be repeated in any future murder trial.

Tricky situation. But, in the end, Veronica Lucan went for it. The court was packed to the rafters with lawyers, police officers, witnesses and reporters. A veritable battery of barristers sat at a table piled high with papers and buff folders. Michael Eastham, QC, represented the Lucan family, his job being to cast doubt on Veronica's evidence. Her own legal eagle was Bruce Coles, QC, with Brian Watling appearing for the Metropolitan Police and David Webster for Sandra Rivett's family in support.

The jury of six men and three women sat to one side,

listening intently as the coroner addressed them at the start of an inquest that would make legal history.

'Ladies and gentlemen,' he began. 'I will explain why you are here. This is not a trial, but an inquiry. The circumstances are very unusual – the death of Sandra Rivett, who was the nanny to the family of Lord and Lady Lucan. She was aged 29, a married woman living apart from her husband.

'There is a warrant for the arrest of Lord Lucan for the murder of Sandra Rivett and the attempted murder of his wife. The coroner's situation, when there is a death, is that he enquires into the cause of death which appears to be violent or unnatural.

'We are here, in a position where you have the person who has been killed and, we shall hear from the evidence, where somebody has been named as responsible. Lord Lucan has disappeared.

'Your function is to decide who the deceased person was, how, when and where she died, and then the persons, if any, to be charged with murder or manslaughter.'

Dr Thurston outlined the situation regarding a wife giving evidence against her husband. 'The one exception is where a man has assaulted his wife – and this is the exception. This is the difficulty we have to untangle. This case has received an enormous amount of publicity. It is my duty to say, as you already know, that you must only come to your conclusions on evidence you have heard in this court.'

In all, 33 witnesses testified before the assembled group. They ran the gamut from the Plumbers Arms barman to the Home Office pathologist Professor Keith Simpson. One hundred and seventeen exhibits were entered. After formal identification and photographic evidence from police and the pathologist were presented, a sudden buzz went round the packed courtroom. Lady Lucan rose to take the stand.

Smartly dressed in a green tweed jacket and skirt, black velvet coat and white turban, she walked slowly towards the witness box, her face pale and tense. Throughout the hearing it was obvious that she was barely acknowledged by her mother-in-law or by any of the Lucan Set. The coroner invited her to sit in the box, then guided her through an ordeal that would last two long hours, first questioning her gently to establish her background and then enquiring into the condition of the marriage.

Lady Lucan described the events of the night in a clear but quiet voice, confirming that she had forgotten to pull the brass safety chain across the front door, to which her husband had a key. She gave harrowing details of the struggle between them on the stairs, how 'he thrust three gloved fingers down my throat, and we started to fight' and how he gave up after she grabbed him 'by his private parts', with both of them exhausted.

Michael Eastham, retained by Lucan's mother, the dowager countess, went straight for the jugular with an opening question that drew gasps from the court. 'The separation was in January 1973, but even before that you entertained feelings of hatred for your husband?' he asked. Before Lady Lucan could answer, her counsel rose to object, but the damage was done.

With that, battle was joined, and the Lucan family squabbles were aired before a fascinated nationwide audience. Barrister Mrs Susan Maxwell-Scott, presumably more at home in the environment than most of the other participants, told the court that, according to Lucan, his wife had accused him of hiring a hit man to kill her.

During the dowager countess's own stint in the witness box, which lasted more than an hour, she attempted to disparage Veronica's mental state to such an extent that the coroner ordered the press not to report some of her testimony.

The dowager countess went to her grave in November 1985 in a Northampton nursing home, defending her son to the last – and, in the words of top crime reporter George Hollingbery: 'taking the secret of her son's whereabouts with her.'

Hollingbery suspected, as did most of those closest to the case, that she knew more than she ever revealed about Lucan's fate.

After three days of testimony, punctuated by two lengthy recesses in which the world had been treated to a mass of sensational headlines, the coroner summed up. The nation hung on his words. Dr Thurston took 70 minutes, carefully outlining all the known facts and concluding: 'It is fairly clear from the letters written by Lord Lucan that there is existing in the family animosity, tension and matters which, if aired, could only be prejudicial and painful to those concerned.

'Simply to turn this into a forum for airing family tensions would be a wrong thing, and I do not think justice would be served by doing so. You have to ascertain the persons, if any, to be charged with murder or manslaughter. On the evidence, you have got to decide whether you can name the person responsible.'

The press ran a book on how long the jury would be out. In the end they took just 31 minutes to decide. When they returned to their seats, the atmosphere in court was electric. The foreman stood up and announced: 'Murder by Lord Lucan.'

There was no sound in the courtroom, not even a gasp or a sigh. Lady Lucan kept her face expressionless. The Rivett family stared at the floor. The dowager countess's face was turned to stone.

The coroner addressed the jury. 'It is a very rare procedure in coroner's courts for a person to be named as you have done,' he told them. 'It is my duty to commit that person for trial to the Central Criminal Court. There is no doubt that if Lord Lucan turns up he will be charged and will appear before the justices.'

Lord Lucan did not turn up.

Shortly afterwards the family silver was sold at auction to offset the debts. The heirlooms were described in Christie's catalogue only as 'the property of a nobleman'. They fetched £30,000. Even Lucan's personal poker chips embossed with his coronet came under the hammer, sold to a Spanish antique dealer for £400 and later put on show in a cabinet in a San Sebastián casino. The Yard traced a secret numbered Swiss bank account to the jet-set ski resort of Gstaad. The £4,000 in it was handed over to the trustees of the missing peer's estate.

Three years after the murder Lady Lucan wrote an open letter to her errant husband, which was published in the *Sunday Mirror* on 23 October 1977. It began: 'Dearest John, I appeal to you to return to the world you love, to the warm world of your family and friends…' Cynics might suggest a cold prison cell was more likely, but the letter was a touching plea and ended in her own handwriting with the words: 'If you can, please come home. Lovingly, Veronica.'

'If you can…' Three little words, but they could be interpreted in more ways than one. Such as: dead or alive? Odd all the same, given her insistence that her husband had died by his own hand immediately after the murder. But this was a case full of oddities and red herrings.

Much later the trustees were 'assisted in dealing with the 7th Earl's affairs' when, on 11 December 1992, he was 'presumed deceased in chambers', which is as close as you can get to being declared legally dead. But no death certificate can ever be issued if there is no body.

Probate was granted on 11 August 1999, issued by the High Court. It read: 'Be it known that the Right Honourable Richard John Bingham, 7th Earl of Lucan, of 72a, Elizabeth Street, London SW1, died on or since the 8th of November 1974.'

Young Lord George Bingham went from Eton and then Cambridge to a banking career in the City, and applied for a writ of summons in 1999 to take his father's seat in the House of Lords. After much head-scratching and legal discussion this was not authorised by the Lord Chancellor. Lucan's son automatically became the 8th Earl when his father was 'presumed deceased', but he chose not to take the title.

One further irony behind 'the manhunt of the century' is that, had the fugitive peer given himself up and been tried and convicted, the worst that would have happened to him would have been a sentence of life imprisonment. With good behaviour he could have been out in ten years or so.

Instead, as I would discover, the world's most wanted man would choose to serve a life sentence of a different kind – in what amounted to an open prison.

With no remission.

PART TWO

CHAPTER 10

THE HUNTER

The dice were loaded against Mark Winch from the start. From the day he was born blind, through a series of operations that gave him partial sight, he was bound for a life of crime. By the time he came into my own field of vision he was already a young tearaway with a prison record, a hard case without a lot going for him when it came to his prospects for becoming a pillar of the community.

Like so many kids who get into bad company too young and too soon, Mark found himself in a downward spiral where one transgression led to a bigger one. When I finally got on his tail and was planning to kick his door down, I had no idea of any of this, and if I had I wouldn't have paid too much attention. A drug dealer is a drug dealer, and that's the start and finish of it.

This was 1991, and Mark was operating big time around the Thames Valley. When the whisper reached me, I had no idea of the extent of his activities, or that he was actually being welcomed into the august halls of learning at Oxford University on a weekly basis to distribute dope among the undergraduates. That would all come out later. For now, we only knew there was a drum to spin, which, as indicated earlier, is the Filth's lingo for searching a suspect's place from attic to basement.

'The Filth', for those who don't know or somehow missed the entire run of *The Sweeney* on TV, is the slang expression that both the uniformed police and the underworld use to describe the Criminal Investigation Department. It may seem strange, but every man and woman who has been a CID officer is proud of the nickname. Maybe there's an odd element of respect in there somewhere. Or maybe not. Regardless, we took the initially derogatory appellation and made it our own.

When Mark first crossed my path, I was on top of my profession. At the age of 31 I had been a cop for the whole of my adult life and even a bit more since I'd started with the Metropolitan Police Cadet Corps at Hendon Police Training School three months before my eighteenth birthday. The MPCC no longer exists but back then it was a way of grabbing likely and eager young men and women below the permissible age of $18^1/2$ to put them on hold until they could join up for real.

A lot of my own determination to join the Met and spend my life stamping out crime stemmed from the example set by my father, Frederick MacLaughlin, himself a George Medal hero. Dad had won his award with 45 Commando when he was shot at the wheel of an ambulance as he rushed to save a wounded civilian in the middle of a Belfast riot, just when the troubles began to heat up once again in the late sixties. Part of the citation read: 'It was found that a bullet had entered MacLaughlin's right cheek, smashed his jaw and lodged in his throat. He refused help, and completely disregarding his own injury drove through the line of fire to the wounded man, and accompanied him to hospital. His selfless conduct was an example to all who saw him…'

So I had something to live up to. My father had taught me to shoot, live rough and survive in the wild. His gung-ho spirit for adventure and clearly defined code of honour permeated every aspect of my boyhood.

It took three officers from the Metropolitan Police who were touring Scotland in search of raw material to fire my youthful imagination and inspire me to a life in law enforcement. After showing their recruitment film at my school in Arbroath, the chief inspector faced us from the floor. 'Unquestionably we are regarded as the world's finest police force, an organisation for which every other law enforcement agency feels admiration and inspiration,' he told the class – and I was hooked.

Starting from the bottom of the ladder actually imbues you with immense self-confidence. I never had the privilege of going to university, to come out with the kind of degree that would 'fast-stream' one for promotion. But it never did me any harm. Even as the lowliest copper in the ranks I recognised it as a privilege to be taught every aspect of police work through and through by experts, from A to Z.

We had our moments. Anyone who has read *The Filth* may recall the passage in which I recounted how, as eager young recruits, we were photographed in a studio at the college – and then fingerprinted with both hands pressed down on an ink-covered brass plate by a tough-looking sergeant. The print was then transferred on to paper, nothing like the way they do it in the movies where they roll your fingertips on an ink pad. 'Why us, Sarge?' I enquired innocently. 'Surely only villains get fingerprinted?'

'It helps us identify you when you get blown up,' was the gruff reply. I never did find out whether he was joking or not, but he might at least have said 'if'.

My quest for upward mobility through the force started even before I was issued with my helmet, more affectionately known as a 'tit', along with my wooden truncheon, a pair of ceremonial white gloves – which I never wore – a torch and an *A–Z* of London. I learned everything from how to handle a spot of road rage between two angry motorists ('Use tact and diplomacy. Remember the Old Testament: "A soft answer turneth away wrath!",' intoned our bull-necked instructor) to bodies on railway lines, armed robbery, court appearances, the vagaries of the legal system, suicides and even what to do after a nuclear explosion.

Yes, even that. We budding guardians of the law had weekly 'nuclear lectures' from a former army officer, a man with a pencil moustache and not a lot of humour, who arrived with a load of maps, marker pens and videos. We dubbed him 'Nuclear Ned', and he put the fear of God into us by lifting the lid on what was once the unthinkable but has become an accepted reality of life in the twenty-first century.

'Basically your job will be to maintain law and order, protect the public by directing them to the nearest shelter and prevent looting,' he told us. 'Those of you with the appropriate training will be issued with firearms.' Presumably, we said to each other later and well out of his earshot, in case we need to shoot looters.

My early years as a fully-fledged copper based in north London and pounding the beat were filled with road accidents, break-ins, missing persons and domestic disputes, the normal daily grind of a policeman's life. But always my interest lay in serious crime, and this would take me into the realm of drugs and violent death. The CID had been my goal from the moment I watched that unpolished training film in my Scottish schoolroom, and fortunately I got there with relative ease.

However, before getting there and while still a uniformed constable, I had to take a final series of written tests, including a number of papers called 'K and R', which stands for Knowledge and Reasoning. This is roughly the Met's equivalent of a taxi driver 'doing the knowledge', and includes questions like the following:

'At 3pm you are patrolling in uniform when you are called to a main road to deal with an accident between a Ford Capri and a fuel tanker. The Capri is trapped under the tanker. The vehicle's occupant is visibly injured. The tanker is ruptured, seeping petrol.

'The driver of the fuel tanker approaches you and says: "He came round the bend like a maniac. I tried to help him out of the wreckage, but he told me his leg is trapped. He smells like a brewery."

'Another officer joins you and remarks: "I'm sure there was a Capri like that stolen on early turn."

'A uniformed bus inspector approaches you and says: "This is a main bus route. If you don't sort out this mess, how can you expect me to ensure the buses run on time?"

'An elderly woman taps you on the shoulder and says: "Look, the petrol is seeping into the drains." You look towards where she is indicating and observe a group of children, some of them smoking, standing on the pavement watching the fuel disappear down a roadside drain. You are aware from local knowledge that schools in the area do not finish lessons until 4pm.

'State fully your action. Give details of any offences disclosed and powers used.'

My answer would include:

'Render first aid to injured parties, and ensure no one else is in the vehicle. Contact police station, inform the Duty Officer. Request ambulance to deal with victims, and fire brigade to treat spilled fuel. Request assistance of other officers regarding crowd control and gathering of witnesses. Request the assistance of Traffic Division as serious RTA (Road Traffic Accident), possibly fatal. Inform NSY (New Scotland Yard) of situation ref. traffic congestion. Have London Transport informed of situation ref. bus routes and potential delays. Ensure a message is sent to Water Board ref. petrol in public drains. Inform local Highways department to deal with residue after fire brigade have cleared away wreckage. Investigate possible offences ref. drink driving and TDA (Taking and Driving Away), quoting relevant Act and Sections. Explain police powers under statute to breathalyse and arrest driver, depending on his injuries, using case law and force instruction to support my answer. Check on children playing truant and smoking, bringing details to attention of Juvenile Bureau to inform parents and school. Seize cigarettes as evidence and consider proceedings against shopkeeper for selling cigarettes to minors if established children's age is below 16, etc., etc.'

There was, of course, a short answer: 'Suddenly remember you have a dental appointment, make your excuses and leave your colleague to sort out the mess'!

Every aspect of the question called for a specific responsive action. I made it through but there were times when it made me feel as if my brain cells would boil over.

There is a reason I have gone into this episode in such detail. What is it? To demonstrate the kind of meticulous thoroughness and attention to a breadth of diverse and seemingly unrelated details that is instilled into every policeman being prepared to face even minor incidents on the streets. It's an attitude that becomes second nature. It might be worth remembering that every time you see a bobby on the beat, they have been put through this mental mangle and come out the other side, tried and tested, or they wouldn't be there. 'Leave no stone unturned' is the name of the game – and it was drilled into me so thoroughly that my ways of looking at the world and processing information were for ever changed.

Now I would be employing those principles to the full as I reopened the file on Lord Lucan and began my own investigation.

In the summer of 1981, three years after my arrival in London, I hung up my blue helmet for the last time, and became a plainclothes officer with the rank of Acting Detective Constable. That was good enough. It was the sharp end, where all the action happens, and that was what I'd hungered for from the first. Before long I was a full-blown detective and a desk was found for me in the CID office at King's Cross. DC MacLaughlin was in his element.

The route map that would eventually end up on a crossroads with Mark Winch can be traced back to May 1989. That was the month when I was transferred to the Central Drugs Squad, and the pace really hotted up. The Drugs Squad, founded in 1963 by Sir Joseph Simpson, then Commissioner, was made up of six teams labelled 'A' to 'F', and was one of several squads that formed part of the Yard's International and Organised Crime Branch.

When I joined the branch, the squad occupied part of the fourteenth and most of the sixteenth floors at New Scotland Yard, with an impressive view of Westminster Abbey and Big Ben through the blast-proof curtains on the windows. Teams E and F had been recently set up to counter the sharp increase in drug-related crime, with a seventh team, known as Operation Lucy, created to combat the menace of the Yardies, a ruthless Jamaican influx who had brought virtual gang war to the streets of London. The teams were made up of 13 men apiece, all of them hand-picked and under the command of an experienced detective inspector.

I was part of the elite E Team, the best of the best, reinforced to become the most successful drug busters in the country. It was here, in the main office which held 60 detectives, each with his own desk, that my eyes were opened and I got my first real taste of what the scene meant, with all its implications for society and the people who use and abuse drugs.

A line of glass cabinets ran the length of the room, stacked full of drug paraphernalia and substances. Curved opium pipes. Thai sticks. Sheets of LSD tabs. Syringes for shooting up, spoons for melting down. Cigarette holders for 'spliffs'. Dark brown slabs of cannabis labelled 'Paki Black', 'Moroccan', 'Afghanistan' and all points east. Hashish leaves and plants. Uppers, downers. All of it seized by the Central Drugs Squad and donated to this unique museum of misery after the trials where they'd been used as evidence were over.

Up to that moment I had only had a few brushes with soft drugs, mainly marijuana, or 'grass'. The cannabis plant produces ten grams of the drug per foot per year as it grows. A four-foot plant can yield 40 grams a year, close to an ounce and a half. Not a lot on its own, but multiply that and it becomes significant.

I had lost count of the number of homes I'd searched after receiving a tip-off that 'gear' was being grown at an address.

Normally a quick phone call to the electricity board would reveal the property's occupants were using enough juice to be a serious drain on the national grid.

A search warrant would be rapidly obtained, followed by an early-morning wake-up call, delivered in the form of a sledgehammer or size-11 boot.

The most cannabis I'd ever seized in a 'spin' like this was 400 plants being cultivated under the eerie blue light of heat lamps in an indoor greenhouse constructed within an attic in a property off the Caledonian Road. The attic had been lined with hardboard and had a thick hosepipe snaking around the interior, punctured with holes to create a primitive irrigation system. Yellow Gro-Bags full of peat, the kind used for growing tomatoes, filled every square foot, and from each sprouted six cannabis plants.

However, on being transferred to the Yard we were discouraged from wasting our resources chasing such insignificant quantities. If we had to get involved in cannabis, a Class B drug, dealers knocking out multi-kilos of resin, rather than horticulturists harvesting indoor farms, were the characters the bosses wanted taken off the streets.

I was wondering when my next seizure of any significance would come along when I heard the first whisper about Mark Winch.

CHAPTER 11

First Hint

In that year and in the years following I took part in a number of high-profile cases, most of them involved with drugs and surveillance. 'Operation Emerge' was a major drugs haul: a huge shipment of cocaine from Venezuela which involved tracking a vessel across the Atlantic Ocean using an American DEA (Drugs Enforcement Administration) satellite, before finally sending in the marines of the Special Boat Service armed with MP5 sub-machine guns and flash grenades to storm the ship when she docked at Greenwich on the Thames. That one made front-page news – with dramatic photographs spread across every national paper in the country.

When it came to surveillance, I was dubbed 'Britain's top undercover cop', which was extremely flattering but gilding the lily somewhat. There were a lot of officers at the Yard equally versed in the subtleties of being seen but not detected. Meaning that you can be a face in the crowd as you follow a suspect in a busy street, and he can look straight over his shoulder at you but never notice you … until you tap him on the shoulder. Or staying immersed in a ditch under a cloak of leaves and branches all night long, not stirring, with binoculars trained on a suspect's home or on the quarry himself – an SAS speciality the guys at Hereford taught us first-hand.

Some of the names I had come up against in high-profile cases will have a familiar ring. Master criminal Kenneth Noye. Kidnapper and murderer Michael Sams. A drugs scam linked to Formula One cars and some big noises in motor racing. The theft of the £6-million Rubens painting *The Dominican Monk* from the County Wicklow mansion of diamond millionaire Sir Alfred Beit. I had also been part of the grim-faced team investigating the terrible slaying, some years earlier, of PC Keith Blakelock, hacked to death on a North London council estate during a night of rioting in October 1985.

I ran a stable of informants, and as part of the protection they needed to stay alive. I bestowed pseudonyms on them, starting with the World Cup winners, then moving on to top Formula One racing drivers once I discovered a passion for the sport during the investigation into its seamier side.

Geoff Hurst, Alan Ball, Bobby Moore, Martin Peters, Roger Hunt and Gordon Banks all did Trojan service and helped put some heavy-duty 'faces' behind bars. Later Eddie Irvine, Damon Hill, Oliver Gavin, Pedro Lamy, Mario Andretti, Eddie Cheever and Michael Schumacher were all on my A-team, and three of them were women. For their efforts they received rewards in the form of fat brown envelopes full of cash, delivered personally by myself in a quiet corner of some anonymous pub. It worked like a dream.

This was directly contrary to police regulations, which stipulate that no informants should have an alias that bears any resemblance to real persons, past or present. But I do know that the Guv'nor of the day got a quiet chuckle out of signing a monkey (£500) to England's top goalkeeper for alerting us to an armed robbery. If others among the top brass noticed, as they signed chits for hundreds of pounds in the name of some of the world's top sporting heroes as 'expenses incurred' for information received, they overlooked it.

All my grasses were professional criminals who had done time for murder, assault, burglary, drugs or armed robbery. As in both the factual and fictional spy stories you read, I had 'turned' them so that they now worked for me. They also knew their lives depended on me not to shop them, because these folks moved in very bad company and would have been propping up a motorway if anyone broke their cover.

By the time the name of Mark Winch fell on my desk, I had chalked up some big fish in my personal file. Mark seemed a minnow by comparison. How could I know that this young man would lead me to the biggest catch in the ocean, the name that every copper in the country would love to mark down in his notebook, along with an arrest warrant, signed, sealed and executed?

Or that it would take more than ten years before we actually faced each other?

From my side of the fence, all that happened in the second week of December 1991 was a call from a snout in west London alerting me to the presence of a dope peddler in the Slough area. He gave me a name and an address.

'How big?' I asked.

'Not very,' was the reply. 'But he's operating from Slough down to Oxford and he's slipped through the net a couple of times.'

'Leave it to me,' I said. 'I'll handle it from here.'

I had more pressing matters on hand at that time anyway and I left it at the bottom of the 'action' file. Two days later the phone rang again. 'That guy Winch,' said my contact. 'He's done a runner.'

'What?'

'It seems the word got out and he heard you might be coming from town to pay him a visit. He got cold feet and scarpered. I thought I'd save you a trip.'

'Know where I can find him?'

'No. He's vanished off the face of the earth.'

There was no point in circulating him as 'wanted'. We would have had to catch Mr Winch with the goods on him and get him, in that lovely phrase, 'bang to rights'. I hadn't even got as far as taking out a search warrant.

'OK,' I said. 'Thanks. I'll keep him on file.'

And I put it out of my mind … for the next decade.

'Right,' I said to Mark Winch. 'Tell me about it.'

We sat in the small, comfortable living room of the terraced house in a Peak District village that had been his home for the past eight years, poring over the photographs. During all that time the pictures had been lying forgotten in the back of a drawer, while I had completed 20 years with the force and finally decided on a change of scenery.

I'd had a good innings, my work frequently taking me out of the country to Europe, America and the Caribbean. I'd even won an award or two, and the Commissioner's High Commendation – for outstanding bravery and devotion to duty – the highest award he can bestow, looked well in its frame in my office. Two colleagues shared this with me, after a fracas on a rooftop in London's Clerkenwell involving a guy with a rifle. The three of us were unarmed ourselves, but we had tackled the gunman and disarmed him, even though he pulled the trigger and one of us had gone down.

'The courage and dedication of the three officers was in the highest traditions of the Service…' ran the citation, presented personally to us by the then Commissioner, Sir Kenneth

Newman. Nice. The icing on the cake for me was that my father was there to see it.

'Well done, son,' he said, raising his glass in the pub afterwards. 'I'm proud of you.'

That was all I wanted to hear.

But all good things come to an end. In 1997 I heard that the specialist units – the plainclothes detectives, mounted branch, traffic cops, helicopter aircrew, even the Underwater Search Unit – were to be returned to uniform, courtesy of a decision by the then Commissioner, Sir Paul Condon. This policy would be rescinded by the new Commissioner on Condon's retirement, but by then it was too late. I had already resigned.

On the personal side, I was divorced, after a 15-year marriage that folded owing to the pressures of the job, which kept me away from home for all hours of the day and night. My ex-wife Beverly had custody of our three kids, son Ashley and daughters Sara and Anna, though I was able to see them whenever I wanted. The main implication now was that for the first time I was able to look around for other employment without any domestic worries to interfere with the job.

My CV was impressive enough to get me work as an investigator for the next few years and travel the world for wealthy individuals, in between writing *The Filth*. The clientele varied from rich businessmen about to get taken to the cleaners by two-timing wives to millionaire Arab racehorse owners needing advice about their personal safety. I gave security advice to Damon Hill – whose father Graham frequently flew Lucan out of the country. In between, I kept my hand in at unravelling complex frauds; often matters the client didn't want brought to the attention of police or, in turn, shareholders. In addition I had carved myself a bit of a niche when it came to tracking down and recovering abducted children – kids taken by one parent or other in defiance of a court order.

I brought with me a virtual lifetime of Yard experience, and had served with both the Central Drugs Squad and the Regional Crime Squad. My training had included courses in firearms, surveillance (both urban and rural), fraud, money laundering, advanced driving to police standards on the famous 'skid pan' at Hendon, and a few other less publicised skills. Finally I was headhunted for the position of Head of Security with a commercial airline based in Scotland and the Middle East, which enabled me to travel widely and top up my suntan in the process. I was doing just fine.

That was when I got the call from Mark.

CHAPTER 12

PICTURE POWER

On the drive north to talk to Mark Winch I had time to reflect on the Lucan mystery. It had fascinated me, along with the rest of the country, ever since I first read the details of the high-society murder and the peer of the realm's vanishing act. I was only 14 at the time it all happened. But over the years the newspapers had kept the story fresh with new 'sightings' and tantalising clues, and had used every anniversary as an excuse to dust off the files.

Within the force, the name of Lord Lucan had cropped up time and time again, with every copper having his own pet theory. The words 'if only...' lurked behind any such conversation, and every sleuth worth his deerstalker and magnifying glass fantasised about tracking down the fugitive aristocrat and bringing him to justice.

And now here I was, staring down at a set of photographs that were sending chills up and down my spine.

The main picture showed a bearded figure slumped in a

rocking chair. The subject of the photos looked just like Robinson Crusoe fresh off the beach or possibly Rip Van Winkle in the middle of his 20-year slumber. I peered closer.

'Christ!' I said to myself. 'I'm looking at history here!'

And I was.

The man in the chair is in a time warp. Wearing only a pair of khaki shorts, he has fallen asleep with his left hand resting on his right, the knuckles showing clearly, a wristwatch gleaming on his left forearm. A massive sandy beard tumbles on to his chest and almost down to his waist, reminding me bizarrely of the kind of stuffing you pull out of cushions. The body is lean and tanned.

But look closer. The face is more noble than nomad. Even though this man is a vagrant, he has a touch of class about him. Somehow he doesn't look like an itinerant, or just any hobo who has wandered out of the jungle on his way to nowhere. The face has an innate presence about it.

Fishing into my briefcase, I pulled out a known photograph of Lord Lucan. The famous picture that had gone round the world of a handsome man with unwavering eyes and a thick moustache, which has been reproduced endlessly ever since. Lucky was in his late thirties then. Now he would be close to 60. Twenty years or more makes a lot of difference in anyone's appearance. All the more so when the outward trappings of life change dramatically.

But the basic features are all there. The broad, aristocratic forehead. The thick black hair springing up from its parting on the left. The distinctive black eyebrows, and the crease that stood out between them. The scar on the knuckle.

'Let's see the rest.' I bent lower, minutely examining six other photographs with the intensity of fiction's most famous sleuth putting an insect under the microscope. This was hardly

221b Baker Street – but I didn't need a magnifying glass to see the striking similarity.

Photograph number two showed the bearded Crusoe sitting in an open bar, still bare-chested, only this time in blue denim shorts, his eyes squinting against a setting sun – judging from the shadows – and wearing an almost comic Santa Claus hat with a white pompom over one ear. A bottle of beer stands on the table in front of him. In the foreground is a bare-chested, dark-haired young man with a cheeky grin, who would turn out to be none other than Mark Winch himself, then aged 26. A poster pinned to the flimsy bamboo wall in the background gives the location away: Goa, India.

So this is where our fugitive is hiding…

Few things can really stun me any more. If I haven't seen it all and done it all in my career, I've come pretty close. But now I found my heart starting to pump like a steam hammer. Could this really be the jungle hideaway of the 7th Earl of Lucan? Whereabouts in Goa is it? And is he still alive? I could hear the jingle of handcuffs already – in my dreams!

Back to the photographs.

Photo three showed the man in full flow in that same bar. Only this time the camera has widened to reveal a group of young people around him, all of them totally relaxed and accepting the hermit-like recluse in their midst with no apparent embarrassment. A laughing blonde woman at the next table is nearer his age. Was it some charming repartee from the man that had amused her?

Photo four was a crowded beach bar. The sea is way off in the distance. Two colourful sheets have been hung from the bamboo roof to keep out the direct rays of the sun, which would be coming from the south-west. So it must be late afternoon. His back is to the camera – and Mark is pointing straight at the camera, seated between a guitar-strumming youth, who looks Indian, and another swarthy young man wearing a necklace.

The other pictures, less clear, were snapshots taken on a porch with Mark and the bearded stranger sitting together outside their rooms.

I took a deep breath.

'All right, Mark,' I said. 'I'm listening. Let's hear it – all of it. Start from the beginning.'

I switched on the tape recorder, and sat back.

CHAPTER 13

MARK'S STORY

Mark began, hesitantly at first, then with more confidence, the words pouring out. 'I was born in Windsor on 16 December 1965, totally blind. Over the next few years I had 18 operations in all. By the time I was three I had managed to regain partial sight – they called it "a non-distinguishable amount" in my left eye, but enough in my right one to get by. Today I have 30 per cent vision in my right eye and 60 per cent when I put in a contact lens.

'My father was a sales manager. We moved to Basingstoke in Hampshire, where I spent my early years. I had to go to a school for the partially sighted because I couldn't read a blackboard from a distance and I needed the special facilities like large-print books. My parents moved from Basingstoke to Seaford in Sussex because they'd found a school I could attend as a day pupil and not have to board. I stayed there until I was 16 and had five O levels, but by that time I was already heading for trouble.

'Being a day boy at a boarding school meant that after four o'clock my mates were "confined to barracks" and none of them could come out to play. You couldn't call me a loner because I tried to fit in. But it wasn't easy.

'I had a pushbike like the other kids and my best friend was my little brother Adam. There were four years separating us, but he was always there for me, like a human guide dog. We'd have races across the golf courses, jumping the bunkers on our bikes, with Adam hurtling ahead up front and me following him.

'At first I tried to fit in as a bit of a prankster to make myself popular with the local kids. But it was easier to be accepted by other young tearaways than by the normal boys who don't have these sort of problems. I joined a gang, a small group of mischief-makers – and that, I'm sorry to say, led to my first court appearance at the age of 11! I was hauled in for smashing every street lamp along one road in the town. Seaford is practically deserted at night and we found this road and lobbed bricks at the lights until we'd totally decapitated them.

'We were all fined £40 each. My father paid my fine – but I wished I'd had enough savings to pay it myself, because he ordered me to do gardening and push wheelbarrows at ten pence an hour to pay it off! Dad made me work every weekend for 18 months to pay back that fine and keep me off the streets.

'After that I was in and out of trouble of one sort and another all the time. Petty thefts, joyriding … but I saw it as just being up for a laugh, to see if I could get away with it. More often than not, I didn't. I got community service, probation, but when I defaulted three times I was rightly looking at a custodial sentence.

'At this point my grandmother Paddy – she was in her sixties, bless her – came down to Lewes Magistrates Court, stood in the dock and said she'd have me at her home in Slough, out of harm's way and the bad influences I'd been hanging around with. She implored the magistrates to give me a chance. They listened to her, then gave me a year's conditional discharge, and off I went with her to a new home. It didn't work. I was a reckless teenager who looked older than I was, so I was able to drink in pubs and clubs. It was during the Sunday lunchtime sessions that I started to enjoy a game of backgammon. I was pretty hot and always up for a game, so much so that my brother, Adam, bought me a small magnetic set for Christmas.

'I was 16 when I started smoking pot, first and foremost to fit in because I found the people around me easy to get on with and non-judgemental. That's how I started dealing. At first I bought the stuff with my own money for my own pleasure, then very quickly worked out that I could make a profit if I sold it on. By the time I was 17 I was smoking the stuff every day.'

Mark paused as the door opened and an attractive woman with shoulder-length blonde hair and a bright smile came into the room with two mugs of coffee. This was Sarah, in her thirties and Mark's partner for the past eight years and the mother of his two sons, aged five and six months.

No intellectual slouch herself, Sarah had once worked at the Bodleian Library in Oxford – while, unbeknown to her, Mark was using the halls of academia to drum up customers among the undergraduates for his dope-dealing operation. She nodded to me, and left us to our coffee. I turned on the tape again and Mark continued:

'Grass is sold in eighths, quarters, half-ounces, nine-bar and kilos. I soon learned that if I bought a half-ounce – at the time the price was £40 – I could sell three of the eighths for 15 quid, and make my own spliff for nothing. It all grew from there. Then I bought an ounce for £75, and not only could I get my own smoke for free, I'd make 20 quid in my pocket. Things went from strength to strength and then it really took off.

'By then I was aware of my own strength and I was also strong-willed. I found it was easier to use my fists than my voice to win an argument. When I moved up to Slough, a much bigger town, I came up against far more conflict than I'd been used to.

'As a rule I don't like violence. Up until the day I moved in with Gran I'd try to avoid fights because of my eyesight. But I'm a big bloke, and maybe because of the raw deal life handed me I had a lot of inward aggression. If I felt threatened I'd defend myself. I'd sooner hit someone first than take a beating. Because I couldn't see them too well, if my first right hook didn't do the job I'd fight more like a wrestler than a boxer. I'd pin them against the wall and then punch them. Or I'd get them in the old "Winchy headlock", which usually saved the day.

'I have to admit that after any violence I'd go away shaking. All my life I felt people had been taking the piss out of me because I had a disability, so I used to react strongly. But, thank God, I've calmed down now.

'The worst time of my life was detention centre. It was the short, sharp shock treatment. Slough Magistrates Court sent me to a detention centre in Gosport for four months after a long string of petty offences – siphoning petrol out of cars, credit-card fraud, various things like that. "Let this be a lesson to you and we hope you learn something from it," said the magistrate, peering down at me through his glasses from the Bench. It was, and I did.

'I arrived at this boot camp in the back of a police van, a cocky young tearaway of 17. Within one minute of the van swinging through the gates, I had a taste of the shape of things to come. Looking back, it was one of those incidents where you might say: "I'll laugh about this one day." Right then it wasn't so funny.

'On the drive down the police officers in the back had filled me in on the camp. One of them said: "You'll like this place.

The 1963 engagement picture of Lord and Lady Lucan.

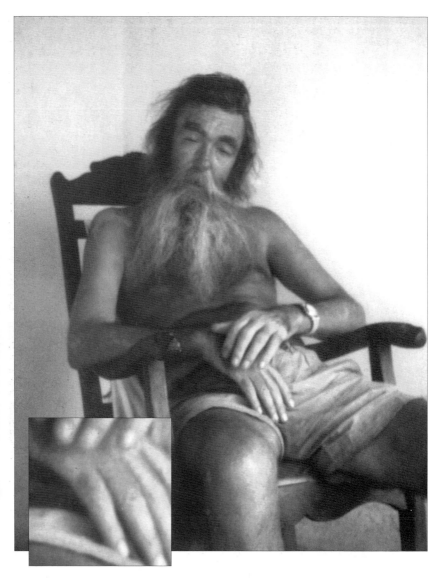

When I first saw this picture I went cold. The similarities with other pictures I'd seen of Lucan (*opposite*) leaped out of the photograph: the broad aristocratic forehead, the thick hair sweeping up from its natural parting on the left, the distinctive dark eyebrows. Even before I started my meticulous research I had little doubt that 'Jungle Barry' was indeed Lord Lucan.

Inset: The scar above 'Jungle Barry's' little finger on his right hand corresponds with the scar on a picture taken of Lucan in the 1960s, which I retrieved from Lady Lucan's website and enlarged using sophisticated police equipment.

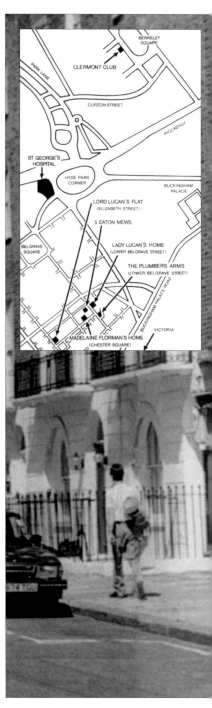

Clockwise from left: 72a Elizabeth Street, Belgravia, the apartment where Lucan lived at the time of his disappearance; a map showing the significant locations of the events of that dreadful night when Lord Lucan murdered Sandra Rivett; beaten and desperate, Lady Lucan fled down Lower Belgrave Street to The Plumbers Arms in her search for help.

Top: Formula One driver Graham Hill. Did he fly Lucan to Portugal in his light aircraft?

Bottom left: The picture, damaged by ants, of Lucan that hung on the wall of Bob's Bar.

Bottom right: Lucan before his disappearance.

Top left: Bob Lawande, owner of Bob's Bar and Lucan's friend.

Top right: The porch at Connie's where Lucan frequently slept in the open.

Bottom: The apartment block in Goa where Lucan died in the bed of his girlfriend.

DEATH

Born 11-3-38 · Died 3-1-96

BARRY THOMAS HALPIN

(JUNGLY BARRY)

DEARLY LOVED AND SADLY MISSED
BY ALL OF US GOOD-BYE OLD COCK

CREMATION on Sat. 13-1-96 12.00 noon
Panaji Crematorium.

Lucan's death notice in the local paper. On my return to England, I conducted
some extensive research.

It's a Naval establishment. They're all sailors. You have a captain instead of the prison governor, and you have officers instead of screws, who are called 'Mate' – as in 'First Mate', 'Second Mate'." OK?'

'I nodded. "OK."

'Inside the camp, the double doors of the van swung open and I looked out to find four marines on either side, standing in line. All for me! One barked: "Stand to attention and look at the guv'nor!"

'Up came an officer. He said: "What's your name?"

'I replied: "Winch."

'He shouted: "Winch, *what*?"

'In all innocence I said: "Winch, mate!" I promise I wasn't trying to be smart.

'The place was just like that *Lad's Army* series on TV, only far worse. Next stop was the barber's. I was sporting a "rat's tail", like a small pigtail, at the back, and I was rather proud of it.

'The barber said: "All right, son. Do you want to keep your rat's tail?"

'I said: "Yes please, guv."

'I heard a *snip* – and off it came. He handed the bit of hair to me, and said: "There you go then." After which he scalped me and left me with no hair at all!

'In my first week I made the mistake of talking in the dinner queue. A screw shouted: "*Get down on your face!*" and ordered me to do 20 press-ups. When I finished I had to do 20 more for some pathetic infringement, like the fact that my feet weren't together. He kept finding excuses to keep me down there and in the end I did 105 press-ups, on the spot. I didn't even get to have my dinner that day.

'It was a tough regime. We scrubbed steps with nail brushes, painted coal, cleaned windows with newspapers. They were trying to break our spirits but they didn't break mine. In the end

I came out as fit as I'd ever been – and not wanting to go back.

'But it taught me something else: I knew I couldn't stop being a rogue – but getting caught was the real crime.

'The most serious offence I have been convicted of was "conspiracy to pervert the course of justice" after an armed robbery because I tried to help out a mate. He had robbed a post office in Eastbourne with a phoney pistol, a replica Colt .45, and made his escape on the back of a moped, of all things. He got away with seven grand – but the stupid berk forgot to change the number plates, so the law were on to him almost before he could get his crash helmet off.

'After he was arrested I went back to his house to get the replica gun so that it couldn't be used in evidence against him. I suppose I felt guilty because he'd told me what he intended to do, and I wasn't able to talk him out of it. He admitted to the crime – and a neighbour saw me coming out of his house, so I was implicated too.

'It cost me 18 months in the Scrubs – and that's when I became a big boy. At that time there were a couple of other prisons where I was banged up as well, for joyriding and stealing cars. Nine months in Norfolk, another time on remand in Reading – where at least I got to meet the film star Stacy Keach when he was in there after being caught with drugs at Heathrow. He ended up serving several months before being released in 1986.

'I got on famously with him. He was a good bloke, very popular with the inmates because he didn't expect any of the "big star" treatment. His only perk was being given the job of projectionist at the Saturday afternoon cinema, which gave the rest of us a huge laugh every weekend.

'I can't remember all the times I've been inside because I've tried to put the past behind me. I know I've done nine prisons, but a lot of that was being moved around the system on remand. Funny thing, somehow I'd always known from the start that I would end up in jail because I laughed at the system. I wouldn't let it beat me. But the fact that I was inside meant it already had, though I only realised it with hindsight.

'I suppose at the time you could call me a career criminal. When I came out of the Scrubs I gave up crime and started dealing in pot full-time. I still don't actually look on that as a crime, apart from the fact that it was against the law! You sold it among your friends, or to people you liked who wanted a smoke. I was never into the hard stuff like heroin or coke, though I did deal in ecstasy once in a while.

'Later I rented a flat near Oxford, on the Cowley Road, and that's when I started getting to know the undergraduates. You know what? I found that at least 70 per cent of them smoked pot. They were always looking for a bit of puff. They're a fine bunch, super people to sell pot to! In the business we call them "joker smokers". You can charge what you like and they never argue because they're not streetwise. These lads were in their second or third year and they wanted to be seen as the cool dudes.

'I'd get a call on my mobile from one of these chaps and go round to the house on a Thursday afternoon where maybe there were seven or eight students under one roof, to see if anyone wanted some hash. I'd find the smartest kid in each house and he'd sell it on to his friends. It was gentleman's dealing, none of it underhand. I'd be invited into the front room and show them the goods, then we'd all sit down together, have a smoke and chill out to some music.

'I lived on my wits. My best scores were the illegal raves in aircraft hangars, warehouses, big barns and open fields. Can you imagine it – 30,000 ravers all having a great time, most of them out of their heads! We were the original "acid house crew" living the underground scene. The revellers were high on pot and ecstasy. The parties attracted drug dealers from all over the country and contacts were made on the spot. No strain, no pain.

'One particular rave in Berkshire I'll never forget. It was in 1988 and began, as usual, after midnight when the word went round. The police tried blocking off the junction to Maidenhead and the whole M4 had a two-mile tailback three lanes wide – total standstill. The party goers were in cars leaning out of the windows with their 1000 watt sound systems pumping out hard bass. The atmosphere was electric, rebellious … everything I loved.

'I had 100 ecstasy pills to get rid of and so did three of my mates. We went walking along the motorway from car to car, selling pills through the windows at 20 quid apiece. We'd paid ten for them. We made £1,000 each in a couple of hours – not bad for a night's work.

'Now? That's all in the past. I met Sarah at the Glastonbury Festival in 1994, saw her, fell for her on the spot, and went up and kissed her. Just like that. We never looked back. From that moment I stopped dealing. It was all down to her.

'She said to me: "I love, you, but I'm not a gangster's moll."

'"That's fine with me," I told her – and I've gone straight ever since. I wasn't born bad. All my life I was always trying to give myself a fresh start. Now I've got it and I intend to keep it that way.'

Mark stopped talking. His coffee had gone cold. I switched off the tape while he went out to the kitchen for a fresh mug. While he was out of the room I thought about all he had said. It made sense and it had the ring of truth about it.

I had indeed intended to take out a warrant to search his home. The authorities had just announced a huge increase in the amount of drugs smuggled into the country: in the first six months of the year, drugs that would have sold to users for more than £35 million were seized at three British airports alone – an increase of 25 per cent on the previous six months.

The message was clear and disturbing: the drug culture was

up and running, and Mark had been in there carving his own small niche. Or maybe not so small. By the time Mark came to my attention, drug trafficking was on the increase across the world. According to a 1990 report by the G7 Financial Action Task Force, made up of representatives from the seven leading industrial countries, sales of cannabis, heroin and cocaine were worth around $122 billion per year in Europe and the USA alone. Compare this with the value of tobacco products sold in the UK the previous year – $16 billion – and you get an idea of the scale of the trade.

A word about search warrants. I was planning to act when the time was right, but there are rules about breaking into anyone's privacy and they have to be obeyed or you'll know all about it in court later. Search warrants are actually two documents, both of which have to be signed by a local Justice of the Peace. One is the warrant itself, which gets the police through the door legally and by whatever means necessary. The other is called 'the Information' and outlines the reason for requiring a warrant. It is retained by the magistrate who has put his signature on it.

Every police station has a list of magistrates authorised to sign, and you can 'go grab' a warrant, to use the vernacular, 24 hours a day – even if it means getting their worships out of bed to oblige. Many is the time I had found myself in the living room of a magistrate's home in the early hours swearing on a dictionary because there was no Bible handy, that the 'information contained herein is basically the truth'.

The power to search a premises for controlled drugs (Class A, B and C) is provided under S.23(2) Misuse of Drugs Act 1971. Search warrants issued under this section are different from all other warrants in that they can be executed at any time within one month of the date of issue. The exact wording on the warrant is very complicated, and never seems to quite make sense, even to me:

'Authority is hereby given for any Constable, accompanied by such person or persons as are necessary for the purposes of the search, to enter the said premises on one occasion only within one month from the date of issue of this warrant, and to search for the articles or persons in respect of which the above application is made on one occasion within one month from the date of this warrant to enter, if need be by force, the premises herein and to search them and persons found therein and if there is reasonable ground for suspecting that an offence under the Misuse of Drugs Act, 1971, has been committed in relation to any controlled drugs found on the premises or in the possession of such persons, to seize and detain those drugs.' Along with the suspects, of course.

Normally we apply for these warrants at the local Magistrates Court. Though Mark Winch lived in the Thames Valley region, after persuading a senior officer that a warrant was needed to spin his place, I'd have obtained it locally in London, most probably at Bow Street Magistrates Court or Horseferry Road Magistrates Court.

Mark came back into the room with his coffee. I switched on the machine and leaned forward for the part of the story I'd driven three hours to hear.

CHAPTER 14

ON THE RUN

'OK, Mark,' I said, 'I know all about you. So tell me all about who you met in Goa, and how you met him. And this time I'm going to ask questions.'

The session went on for the best part of an hour. The following is the transcript:

Q: How did you come to pick Goa?

A: I left in a hurry and you know why. It was December 1991. Insiders in the business had a saying: 'The "Who's Who" in the drugs fraternity spend Christmas Day on Goa beach.' It was a known fact that the really big boys, the cream of the cream, all took their Christmas holidays out there in the sun. I thought: I'm one of them. So why not? I'll join them! And I did. I even had the name of the place to make for: Ximera, a border shanty town on the coast. That's where it all happened.

And you know something? The grapevine was right! The place was buzzing. I tell you, it was one big party on 25 December, with everyone in the beach bars passing spliffs round like there was no tomorrow. I met a few faces I knew and some I didn't. I was proud to be one of them – spending Christmas Day on the beach!

Q: How did you get there, and what did you live on?

A: I had enough dope money on me to stay a year if I'd wanted, around £2,000 in hard currency. Out there you can live like a king for 30 quid a week. In the end I would stay for just seven weeks.

I knew through the grapevine that this would be a safe place to hang out while the heat died down at home. I'd got a visa within 72 hours, and took off from Heathrow to Bombay with just a rucksack and a few clothes I'd slung in. I knew it was going to be hot out there, around 80 degrees every day, so I travelled light. I looked like a student and played the part to the hilt. I even had my pocket backgammon board with me.

This was long before the days of tourism, remember. With me was my mate 'Gentleman Jim', a guy in his fifties who operated as a mule in the drug game. He was a seasoned rogue who took the stuff from country to country and was paid handsomely for the risk. To look at him you'd think he was a real gent, hence his nickname. And he was the type no one was likely to suspect. Sadly, Jim's no longer with us. But he was great company.

It was a long haul to Bombay but once we'd taken off from Heathrow I heaved a huge sigh of relief and knew I'd got away with it. I was clean, anyway. No drugs on me, just a big wedge of notes which would be useful for bribing anyone who asked awkward questions. I'd heard that's the way things get done in that part of the world.

Q: How did you find your way to Ximera?

A: Jim and I took a creaky old bus from Bombay all the way down the coastal highway to Calangute, which is now a popular tourist spot. The neighbouring village is Candolim, and Ximera is in no-man's-land, on the border between them. The bus took 24 hours. It's a distance of around 400 miles, the roads were rough and the whole area looked like a good place to lose yourself. The driver also had to avoid the odd sacred cow at all costs unless he wanted to get lynched.

When we finally trundled in to the terminus, we were so stiff we could hardly move. Our first sight was a massive elephant with half a dozen guys in orange robes walking alongside it. They were in the main street within feet of the stalls and the shops. The noise was unbelievable. Hooting cars and taxis, bicycles with their bells ringing – it never stops. I felt that if I wasn't stepped on by that elephant I'd be run down by a scooter!

We headed for the beach and set off on foot along the sands. We walked for about a mile, asking the locals if they had any huts for rent. The beaches in Goa today are wonderful if you're on holiday. But if you're not it's nothing but sand, scrub and jungle, with the occasional sandy track leading off inland into the bushes. There were no signs of beach umbrellas or sun loungers, just the odd primitive bamboo bar – the tourists were all down south and this was up the coast north from the capital, Panjim, virtually unexplored territory.

Neither of us had any idea where we'd end up. But after walking for over a mile along the beach we came across a group of hippies sitting around on the sand smoking pot. I asked them if we were near Candolim. They looked spaced out but one guy jerked a thumb inland. I looked at Jim. 'Come on. Let's try it.'

We followed a track up through the bushes and cactus into the jungle until we came upon a few ramshackle buildings dotted around a clearing. The first decent shack we stumbled on belonged to Connie, a motherly woman who was scrubbing out clothes on a washboard on her porch. She rented out about a dozen rooms to the few adventurous travellers who came her way, but the place bore a strong resemblance to a hippie commune with the rooms set out in pairs which she rented out for next to nothing. The rooms were basic, each having its own veranda. I decided to hang a hammock on mine for some quality relaxation as the beds were hard as rock. Inside, all they had was a bed, a cupboard and a small window. No washbasin, no running water, no shower, no loo, but at least there was a fan in the ceiling. To brighten my room up I decorated it with locally bought batik pictures, a woollen Kashmir tapestry and a beautiful Indian silk carpet depicting the Tree of Life. I bought the carpet in Bombay for £120. It had 800 stitches per square inch which gave it amazing detail and when I returned home I had it valued at £800 by a local expert. I added brightly coloured throws to the bed and placed sandalwood carvings on every available surface which gave the room a lovely aroma. During my stay, I added to this with other ornaments which I intended to take home as gifts for my friends and family.

The commune was just a scattering of shacks in the jungle. There were about a dozen of us, mostly backpackers who came and went all the time. We'd sit around in different rooms, talking, drinking and smoking. But never in Connie's house, which was a proper home, simple but comfortable, where she brought up her family. We respected her privacy.

I never bothered to find out Connie's other name, but her smile was brilliant and she was so warm and welcoming that I knew instantly: *this is for me!* She let us have a room for 100 rupees a day, which was worth about £2 in those days. Today the rate is more than 70 to the pound, so a tourist does much better on the exchange rate. The economy is crazy anyway and everything changes from day to day.

The place was really primitive. Washing hung out between the trees, open fires smouldering, small children running around barefoot. There were wild pigs rooting in the undergrowth but not dangerous and not very big animals either.

They just cleaned the place up! We had to have 'bucket showers' – all the water came from a well 50 metres away that everyone used, and we'd drag up a bucket and empty it over our heads! Sometimes Connie and her family would make a human chain and fill up a water butt where we could help ourselves. Or we simply went into the sea, down the track 100 metres away.

Q: What about other facilities? It all sounds terribly basic.

A: It was. Going to the loo was something else. We used a 'pig toilet' – I'd never heard of them but there are thousands of them all over India. You've never experienced anything like it. There's no water to flush with – you just leave it to the pigs. They keep it very clean.

Q: What was the atmosphere like?

A: There was a wonderful feeling of freedom in the air – as well as the smell of marijuana. That smell is so thick you can reach out and grab a handful of it! The place was full of hippies, many of them from the flower-power generation back-packing through India. They would spend their evenings sitting around camp fires playing guitars, or in beach shacks with the music of three generations filling the air, creating a wonderful ambience, before going on to Nepal to sample the world's finest hash known as 'Temple Ball', or down to Kerala in Southern India to smoke the grass. Some of them would buy local crafts, silks or even drugs to finance the next leg of their journey as they bummed around the world. Many European Buddhists would travel down from Nepal for the Indian summer, meditating at dawn and dusk and searching for inner self-awareness. One phrase somebody said stuck in my mind: 'The difference between a wise man and a clever man is that a clever man can get himself out of situations that a wise man would never get into!'

Nobody cared who or what you were, or asked awkward questions. There was no sign of the police, but I had my passport with me and I didn't think Interpol was after me. It was just a great place to chill out and I was on a high all day, every day.

This is the way the man called Barry had lived for almost 20 years when I met him.

CHAPTER 15

ENTER 'JUNGLE BARRY'

Q: So, how did you meet this 'Barry'?
A: I first set eyes on Barry when he challenged me to a game of backgammon. On the second morning I was sitting by myself on the porch with my magnetic set in front of me, when this tall man with long hair and a beard, very tanned and wearing only a pair of shorts and sandals, appeared from nowhere. I put his age at around the late fifties, though the beard made him look as old as Father Time. My first thought was: where the hell did this guy come from?

Connie introduced us. 'Mark, this is Barry. He's in the room next to you.' She gave her infectious laugh. 'We call him Jungle Barry! That's where he came from.'

The hermit-like figure nodded gravely in my direction but did not proffer his hand. He was occupying a room on the end of one hut, nearest the main house. He also had a habit of moving very quietly and unobtrusively. I noticed he was carrying a bottle of the local Honey Bee brandy and it was still only just after breakfast. He was always just 'Barry'. If he had a surname, he never used it.

Fair enough. I immediately gave him the nickname of 'Barry the Wildebeest' because of his appearance, though I kept the thought to myself. I was looking at Goa's answer to Grizzly Adams! To outward appearances, he looked like a tramp. But in fact he was very fastidious about personal hygiene. He even used to clean his nails with a small piece of wood.

The first thing he said was: 'I'll play you for a drink! Beer money…'

Beer money? Barry drank more than beer. He started before breakfast with Honey Bee brandy and Kingfisher beer, then moved on to the local firewater called *feni*, fermented coconut juice, quite colourless, but 180 proof and with a kick like a mule. I tried a sip, and it made my eyes water. After that I stuck to beer.

'OK,' I told him. 'Let's play!' And from then on we played three or four times a week. Barry was very good. But I'm pretty hot too, so we always had a close game.

His voice was cultured, rather gruff through the beard, but quite distinctive. As I got to know him, I found a lot of inconsistencies about him. Of course, I had no idea who he might be or what he might have done. When the Lucan business happened I was only nine years old, and I'd never even heard the name.

Q: Did he tell you how long he'd been there and where he came from?

A: Yes. It was one of the first questions I asked and that was one he didn't seem to mind. It's the sort of innocent thing you'd ask anyone, isn't it? 'Seventeen years,' he said. Not 'almost 20' or 'more than 15'. He was quite specific. That would make it 1975. As for where he came from, all he said was: 'Ireland.' Then he clammed up and I didn't press him any further.

Over the next seven weeks I saw Barry almost every day. Sometimes he would stay in his room not speaking to anyone. Other times he would emerge to join us all on the main veranda, where Connie would serve meals for anyone who wanted them. It was all very free and easy and she served up marvellous chicken curry, which I've been hooked on ever since. In return we'd give her a few rupees, if we had them.

Those who didn't have any money to spare would help out around the place, chopping wood or repairing things that needed fixing. But mostly people spent the time sitting around a big banyan tree drinking beer, strumming guitars, smoking pot and talking the hours away in a haze of cannabis. All the blokes hired Enfield Bullet motorbikes and rode around in shorts while the hippie chicks shopped at Anjuna market for all the colourful silk sarongs.

Q: Wasn't Barry out of place in that company?

A: Barry was certainly the oldest in the commune. He was old enough to be everyone's father, but he was accepted as part of the group. Sometimes when he sat with us he would stay in his shell not speaking for hours, but that was OK too. You just did your own thing and people left you alone.

Barry would go for a daily swim in the surf. When I saw him on the beach I couldn't help thinking of Robinson Crusoe – he looked just like a castaway! But when he threw back his head and laughed at something, it was with the air of a confident, authoritative man, and a completely new personality emerged.

If we were at Connie's we used my pocket backgammon board. But I'd also find him in Bob's Inn, his favourite hangout – 'My second home,' he'd call it – half a mile inland on the main road from Panjim to Calangute. Every bar in

Goa has a backgammon set for the customers and Bob kept a board behind the counter. Barry would bring it out and sit with it in front of him, challenging anyone to play. Just like I used to do back in Slough in my other life.

There was a long table where all the regulars used to sit. It could take around 16 people. Barry would be there in the middle, holding court when he was in the mood to anyone who would listen. Other times he just sat there nursing his glass, staring into space.

Whenever I won I chalked it up on a slate and wiped it off later because Barry had no money. When *he* won, I'd give him rupees for a bottle of Honey Bee, which he really enjoyed. It's a special kind of brandy, very smooth with a honey flavour and you can get through half a bottle before you know it. The stuff was also dirt cheap – less than a pound a bottle in those days.

Often when he lost he'd call out: 'Double or quits!' and keep going until he won. Typical gambler! He used to say to me: 'Have you got the gambling dice?' These are special dice with the numbers 2, 4, 8, 16, 32, 64 on them and it's a very quick way of losing money. I never carried gambling dice because I didn't like the odds. But if you're playing back-gammon it makes the game more exciting. It changes the odds dramatically – and raises the stakes. It gave me an insight into Barry's character. Here was a real high roller!

We also played cribbage and since we didn't have a board I'd write out the moves on a notepad. It worked all right. He was good at that, too. But my granddad taught me cribbage when I was a kid, so I could more than hold my own.

I learned later that when Barry first arrived the road was only a dirt track. In fact the first shack he stayed in had been with Mama Cecilia, one of the legendary figures of the area. Everyone knew Mama, and her restaurant-bar, Cecilia's, was the first to open down on the beach at the end of the track. I met her a couple of times but only when I dropped in to her bar for a beer.

I soon found that Bob's Inn was the place where all the dealers gathered. There were some nasty people in there. The local pot was crap – 'camel shit' we used to call it. Smoking was a huge culture and the drug runners were bringing in excellent stuff. The place was a transit camp for drug smugglers bringing gear in from the north – Tibet, 'Afghanistan Black' grass from the border, hash from Kashmir. Other stuff from Thailand, Cambodia and Malaysia to the east. It was all coming through.

The guys in that bar would pass spliffs around like there was no tomorrow. They were all ages and they came from all over the world. I met villains from the Middle East, Europe, Russia, from everywhere. I met kids from California and backpackers from Australia and Scandinavia.

I'd often join in with the younger backpackers who would spend their evenings partying on the beach all night, dancing to rave, trance and European techno music till sunrise before going on to Nepal to sample the world's finest hash – known as 'Temple Ball' – or down to Kerala in southern India to smoke grass. In those days everybody smoked. If you didn't you'd be ostracised. Unless you were part of the circle, that was *it*. They could smell a suspicious stranger a mile away, and make it clear he wasn't welcome.

I was proud to be accepted as one of them. Like I say, spending Christmas Day on the beach was a high and a memory I'll never forget! Nobody asked me any questions. Nobody cared – or if they did they kept their thoughts to themselves.

Barry was part of the inner circle, though I have to say that I never saw him smoke. I'm told he did take the odd puff when it was handed to him, just to be sociable, nothing more. But everyone had accepted him by then anyway. He had nothing to fear because he was part of the furniture. All he liked was to drink. He was pissed out of his head most of the day, drinking himself to death, and no one was going to stop him. Maybe he was just bored.

He had a taste for music and when he was drunk enough he'd produce a flute or a guitar and start playing them to entertain the crowd. He was actually rather good.

After a morning drinking session with us, Barry would suddenly say: 'I'm off for my afternoon nap!' Nobody else ever used that word. He had a certain dignity about him as he disappeared off into his room or stretched out on a bench or on a rug on the stone porch. He'd be out like a light. At other times he would fall asleep in a drunken stupor in his rocking chair on the porch and stay there for hours.

For the first few weeks I was careful not to photograph anyone, Barry included. I could have got myself into serious trouble, especially around Bob's bar. But one day, when I'd been there more than a month and felt I was part of the scene myself, I took out my camera and fired off a couple of shots of Barry with the group, purely for my scrapbook. It was a Canon Sureshot – nothing special.

Suddenly he looked up and saw me. 'Put that bloody camera away, will you?' he said sharply. He was really annoyed. Then he stomped off to his room and slumped into his rocking chair on the porch and passed out. Because of what Barry had said to me in front of everyone, I thought I'd take the piss out of him. So – *click!* I took a shot of him and got the picture of a lifetime without even realising it.

Q: Did Barry have any other way of making money apart from gambling?

A: There were a couple of times when he disappeared for three or four days, taking tourists on foot into the jungle to earn himself an extra crust. He called them his 'jungle safaris'.

I never went with him. Some of them told me afterwards how they stayed in rest houses along the way in the villages and ended up sleeping on rocks under a waterfall. Barry charged 200 rupees a trip – plus 'expenses'. This was a joke. Expenses meant stopping in every bar along the way. The treks became Barry's pub crawl! But the man had immense knowledge of the local area because of the years he had been there.

Q: You had seven weeks with this man Barry in the jungle. How well did you get to know him?

A: Over our games of backgammon, he started to unwind – though not much. We talked about all sorts of things. He was extremely knowledgeable about some of the cultural aspects of England, which for a guy living in the jungle I felt was quite unusual.

I have a passion for cars myself and he could talk about Bugattis, Lagondas and Bentleys like an expert. Where his knowledge came from, I couldn't say – then.

He was quite happy to chat about general things, but if I started probing too deeply he would just tighten his lips and say nothing. Occasionally I asked him questions out of sheer curiosity, like: 'Tell me, Barry, what's a bloke like you doing here?' Always he'd give me a cryptic answer, or simply evade the question. He never actually said: 'Mind your own business!'

Barry was obviously a highly educated person and had a very good vocabulary. He liked word play and I remember one curious expression – he always used the word 'motion' before heading off for the pig toilet! Like: 'Excuse me, I'm off for a motion!'

If I became too curious, he'd clam up. Not rudely, just change the subject or stop talking altogether. But once, over the backgammon board when he'd got through almost a bottle of Honey Bee, I asked him outright: 'Are you on the run?' I know a fugitive when I see one, people on the dodge – I've met a few in the past.

Barry stopped playing, paused for a long moment, then replied: 'Isn't everybody?'

I said: 'Well, to a certain degree.' I was thinking of the Yard breathing down my neck at the time. The thought crossed my mind that he might be one of the Great Train Robbers. There was something not quite right.

'Where are your family from, Barry?'

And the evasive answer: 'I don't have a family.'

One odd thing he said that has stuck in my mind all these years was when I asked: 'What did you do in the days back home?'

He stared at me fixedly for a long time and finally replied: 'I am an historian.'

Somehow it was rather poignant the way he said it. I pursued it: 'What do you mean, historian? Are you a curator? Did you work in a library?'

He said: 'No. I am part of history!'

I never found out any more. But I can hear him saying those words to this day.

Q: Physically, what was his condition?

A: I can tell you that Barry was a fit man, even at that stage of his life. He had actually learned to climb coconut trees! Not the towering 60-foot trunks, but smaller ones where the fruit is in clusters 20 feet above the ground. I only saw him do it once but he shinned up this tree like a man going up a telegraph pole – with his ankles tied together with rope and a machete in his belt.

Coconut trees are often curved and this one gave him no problems. He took it slowly, using gashes that had been carved out of the trunk like steps to help him climb. Then he chopped the coconuts off their stalks and they were caught by some kids below. We all applauded him when he climbed down again and he took a bow like a music-hall entertainer.

We were all hugely impressed. I remember saying to him: 'Christ, Barry! You really have gone native!' He just smiled – and handed me a coconut.

Q: Did he have a sense of humour?

A: I'd say Barry had a dry sense of humour. He liked puns and would come out with them when you least expected it. There was a curious mix about him of someone who wanted to be among people and yet remained a loner, never really giving himself away.

Q: What about his possessions?

A: He had absolutely nothing. As far as I was aware, all he owned were the clothes he wore – and a watch. I never saw anything else, though he may have had a few belongings in his room. He also had a walking stick, which he used for beating a path through the undergrowth or waving at the odd wild dog.

Q: When did you finally come back?

A: I gave it seven weeks and by February 1992 I'd had enough. Every day was in the nineties and frankly I was getting bored out of my skull just sitting around drinking and smoking. How Barry stuck it for so long I'll never know. There was nothing else to do except go for a swim or walk on the beach for a bit of exercise. I felt the coast would probably be clear back home and I thought I'd chance it and make sure I kept out of trouble. I still had £1,000 in my pocket – and I reckon I'd been overspending. Most of it on grass.

Q: When was the last time you saw Barry?

A: I got a taxi to Goa airport. My final view of Barry as I headed away from the shacks was of him sitting in his rocking chair on his porch, just the way I'd photographed him. He waved a hand but he didn't call out goodbye. That's the last I saw of him and that's how I'll always remember him.

Mark finished speaking. I switched off the tape recorder and put my notebook away. It was time to go. There were more questions to be asked – and answered – plus a lot of digging to do before I reached the stage where the next logical step would be to fly out to Goa for an on-the-spot investigation.

For the moment I had a lot to think about.

CHAPTER 16

TRUE OR FALSE?

I stared unseeingly at the passing countryside, driving on automatic pilot, my brain seething with the ramifications and possibilities of all I'd learned since leaving home that morning. I had deliberately taken the long, slow route home, using the A roads rather than the monotony of the M1. I needed time to think, time to get everything in proportion. Calm down, Duncan!

First and foremost, I wanted to believe it. That was the trap. Wishful thinking. I recognised it and that recognition made me extra cautious about jumping to any conclusions. Of course, Lord Lucan could be long dead, either through suicide or at the hands of a hit man he could have hired to do the job for him of killing his wife. The first went totally against his nature. From everything I'd gleaned, he was far too self-important and absorbed a character, as well as being too fastidious, to take the necessary steps to end his own life. The second was surely too remote and far-fetched a possibility to even consider.

As the years passed and the elusive earl became a figure of

folklore, many of my former colleagues had become more and more convinced that the quarry had stayed alive and gone to ground with some imaginative subterfuge to hide him from discovery. I could buy that.

So what did I really think about Mark's story? Either it was true or it wasn't. There were a number of intriguing options open. And each one would have to be investigated thoroughly before I did anything dramatic and headed out for India.

First, was Mark Winch telling the truth? Or was he a raving fantasist who simply wanted to get his name in the papers? Like any seeming contradiction in terms, his story was so incredible I felt it had to be true.

The timing was tantalisingly close if the dates were correct. I would have to pin down the exact time that this man Barry materialised in Goa, because Mark hadn't pushed him that far. The backgammon was a massive plus factor. So was the cultured voice, the man's deportment, his whole manner and bearing – as well as his secretiveness and the fact that the only time he'd shown any agitation, indeed the only sign he'd shown of having strong feelings about anything in the weeks he and Mark had reportedly lived side by side, was when he realised his photo had been taken.

And the things he had said, if Mark had reported them accurately. 'Take an afternoon nap', '*an* historian'. This was no illiterate tramp. Or his 'cultural knowledge' and the animated discussions on the merits of Bugattis and Bentleys.

As for the physical proof itself – were the photographs real or fake? Could Mark have doctored the prints, digitally enhancing them to back up his entire fabrication? No, because before I left I had asked to see the negatives and examined them under a magnifying glass. Unless there is some amazing new technique hitherto unknown, negatives can't lie. And as any lawyer will tell you, the most unreliable witness in a court of law is not a man who is lying but one who honestly believes he is telling the truth and is mistaken.

Presuming that 'Jungle Barry' existed, was he still alive? Ten years had passed. If he was and I found him, how could I positively identify him as Lucan? The surest way would be a DNA test to be compared with a blood sample from his son Lord George Bingham, or from one or other of his daughters. But that would require their cooperation. Would they play ball knowing that it would almost certainly reopen the whole sordid can of worms? Or would they resolutely insist on letting the ghosts and scandals of the past remain undisturbed? That is, of course, assuming that their father was wholly a figure from the past for them and that their last contact had been on 7 November 1974, rather than someone they'd regularly travelled to visit in the ensuing 28 years, as some camps had always believed.

There is a difference between evidence and proof and I was well aware of it. Proof would be a DNA sample, a fingerprint or possibly handwriting comparison with a letter from Lucan – like the one to his friend Michael Stoop – that would be on file at the Yard. Although writing can be forged, it's tough to fool an expert in the field.

Personally speaking, I had my own reputation to think of. Even today there are still between 50 and 60 'sightings' of the errant earl logged at the Yard from all over the world each year. The body of evidence would have to be as conclusive as was humanly possible.

But juries can and do convict if the evidence is so persuasive that they have no doubt in their minds as to the guilt of the accused. In this case the public, as well as my former colleagues, would be both judge and jury.

Of course, bringing in Lord Lucan, alive or dead, would be a crowning achievement for any investigator. That potential, coupled with my gut feeling about the details Mark had just provided, were good enough for me to know I wanted to follow the trail.

Back home I poured myself a drink and sat down to collect my thoughts. Mountains of paperwork had built up around the Lucan mystery since 1974 and as the years went by the slopes became steeper. In 1992 he would have been 58. Today he would still be under 70 and could easily be alive. My pulse rate quickened again.

If Lucan had reinvented himself and lived so successfully for almost 20 years before Mark crossed his path, there was no reason why he could not still be living out his audacious charade, safe in the camouflage of his jungle lair. There was the aspiring actor in him that would have relished the challenge – hadn't he once seen himself as James Bond and even auditioned for the part?

Something nagged at the corner of my memory. Police training gives you a number of skills which you can put to good use in everyday life: a methodical way of doing things, endless patience, a tidy mind and a sharp eye for detail. I had all these and I was proud of them. My brain cells started whirring, struggling to make the connection.

Lucan ... India ... Eddie Irvine ... that's it! Now it all came flooding back. Throughout the eighties and nineties one of my 'Formula One' informants, known by the pseudonym Eddie Irvine, had been active on the London social scene. She was a regular at parties in and around Mayfair, Kensington and Chelsea, rubbing expensive shoulders with the smart set. Yes, my Eddie was a woman, and a very useful one too. She had furnished titbits of information on Lucky Lucan's friends in the past, so much so that I was instructed by a senior detective attached to Specialist Operations at the Yard and who held the Lucan file to encourage my source to dig deeper.

In July 1996, included in a verbal report to me regarding the movements of an LA-based international drug dealer, Eddie had added a brief comment that Lucan's bolt hole 'was believed to be in Southern India, where he had settled'. Very general, nothing specific. But ... he had also 'received regular visitors' from the UK, as well as 'financial aid'. I passed this piece of information on as part of an official report to the department at Scotland Yard holding the Lucan file and awaited developments. There were none. The report was filed, and forgotten. Rightly or wrongly, however, I kept a copy.

Strangely, India as a destination had never been on the list of Lucan sightings. In fact Goa remained conspicuous by its absence on the world map of these. On impulse, I checked the Internet. And there, tucked away amid page after page of Lucan memorabilia, a name I recognised from the afternoon's tale sprang out: 'Bob's Inn, a well known travellers' hangout. Apparently Lord Lucan was spotted here.' Just one line mentioning a possible sighting and that was that. Christ! I thought. Could the snippets of information truly be turning into gold nuggets?

I reached for a second Scotch, downed it and headed for bed. It had been a long day and my head was spinning. My last thought before I drifted off into an exhausted sleep was that, when it came to Jungle Barry, even my personal jury of one was still out.

The next week I started making my preliminary enquiries.

It took three months before I was ready for the big move because I still had my full-time job. This involved trips to Dubai and various parts of the Far East, none of them day returns. Summer came and went. But every spare minute that I had was put to good use on research, and on creating my own special file on the missing earl.

I studied the Internet, printing off page after page of information, a lot of it spurious and repetitive. I went to newspaper archives and buried myself in volumes of cuttings, finding isolated factors that had been passed over as unimportant suddenly taking on new significance. I pored over the psychological profiles of both Lord and Lady Lucan. This last was particularly illuminating.

Two phrases from the three letters Lucan wrote immediately following the dreadful events of 7 November 1974 stood out. The letter to his friend Michael Stoop ended: 'When they [the children] are old enough to understand, explain to them the dream of paranoia, and look after them. Yours ever, John.' Now just what, if anything, did he mean by this flowery, almost romantic language? 'Dream of paranoia'. To what could it refer? He had also mentioned how: 'A crooked solicitor and a rotten psychiatrist destroyed me between them.'

And the other phrase, in one of the letters to Bill Shand Kydd? 'I will also lie doggo for a bit.' Both letters were written on the same night. Both, presumably, when Lucan was in a state of some shock since everything had gone so disastrously wrong for him.

Put the two together, and what do we come up with? Lucan had tried the legal road to recover his children from his wife. He'd gone through the courts and failed. All he had to show for the exercise was a bill for £40,000, total lack of funds to meet it and what appeared to be delusions of persecution that inflamed his mind to the brink of insanity.

Paranoia is generally a hopeless affliction from the point of view of recovery. As has been frequently stated, the subjects of most forms of paranoia are liable to commit crime, usually of violence, which may lead to their being tried for assault or murder.

Perhaps the studies on mental illness found in Lucan's basement flat had been for him as much an aid in understanding his own state of mind as in providing information about his wife's condition. Initially everyone had assumed it was the second.

And 'lie doggo for a bit'. Those were hardly the words of a person intending to commit suicide. To me it sounded more like a person planning to flee to a place of relative seclusion where he could lie low and wait for the storm to pass before deciding on his next move. And he'd have been planning, of course, on a storm that could take months or even years to blow itself out.

The 'dream of paranoia' could take him to the farthest corner of the globe to evade his tormentors. Intriguing. You didn't have to be Freud or Jung to deduce that here was a disturbed mind desperate for an avenue of escape. But to which point of the compass did he head?

Questions and more questions. I tracked down no fewer than seven books written over the years: *Trail of Havoc: In the Steps of Lord Lucan* by Patrick Marnham, *The Troops of Midian: The Story Behind Lord Lucan's Escape* by 'Richard Wilmott' (an amalgamation of several writers and researchers), *Lord Lucan: What Really Happened?* by James Ruddick, *Looking for Lucan: The Final Verdict* by Roy Ranson, *Lucan: Not Guilty* by Sally Moore, *The Lucan Mystery* by Norman Lucas and *Lucan Lives* by David Gerring. All with a genuine desire to get at the truth, all with one thing in common: a lot of fascinating and plausible theory, but nothing tangible. No real proof. Above all, with no body and no photographic evidence to support the speculation. I hoped to provide both.

As for Lady Lucan, I found to my surprise that she has a website (www.ladylucan.co.uk) and an e-mail address which anyone can access: countessoflucan@eudoramail.com. Part of the site reveals the bitterness she still feels towards the Lucan family: 'The extraordinary behaviour of my blood relations in supporting a belief in my late husband's innocence, and attempting to cast doubt on my sworn evidence and somehow portraying me as the offending party, has been confirmed to me by members of the media who have interviewed them. It was, however, to be expected that my late husband's rather uncivilised blood relations would make futile attempts to clear his name. No informed people believe the 7th Earl to be alive. I have publicly stated since 1987 that my late husband is not alive, and I sometimes use the prefix "dowager" to make my position clear, which is that of a widow.'

In 1994, talking directly about the murder, she was quoted as saying: 'It was purely about money. He was about to go bankrupt, and he had to save the family reputation. The only way he could do that was either to win a terrific amount at the tables, or to get hold of the house and sell it as fast as he could. Since I was firmly in place he had to get rid of me. It was a calculated act. There was no personal feeling involved.'

And, significantly, she declared in a recent interview: 'My husband was a heavy drinker who would surely have been dead now even if he hadn't disappeared at the bottom of the Channel.' She added, in a website posted on 13 May 2003: 'As far as I know, there was no DNA of my husband's available, and even his blood group was not known.'

If my investigation turned up the evidence I hoped it would turn up, what on earth would Lady Lucan say when I showed her the pictures of her husband that were currently burning a hole in my office safe, Mark having by now entrusted them to my possession? Now in her sixties, the poor woman had for so long clung doggedly to her belief that he was dead that it would be hard for her to come to terms with his new identity. Well, that could wait. There was a heap more digging to do.

The thought that my quarry could be somewhere out there in a lawless enclave in the jungle was simultaneously frustrating, tantalising and a little scary. It was enough to keep me permanently on edge and I was hard put not to jump on the next flight to Goa. Not only was the thought of conclusively solving one of the world's greatest mysteries compelling me, the possibility that someone else could stumble on the truth after all the legwork I'd done was downright maddening. But I held myself in check while the dossier grew thicker by the day and I began to feel that I was getting to know Lord Lucan almost as well as he had known himself.

There was gold dust in the archives, waiting to be panned and sifted by an energetic prospector. I unearthed a photograph of Lucan taken on one of the Venice canals during a holiday. The picture showed the earl lying back in a gondola, smiling and relaxed, while a gondolier serenaded him from the stern. (At the time of writing, this picture is available for inspection on Lady Lucan's website.)

But my eyes went straight to his hands – and the scar clearly visible below the knuckle of the little finger on his right hand. The next step was one phone call away – to a friendly scientist I'd kept in touch with from my days in the Drugs Squad. John (not his real name) agreed to see me in the Met's forensic science laboratory in Lambeth 'after hours'. With rising excitement I took the two photographs with me, the one taken in Venice and one of Mark's pictures showing Jungle Barry on the porch, and laid them out on his desk.

My tame boffin set up both pictures on a large screen, side by side, homed in on the hands to enlarge them ten times over, and spent several minutes comparing them minutely. Finally he looked up, and nodded.

'You've got it,' he said. 'They're the same.'

The scar on Lord Lucan's hand was identical to the mark on the hand of the man in the rocking chair.

CHAPTER 17

IF THE FACE FITS...

It was time to bring in the heavyweights. Identikit drawings are all very well, and in the immediate aftermath of a murder or a terrorist atrocity serve to jog the public memory. An artist's impression of the 'Have You Seen This Man?' kind certainly produces results, just as *Crimewatch* scores so highly on television.

But when it comes to a legal identification, we are swimming in deeper waters. I needed the services of a forensic anthropologist, those academics who specialise in human identification and are called on to give evidence in criminal trials and coroner's courts. Basically this means they dig up bodies and help the police to try to put a name to them. They tend to use long words like 'morphological' (which relates to the biological study of the form and structure of organisms) but their experience in this complex area is invaluable.

When it came to photographs and a forensic artist's evaluation, I knew who to approach. Professor Sue Black, OBE,

BSc, PhD, DSc is an extraordinary person. She currently holds the impressive title of Professor of Anatomy and Forensic Anthropology at Dundee University.

Sue Black was awarded an OBE for her work in Kosovo in 2002 with the British forensic team. The last I heard of her, she was out somewhere in the scrub and desert of Iraq, employed by the CPA (Coalition Provisional Authority) and our Foreign Office, with the grisly task of examining mass graves that had been found after the 2003 conflict, and dispensing her services for the US and British military as Director of the Centre for International Forensic Assistance.

With 22 years' experience at the sharp end, Professor Black has worked for the British government, various European and other countries' governmental and police forces, as well as for the United Nations and in alliance with the FBI. In other words, this is one special lady, with a book inside her that must surely be written some day – when she has the time.

Our paths had crossed occasionally, and I had the utmost respect for her opinions. The story I like best about Sue concerns the mission she was on in Sierra Leone. It was a war crimes investigation into the deaths of four UN soldiers, two from Nigeria and two from Zambia, who had been involved in a firefight at Rogberi Junction. A witness had said that the soldiers had had their hands tied behind their backs. If they had been shot with their hands bound, it was a war crime and not a war death. If the ruthless rebels responsible had simply slung the corpses on a pole by tying their hands to take them back to camp or for some similar reason, then it would not qualify as a war crime.

Professor Black's job was to go in with her six-strong team of forensic experts and examine the bodies *in situ*. Because of the volatile situation, with an unseen enemy close by, she was escorted by a contingent from the Indian Army to guard the possible crime scene and provide security. The rebels at the time would have loved to gain a British hostage, and for that hostage to have been female would have been even more satisfactory for them.

The troops fanned out to form a wide protective circle in the jungle so she could get on with her work. There was intermittent gunfire. Sue and her team worked throughout the morning, keeping their heads low. Beyond the soldiers was a second outer 'ring of steel', comprising helicopter gunships strafing the jungle to discourage the rebels from coming anywhere near the team that was working literally under fire. It didn't take long. Within a few hair-raising hours they established that they had been tied up *after* their death – and thus that it was not classified a war crime. Professor Black and her team earned their stripes that day.

I e-mailed her four of Mark's photographs, along with half a dozen file pictures of Lord Lucan taken on a tour of Italy, and waited for results. I didn't have long to hold my breath. Two weeks later a buff envelope dropped through my letterbox.

Professor Black's report was comprehensive, to say the least. It came in four sections:

'*Introduction*: I was contacted by Mr Duncan MacLaughlin regarding some archived photographs of a missing person and more recent images of a person believed to be one and the same. Mr MacLaughlin asked if I would look at the two sets of images and offer my professional opinion regarding the possibility that both sets of images represented the same person with approximately a twenty-year difference.

'I agreed, and the images were transferred to me by e-mail. The missing person was identified as Lord Lucan, who disappeared from the UK in 1974 aged forty years following the murder of Sandra Rivett, the nanny.

'Despite Lady Lucan's repeated assurances over time that her husband committed suicide, I am not aware that any remains have been positively confirmed as Lord Lucan and he is therefore still technically a missing person. The photographs of the unidentified male known as "Barry" were taken some eighteen years later in 1992 in India.

'"*Barry*": Four photographs were available to me taken of the gentleman identified as "Barry". One was of particular value, and shows a middle-aged male wearing only shorts, slumped in a wooden chair. A morphological summary of the person as witnessed from these four pictures is as follows:

'This is a male of mature years, probably between fifty-five and sixty-five years of age. He is Caucasian and most likely of northern European genetics. The proportions of his limbs and torso suggest that he may be a man of moderate to tall stature. His general appearance is unkempt, and his length of hair and beard in particular suggest a number of years of unfettered growth.

'His hair is naturally dark as witnessed by the colour closest to his head, his eyebrows and hair on his hands and on his legs. The blonde coloration in his beard and moustache may well be as a result of bleaching by natural sun. He has a relatively low fat mass, but muscle development is not particularly pronounced and he shows a tendency towards a mid-waist paunch.

'He wears a watch on his left wrist, which can often indicate right-handedness – but it is not necessarily always conclusive. There is no evidence of any other jewellery, e.g. a wedding ring.

'He has an alcohol problem as witnessed by his tendency towards gynaecomastia (female type breast development most obvious in the swellings around the nipples), oedematous swelling of the end of the nose and rheumatoid swellings around the knees, knuckles and joints of all his fingers. These symptoms manifest following prolonged alcohol abuse.

'He shows a number of patches of pale skin that contrast

with the dark tanned colour of the rest of his skin. The largest patch is on the tip of his right shoulder but smaller areas are also visible on his right shin, left forearm and possibly on his right cheek. The origins of these are not clear, but may indicate burns or a dermatological condition.

Comparison: The comparison between "Barry" and Lord Lucan is made using material that is not of a particularly high quality resolution.

'Hair: The tanning of Barry's skin clearly indicates that he has spent some not inconsiderable time in the sun, and as a result his hair is probably bleached several shades lighter than its natural colour. His beard is very blonde, but his eyebrows and body hair are dark. His hairline is not dissimilar to that seen in the photographs of Lucan, and I suggest that in fact the hairline as seen in Photograph 1 is virtually identical to that seen in the photo of Lucan taken in Rome.

'Barry's hair is certainly longer and therefore higher on top, but the basic sweep of a curve across his forehead passing up towards a peak to either side is very similar and therefore cannot be discounted.

'The eyebrow shape is not dissimilar between the two men, although they are much bushier in the pictures of Barry. This would not be considered a problem, as continued eyebrow growth in men with advancing age is a well-recognised phenomenon. Hair patterning on the hands and fingers are also consistent, but this is a well-defined and not exclusive male pattern.

'Hands: A comparison of hands as seen in Photograph 1 of Barry and that of Lord Lucan on the gondola in Venice do not show any particular dissimilarities. There is a suggestion that Lord Lucan may have a scar on the finger of one hand, but this may well be a defect in the photograph or an anomaly.

'Forehead: The shape, depth and width of the forehead is similar in both men. The crease patterning is also consistent.

The forehead in both cases shows a slight slope with mild glabellar development and a lack of marked supa-orbital ridging. In both cases there is a slight overhang from the glabella on to the nasal bones and the bridge of the nose is pinched.

'Nose: Little can be usefully compared in the nose because of the destructive effects of alcohol abuse. The junction with the glabella is however similar in both men, as is the bridge of the nose.

'Cheeks: This is again an area that is very difficult to compare over a twenty-year span especially in the aftermath of alcohol abuse, as there is a restructuring of the buccal (cheeks and mouth) area due to increased surface vascularity. However, there is no evidence to indicate that these two men do not compare reasonably favourably in this region.

'Eyes: The eyes are not clearly defined in any photograph of Barry, but the overall shape and slope are similar in the two men.

'Mouth, ears and chin: Unfortunately these areas cannot be compared as they are covered in every photograph by hair. This also ensures that a full comparison of face shape is not possible. It can however be confirmed that the upper face compares favourably in shape between the two men.

'*Conclusion*: Whilst it is my professional opinion that there are no clear areas of *dissimilarity* between these two men, there are equally no unequivocal indicators of positive identity. Therefore whilst it is possible that they may indeed be one and the same man, it is not possible to confirm this with any conviction based on the current photographs.

'This report forms the basis of my examination and whilst it is my true and honest opinion that the information enclosed is correct, I reserve the right in the light of further investigations and information made available to me to alter these findings. Attested on soul and conscience.'

In the carefully phrased language of the Home Office, to which I had been witness for many years at the Yard, this was as close as a pathologist dared go to confirming: 'That's him!' And if two negatives make an affirmative – 'no clear areas of *dissimilarity*' – then I found Professor Black's honest appraisal good enough for me to cut to the chase. How could anyone in her position claim to be 100 per cent certain anyway, given the fact that these were photographs and not flesh and bone? I couldn't have asked for more from anyone in that position. The eminent professor had said enough for me.

My final step before taking the plunge was to approach Lady Lucan – treading, very, very carefully. I made contact by e-mail, explaining that I wished to ask some personal questions that were not dealt with in any of the books or press cuttings I had read. Surprisingly, the countess reacted positively and without any curiosity about the reason for my enquiries. Over the years she must have been inundated with questions from complete strangers and had probably given up querying them. Her website certainly raised her to celebrity status, and also provided a defence mechanism for her to see off unwanted intruders into her privacy.

I began by asking her about any distinguishing features or scars that she could remember. Her reply: 'My husband had a boil mark on the back of his neck.'

She also revealed that he had a hairy chest, that his waist size was '34 to 36 inches', his shoe size was 'about 10', and that his dentist has died and she had no idea whether any records had been kept. Lucan's religion was Anglican and he was not a Freemason. To this information she added: 'He showed very little interest in religion, but said to me once that one might as well go along with it as it might be true.'

I left it at that as I didn't wish to probe too deeply at that point. There would be time to make further contact later. For now, I had all I needed – and plenty to proceed on.

It was time to book my passage to India.

CHAPTER 18

PASSAGE TO INDIA

The one thing I did not need was to find myself embarking on a wild goose chase. The only goose I wanted in my hands was the one that would lay the golden egg. Facing facts and separating them from fantasy and wishful thinking, I felt the odds of tracking down Barry had to be at least 60/40 in my favour. And the odds of him being the fugitive earl? Probably nearer 70/30 – again, for. Up to now all the Lucan hunters had been chasing shadows. I was the first one to be chasing substance. Good enough.

Go for it, Duncan!

So I went for it.

There were plans to be made. I set aside three weeks for the on-the-spot investigation but prepared myself for longer if necessary. This was uncharted territory and even with Mark pointing the way the future was one of total uncertainty, full of imponderables. The situation could well be extremely dangerous if I was going to walk into a lion's den of villainy and start asking the wrong questions in the wrong places.

There were four possibilities. One: Barry was indeed Lord Lucan and he was alive. If so, I'd find him in a drunken stupor on his porch, holding forth at Bob's Inn or propping up a bar somewhere in Goa. What would happen after that would depend on the circumstances. I could only take each moment as it came.

Two: Barry was Lucan, and he was dead. If so, I'd want to find the body or determine what happened to it.

Three: Barry was not Lucan but an eccentric hobo who'd gone native and was drinking himself to death on jungle juice. If he was alive, I'd have a chat with him.

Four: Barry was not Lucan and was dead. In which case I'd forget both the chat and the case and get a suntan on the beach.

They say we live most of our lives in the future or in the past – having an ongoing series of inner conversations about what we're going to say or do to someone, or what we wished we'd said and done five minutes or five years ago. Certainly I've actually seen people's lips moving as they walk along a street or stand in a bus queue, having a little chat with themselves. Right now this theory certainly was true for me. Rarely had there been so many diverse possibilities swirling around inside my head – with so much riding on their outcome.

The screw tightened another turn. Never having set foot in India added to the mounting tension – and to my insomnia. I'm only human. There was too much at stake now and I was starting to have sleepless nights. When I did finally drop off, usually somewhere in the early hours, I began having vivid dreams. Not so surprising, really, considering that Lord Lucan was the person I thought of last thing at night, and was back again to haunt me first thing in the morning – and whose head I had spent countless daylight hours trying to get into over the past months. Nonetheless, this had never happened to me before, even on my toughest cases.

They weren't bad dreams, exactly, just weird ones. Barry's face swam out at me from behind a maze of green foliage, dripping with fresh rain. Small, aggressive pigs came squealing out of the shrubbery at my feet, gnawing at my ankles. Barry again, hunched over a bottle of beer and a game of backgammon, grinning up at me through his beard. Barry suddenly opening his eyes wide in the rocking chair and laughing in my face.

Was I getting spooked? Christ, the man was getting to me, and I hadn't even set eyes on him!

Business was temporarily quiet on the commercial aircraft front, owing mainly to the global economic climate, the ripples following 9/11 and the noises about impending war in Iraq. So I was able to extend my leave to a month, giving myself an extra seven days' leeway. In the weeks leading up to our departure I buried myself in research. I had one big asset: my police training had hammered into me the vital importance of 'procedure', the dogged groundwork essential before embarking on a surveillance job or a pursuit.

The plan was to fly out in late November, before the Christmas rush that would quadruple the number of tourists on the beaches and double the cost of getting there. High season in Goa extends over the winter months, December to February, and into early March for the hardy tourist who can survive temperatures soaring regularly into the high nineties. After that it's just too hot for comfort.

The heaviest monsoon months are June and July, when the drought breaks and the rains come. When Mark had made his hurried departure a decade previously, he had queued for a visa at India House in London's Aldwych and headed for Bombay. In ten years a few things had changed. Bombay had become Mumbai. Today it can take up to three weeks to get a visa by post and personal application means queuing for hours amid a mass of surging bodies to get through the doors. The only plus is that it gives you a taste of things to come: like most Third World countries, Indian bureaucracy loves its red tape and pen-pushing. I'd be getting my fill of both in the very near future.

At least there should be few problems with communication. A guidebook from a shop in Charing Cross Road proved a mine of information. 'With a population of one thousand and twenty-seven million, and over sixteen hundred languages and dialects in India, it is not surprising that English is still widely spoken fifty years after independence. Eighteen other languages are constitutionally recognised, with Hindi being the most widely spoken of these.' So that was all right, then. English I could manage.

Personal safety: 'India is generally safe for tourists, apart from the north-western states of Jammu and Kashmir. Be on your guard in major cities and in markets. Swimming in Goa can be dangerous in places – be aware of undertows and strong currents, and avoid deserted beaches.' I didn't think I'd be getting too much time for sunbathing but thanks for the warning.

As for health, a leaflet made it sound as if I was facing plague and pestilence: 'Immunisation is usually advised against the following: Diphtheria, Hepatitis A, Poliomyelitis, Tetanus, Typhoid. Staying over one month: add Hepatitis B, Japanese B encephalitis spread by infected mosquito bites, Rabies, Tuberculosis and Malaria.' After all that lot I'd be like a walking pin cushion!

A reassuring note added that Goa was one of the safer places in the country and most of the above were optional. If I ventured further into the interior, other hazards would rear their ugly heads. I didn't like the sound of dengue, leptospirosis or filariasis, which sounded more like something you order off a menu than conditions that had a good chance of sending you into a hospital bed or the mortuary. I settled for four of the vaccinations on the list and a course of malaria tablets and paid for the privilege at the British Airways Travel Clinic in Regent Street. Emerging into the crisp autumn sunshine of Piccadilly, I was thankful how fortunate I was to live in Britain.

Goa is a tiny bite out of India's waistline, midway down the west coast, measuring 65 miles long and 40 miles across at its widest point, with a total land mass of 1,400 square miles. Getting there is not as easy as it sounds, as many a tourist has found. The main airlines don't land at Dabolim airport, 20 miles south of Panjim, which is officially classed as a domestic terminal but still capable of taking the big charter flights.

You can fly British Airways or other 'heavies' to Bombay or Delhi, and it takes approximately ten hours. But then comes a problem: all the planes land at around nine o'clock in the evening and there are no onward connections. I didn't fancy spending all night kicking my heels in the airport lounge at Bombay before the first local internal carriers like Indian Airlines or Sahara Airline take off at 7am next morning for the 45-minute flight to Goa.

The answer was obvious: a charter flight, direct to Dabolim. A package holiday came with the deal. Mark was unable to recall any hotels from a decade ago, or even if he'd set eyes on one, and I couldn't blame him. Think back ten years and see how much detail *you* recall of your summer holiday. After thumbing through the brochures I booked the two of us, along with journalist William Hall and photographer Mike Maloney, whom I was bringing to record the investigation, into the Valentine Retreat in Candolim. It was quiet, without being monastic, and looked as if it would suit us well.

Thursday, 28 November found the four of us at the My

Travel desk at Gatwick checking in for Flight No. MYT049 to Dabolim, leaving at 18.35 and arriving 11 hours later at 7.30am local time.

The visas extended for three months, surely time enough to wrap up the case. I had packed with extra care. Camera, tape recorder, a fresh box of 90-minute cassettes, notebooks, felt-tip pens, Maglite torch, RayBan sunglasses, sun cream, mosquito repellent, swimming trunks. A minimum of other clothing, but I did include a pair of hiking boots. We were travelling light because we had no idea what lay ahead or if we would have to take off somewhere in a hurry.

'This is what you call going out on a wing and a prayer,' I muttered to the others, as we shuffled forward in the queue.

I'd thought about a pair of handcuffs, but decided they might take a bit of explaining at the immigration desk at Dabolim if my luggage was searched. Most important of all, I had the famous black-and-white 'wanted' photograph of Lucan that the police had issued at the time of the murder. It was almost 30 years old now but this must be close to how he looked when he arrived in Goa. I hoped it would strike a chord with witnesses if I couldn't locate the quarry myself.

It always amazes me how some people just don't do their homework. As we neared the check-in desk, an argument broke out at the counter. A couple were being turned away for the simple reason that they had forgotten to get themselves a visa. Can you believe it? I looked at my travelling companions and shrugged. The couple had their tickets bought and paid for, their luggage was unloaded from the trolleys and on the conveyor belt beside the desk. Ready to roll. And then – oh, dear!

'You don't appear to have a visa, sir.'

'What visa?'

'You must have a visa for India. You can't take off without one.'

'Nobody told me. Can't I get one when I land?'

'Not any more, sir. We can't allow you to board the aircraft without one.'

And off they went back home, those poor souls, to unpack their luggage and presumably make furious phone calls to their travel agent or whoever had booked their tickets and neglected to apprise them of this rather crucial piece of information. And then another call to their insurance company: now *that* would be an interesting one to listen to as a fly on the wall.

The agent took our tickets, checking the colourful visas in English and Sanskrit that filled a whole page of our passports, complete with a bright-green stamp. 'It happens all the time,' she said wryly. 'Someone should have checked.'

But now at last, with any luck and the wind in the right quarter, the four of us at least were on our way.

The prospect of venturing into one of the notorious drug centres of the world to apprehend a wanted fugitive without any real back-up is a challenge, to put it mildly. Normally I would have a team of experienced officers behind me, each one fully briefed and raring to go.

In fact, this wouldn't be the first time I had been involved with India and its notorious narcotics culture. Ten years previously, just after Mark had fled the UK, I tangled with Indian smugglers on what turned out to be a drugs bust of massive proportions. It was called 'Operation Dakota'.

My stable of informants was up and running by then, and that's how I'd been put on to Mark. In fact, the main reason his information had gone to the bottom of the stack was that grasses usually brought me bigger fish. One of the most useful was an attractive Asian lady named Usha. She was a postmistress in a small sub-post office in east London, but the circles she moved in after work were far less staid. Though Usha didn't touch illicit substances herself, she knew people who did. In fact, she knew all the drug dealers in the community. Usha's cover name was Damon Hill, one of my Formula One team.

With the Yard's approval I accompanied Damon to an evening reception at a hotel off the A4 near Heathrow, following the wedding of an Asian couple in Hounslow. She had told me there would be some major players and 'faces' from the Indian drug cartels, from the Golden Crescent (the area around Afghanistan, Pakistan and Northern India) among the guests – and she wasn't kidding.

Looking around, I couldn't help noticing that I was the only white person there. I stood out in the crowd, so I had to be extra careful to not put a foot wrong. I could have ended up face down in a gutter if anyone among the ungodly suspected who I was, but I was confident that my training and experience would see me through.

Usha and I had rehearsed our story until I knew it backwards. My own cover was simple: I was a deserter from the military, now making a living moving gear from Holland to England. Some of the assembled brethren in the flower-bedecked function room eyed me rather suspiciously but Damon assured them: 'He's one of us' and, thank God, they believed her.

My instructions from the Yard were simple. Keep your eyes and ears open and gather as much intelligence as possible. I would then be in a position to help a colleague from SO10 (the Covert Operations Group) go in deep at a later stage.

It worked. The place was like a scene from a Bollywood version of *The Godfather*. Over a lavish buffet supper I got talking to several big hitters who warmed to me because they really thought I was AWOL. With the information I'd gleaned as a result of my father's service with the Royal Marine Commandos during his illustrious career, I was able to flannel my way through all the military jargon and convince them I was on the run.

One particular woman I got talking to, whom I will call Madam X, was actually serving a lengthy prison sentence for heroin distribution and was on weekend release for the happy occasion. Ironically, she let slip that she had been nicked by my own squad some eight years previously, fortunately prior to my tenure. Even though she was spending her days inside, this lady remained a major link to the Golden Crescent back home in India, presumably making her calls and conducting her nefarious deals while she was 'on leave'.

Madam X told me her cartel was having problems getting the drugs into the UK. 'It's easy to get through to Europe from India. There's the Balkan route, or Iran and Turkey. It's all land until you get to the English Channel and that's when we hit our most dangerous hurdle,' she complained.

'Then I'm the person you need,' I told her. I'd spotted the Achilles heel in the set-up. I went on blithely: 'Listen, I do a lot of parachuting. And I've got access to several pilots with light aircraft who do things for money and don't ask questions.'

I played my trump card. 'If it comes to the worst and you're worried about a reception committee from Customs and Excise when you land, I can always do a free-fall parachute jump with the gear over south-east England before it gets there.' This high flyer could, too, with numerous jumps to my credit – though right now I rather hoped it would never happen. I hadn't sky dived from a height of 12 grand for several years and the thought of doing so ever again, particularly with a parcel attached to me, didn't appeal. In fact, I'm man enough to admit it scared me. Remember, I was a father of three. I'd pushed my luck long enough. I had no desire to become a permanent feature of the Kent countryside, embedded in a farmer's field.

When Damon and I left the party that night I could positively hear the tongues wagging. The following day they took the carrot. I effected an introduction to a handful of undercover police officers, and then faded rapidly offstage.

Operation Dakota came to fruition some seven months later – and led to the seizure of literally tons of cannabis, kilos of heroin, false passports and a large amount of 'funny money', otherwise known as counterfeit banknotes. It was a massive sting worth millions in street value, with undercover cops flying the bad guys to remote airfields – and a reception committee they weren't expecting inviting them to be Her Majesty's guests for the foreseeable future. It didn't end there. I had given the Yard the key to penetrate the Asian crime scene and over the next months they would put villains away by the prison van load.

As for me, spurred on by a comment made by one of the undercover pilots that only fools jump out of aeroplanes, I decided to learn to fly. Two years later I was the proud possessor of a pilot's licence.

As a postscript to the operation, I took the fragrant Damon Hill out for a celebration dinner. Curry, what else?

Fast forward to the present day. In my front-row seat on Flight MYT049, I sat and wondered what lay ahead after our wheels hit the Indian tarmac. Unwittingly I found my thoughts drifting back almost 30 years to the anguished words of Sandra Rivett's mother, Mrs Eunice Hensby. Somehow those words had stayed with me long after I had researched the inquest. There I had been introduced to all the players, who had emerged like actors on a stage to recite their piece and retreat again into obscurity or the world stage of their jet-setting lifestyles.

'I like to think he is dead and rotting in hell. If he is still alive, I pray this will stay on his conscience for the rest of his born days...' That's what Eunice had said, and she meant every word.

On the flight I had several hours to get to know Mark Winch better – and I found that my newest informant nearly didn't bring back the sensational pictures at all. It seems that on his final day in Goa his drug-running friend, the mule known as Gentleman Jim, stole his Canon Sureshot with the precious film inside it and buried it in the sand outside the shack they both shared with Jungle Barry. Mark discovered the theft only minutes before the taxi was due to take him to the airport for the flight home to Britain. Somewhere over the Arabian Gulf, the story came out. Mark recalled the 'betrayal of friendship', his eyes suddenly cold and hard.

'I was all packed up and about to say my farewells to the group. Suddenly I realised the camera had gone missing. Jim was sitting on the porch as I came storming out of my room with my rucksack. He was high on pot and out of his brain. I grabbed him and demanded: "Where's my camera? What have you done with it?"'

'He started taunting me, God knows why, saying: "You've done nothing but take photos!" In fact all I'd done was take a few snaps, some of them of Barry with the group and the one of him in the rocking chair. But no more than that, apart from a few holiday shots of the beach.

'Jim denied it but I could see he was lying. His eyes were all screwy and he wouldn't look me in the face. I yelled: "Where is it? I'm going to ask you one more time!"'

'He shook his head and laughed like a lunatic. "I don't know!"'

'So I punched him in the face. Then I asked him again: "Where is it, you bastard?"'

'He continued shaking his head, with an idiotic smile on his face. I was so mad, I laid into him. I beat him up. I'm not proud of it but I wanted my camera. Jim was on the floor shouting for help. When I hit him again and again, he finally gasped: "Over there! Over there!" He was on his hands and knees in the dirt outside the hut, so he crawled over to a sandy patch and dug down with his fingers. And there it was, buried in the sand.

'Unfortunately, the fight had taken place in front of Connie and Barry, and it was a nasty thing to witness. There was a lot of blood, none of it mine. So I left on a bad note. But what was in the camera were the memoirs of my first-ever trip to India and, even though I had no idea of who I had photographed, I wasn't going home without it.

'The weird thing is that if I hadn't beaten a confession out of Jim, the world wouldn't be seeing these pictures today. Out of sheer guilt at what I'd done, I turned round and threw £200 at him as I left for the taxi, which was a lot of money to leave in India. I remember saying: "I'm sorry, Jim but I don't know where you're coming from..." Then I walked away.

'I didn't want it to end like that but there was no other way. Nobody waved me goodbye – except Barry, who flapped a hand at me from his chair. He was drunk by then anyway, pissed out of his mind and past caring.'

End of confession. Mark stopped talking, took a drink of beer and had a look of contemplation on his face as he stared past me out of the window. We would be landing in Bahrain soon for an hour's stopover to refuel. I sat back in my seat, gazing out at the endless brown desert passing far below and reflecting on all the 'what ifs' that had already marked this complex puzzle I was trying to piece together.

A stupid practical joke, or would-be theft, had almost ruined it. But Jim was long dead according to the word Mark had received on his own private grapevine – where or how, he didn't know.

What interested me now was whether the man I was hunting down had joined Gentleman Jim in the hereafter.

CHAPTER 19

ON THE SCENT

It is Thomas Edison who is credited with the famous statement: 'Genius is one per cent inspiration, 99 per cent perspiration.' If the American inventor had been more familiar with detective work he might have said much the same about this, too.

I'm not sure how much genius there is in my chosen profession. But the truth of the other part of the equation hit home with a vengeance when I stepped out of the air-conditioned comfort of the Airbus A330 and into the heavy, cloying oven that was Dabolim airport. Sweat sprang up, soaking my shirt before I had walked ten paces. The sun was a glaring white ball above the palm trees, heat shimmered off the tarmac and even at 7.30 in the morning the temperature was heading up through the seventies. By noon it would be in the nineties.

Mentally I prepared to spend the next few weeks in a lather.

It was already abundantly clear that I was dealing with a new culture as soon as we joined the queue to get through

Immigration. As noted previously, India loves officialdom, and officialdom thrives on form-filling. Forms were stamped and stamped again. The final hurdle was an immigration officer in a smart blue uniform beckoning me over to his desk.

'Your reason for being here, sir?'

My reason? For one wild second I was tempted to reply: 'I'm here to track down and hopefully arrest the world's most wanted fugitive, who is currently hiding out in one of your drug-ridden bolt holes!'

Instead I said: 'I'm here for sunshine, sea and sand.'

'Thank you, sir.' The stamp thudded down again. 'Welcome to Goa!' We were in.

It took nearly an hour for all the passengers to be cleared through to the baggage-reclaim area and another half-hour after that for the four of us to find our bags and head out into the open air ... and chaos.

So this is Goa.

Dabolim itself is a small, functional airport close to the sea, struggling to come into the twenty-first century. Inside, modern check-in counters below the arrival and departure boards handle both charter passengers and internal flights, and the two occasionally get mixed up. But the staff are friendly and the air-conditioning works well enough to keep the passengers relatively cool while things are sorted out.

Outside, the scene probably hasn't changed in half a century. Baggage handlers grab for your luggage, even when you're pushing the trolley yourself. Cab drivers, hungry for business, teem around the exit, tugging at the sleeves of arriving travellers in the hope of gaining their patronage through sheer force of will. Sweating tour operators wave clipboards and check off new arrivals as they direct them to their various buses. The prices for taxis, listed by destination, are displayed on a board by a ticket office, which saves a lot of haggling at the end of the ride. Things have improved since 1988, when the first tourists were counted in from the UK on an Intasun charter flight, but the arrival is still pandemonium and gives one a taste of things to come.

In the sixties, Goa was internationally recognised as the pot of gold at the end of the rainbow for the flower-power generation. Well – certainly pot. It was a rite of passage for backpackers and students from Europe, California, Scandinavia and Australia coming of age in the Age of Aquarius to spend time on a Goan beach as part of their travels. The primary magnet for the crowd was the weekly 'hippie gathering' at Anjuna, a sprawling flea market on the beach where they could meet like-minded fellow travellers and get stoned together on some of the world's best grass. Goa was dubbed 'beginner's India' and the phrase stuck. It was the embodiment of the peace, love and tolerance that hippies worldwide sought as their birthright during that era. These days, things have changed somewhat, with more than 100,000 holidaymakers from Britain alone hitting the idyllic beaches every year. But the essence of Goa that has woven its magic around visitors since the beginning of time – and even lured the gods to its golden shores when the world was new, according to local legend – remains unchanged.

The history books will tell you that the Portuguese arrived in 1498, courtesy of their globetrotting seafarer Vasco da Gama, who set foot in the southern Indian port of Calicut, the first person to travel to India directly via the sea route from Europe. The most significant date for Goa itself is 1510. That's when another Portuguese gentleman, Alfonso da Albuquerque, established a settlement there. A trading post made it the hub of Portugal's vast maritime empire stretching from Africa to Malaysia.

Impressed by the 60-odd miles of soft sands lapped by the

Arabian Sea, the Portuguese decided to stay a while – close to 500 years as it turned out. In those heady days Goa was dubbed 'the pearl of the Portuguese empire', well worth hanging on to for half a millennium. The cultural conquistadors finally threw in the towel in 1961, leaving behind stunning architecture, beautiful white churches, an advanced culture and a population that is 30 per cent Catholic.

Since no treaty was signed, the status of the Goans – neither Indian nor Portuguese – has remained in question ever since. The populace, it has been said in a telling phrase, are 'quite conscious of their uniqueness'.

There had been no travel books on Goa in Lucan's basement flat in Belgravia amid the rather bizarre collection of Hitler's speeches, tomes on psychiatric illnesses and detective novels. If there had been, he might have read: 'Goa is in a unique position of being a place where East meets West. It is distinct from any other part of India or the world. Goans are a happy and tolerant people, largely honest, peaceful, gracious and hard-working. Portugal was a part of their lives for over 400 years, and Portuguese genes run though many Goans.' Now there's a juicy carrot to dangle in the face of a potential fugitive with a love for all things Portuguese.

Old Goa was the richest and most opulent capital city in Asia during the early seventeenth century. The population moved 20 miles downriver to Panjim, now the bustling capital and a major port at the mouth of the Mandovi estuary. Marooned in the jungle, Old Goa's main attraction is the tomb of the sixteenth-century saint Francis Xavier, reposing in a glass coffin high above the altar of the world-famous Basilica. I'd have to give that one a miss. Some other day.

What neither the history books nor the brochures prepare a newcomer for is the culture shock of stepping into what literally seems another world. Crammed into a taxi that looked like a bright-yellow bug on wheels, I stared out in disbelief at a scene where the lunatics had surely taken over the asylum. The driver, proving himself more agile than the rest, had introduced himself as Rudi, grabbed our bags and hurled them aboard, waving us to follow them into the cab.

The ride north to Candolim took 40 minutes, bouncing along a bone-jarring highway teeming with packed buses, stuttering lorries, scooters, bicycles, clapped-out old bangers and trucks groaning with vegetables, fruit and live chickens. An open van loaded with water melons like green rugby balls lurched up a hill at ten miles per hour, daring anyone to pass. At least a sign on its rear bumper said: 'Overtake Horn OK.' Our driver obliged, adding to the general cacophony. The only safe creatures appeared to be groups of sacred cows meandering placidly down the middle of the road, serenely confident of their protected status and local nickname of the 'Goan Traffic Police'.

Motorcycles had whole families riding on them, the children tucked in front of the driver, no one bothering with crash helmets. Vivacious girls rode pillion on scooters, sitting side-saddle, their brightly coloured saris hoisted like sails, long black hair streaming behind them in the wind and hands clutched in a vice-like grip around their man's waist, seemingly uncaring that they were in a potential sequel to *Death Race 2000*. There is talk of a law coming in 'one day' to make protective headgear compulsory – but then pigs might fly too.

I was reminded of those arcade games where you hurtle along a road, missing obstacles by inches – and usually end up with a flash and a bang and a pile of wreckage on the screen. Game over!

'This is madness,' I shouted to the driver.

A beaming smile lit up his brown face in the mirror. 'No, everything OK,' he called back. 'One crazy driver, plenty of accidents. Here, everyone crazy driver – no accidents!'

I made a mental note to pass on this philosophy to someone at the Department of Transport if I ever got home.

In spite of the pandemonium, the scenery took my breath away. Vast tracts of forest surged inland from the coastal road, merging into a carpet of green jungle unrolling to the distant horizon and beyond. Banana and coconut palms spread like a dancer's fan, jostling with the indigenous betel plant, whose leaves, when chewed, induce both stimulating and narcotic effects. Our driver, happily taking on the additional role of a tour guide, pointed out pineapple, grapefruit and mango trees. 'One mango, over 1,800 fruits.' I believe you, Rudi.

We crossed over a causeway straddling an inland waterway, where Rudi took one hand off the wheel to gesture at the banks thickly forested with mangrove trees. 'Plenty crocodile,' he said. 'You want tour, you call me.' On cue, a business card slid over his shoulder with practised ease.

In the distance I glimpsed a dazzling building shimmering in the sun like an ornate brilliant white wedding cake. Then it had gone and I was left with a vision of one of the most beautiful churches I had ever seen. The Portuguese, of course. Those seafarers knew a thing or two about architecture, and for a moment I could understand how Lord Lucan had been drawn to the country. With that thought of the church came another: the famous prayer of the agnostic: 'Lord I believe. Help thou mine unbelief.' I wanted so much to believe that we were on the right track, that the 7th Earl really was waiting for us at the end of the line. But the cynic in me held back. You could hardly call it divinely inspired intervention, but that little prayer just about summed it up.

The villages of Goa have one thing in common. In this tiny monument to European civilisation clinging to the western shore of the Indian subcontinent, you will find that each of them has at least one church with a square in front of it that the locals conscientiously attend each Sunday, the older men in sober dark suits, the women with headscarves. Our taxi bounced on.

Candolim. The first sight of where our quarry might be hiding out did nothing to calm the butterflies fluttering in my stomach. 'I'm here, Lord Lucan! Where are you?'

The geography of the place was just as Mark had described it. The long coastal road had been carved through the jungle, a main artery running parallel to the shoreline with veins of sandy tracks leading off through the trees to the beaches 200 metres away. The twin-towered Church of St Alex stood guard imperiously where the road forked, one branch heading for the coast to the left, the other circling inland. In Barry's early years there, that road had been a dirt track with only a few ox-drawn carts and the odd bicycle passing along it. Now every day is a logjam where the weakest go to the wall.

This is all thanks to Mrs Indira Gandhi and a Commonwealth conference she hosted in New Delhi for 43 heads of state in 1983. After all the talking was done, the delegates were invited to a 'retreat' for a spot of rest and relaxation. With many of the world leaders on her doorstep, the premier wanted to show them that India was not all grinding poverty and that the country could put on a show if it wanted.

Mrs Gandhi chose Goa as the place that would have the honour of making this point. The attending world leaders were housed in the isolated Hermitage Hotel, close to the sixteenth-century Fort on a spectacular headland overlooking Aguada Bay. A helicopter pad was constructed on the cliff top and with it several minor connecting roads. Most significant for the denizens of Ximera, a tarmac road was laid down over the existing dirt track – past the front door of Bob's Inn.

That road is Chogm, pronounced 'Chog-hum', an acronym that stands for 'Commonwealth Heads of Government Meeting', though it's hard to find a sign anywhere that identifies it these days. Postal addresses are mainly box numbers, with mail collected from local post offices by the recipients.

The resulting spin-off of the conference and its weekend 'mini-holiday' opened up a whole new area of uncharted territory to tourism, and the place changed almost overnight.

I stared out of the taxi window and realised my breathing had quickened. I could suddenly see how Lucan had managed to disappear so effectively from the world into this remote haven where the law never reached, establishing his new identity until he lived, breathed and believed it.

The one-time Richard John Bingham, 7th Earl of Lucan, and his new-found friends in this 'land that time forgot' doubtless felt a nasty chill as the coaches started rumbling past their doors, for up until then oxen, cart and pushbike had been the most favoured forms of transport. More tourists meant more likelihood of recognition and probably even more law enforcement. Lucan must have been concerned that sooner or later, even after more than eight years of successfully blending into the scenery, someone would point the finger. But no. It looked as if our man's disguise had remained rock solid even as the make-up of the crowds around him changed so dramatically.

Main Street, Candolim. The humid air is cloaked by a pall of dust from building sites from which new hotels to provide for the ever-increasing tourist trade will eventually tower above the palm trees. Development is going on everywhere. The clash of picks and shovels resounds through what was once virgin jungle. None of it seems coordinated or planned.

Ramshackle buildings nestle like poor relations between

shop fronts garishly lit with naked bulbs. Abject poverty and opulent wealth make odd neighbours – but the influx of tourism is bringing work to 20 per cent of the population.

A road-side vendor is selling sugar-cane juice from a tricycle like an ice-cream salesman, the long strips of cane being fed into the oil-black teeth of the grinder at one end and coming out crushed into a refreshing juice at the other. A lime is squeezed into the cloudy white liquid for good measure and it's yours for five rupees. Stalls hawking everything from pocket chess sets and backgammon boards to silk saris have staked a claim between barber's salons and chic jewellery stores. Open-air fruit stands list seven local varieties of bananas among their wares. Restaurant-bars with the day's special chalked on blackboards whet the palate of passing holidaymakers.

The Snow White Laundry. A corner-shop mini-market. There is even a pharmacy that, on further investigation, appears to sell everything that even the most confirmed hypochondriac could possibly crave: from headache pills to sunburn creams – and the essential yellow Loperamide capsules for 'Delhi belly', the predictable side effect for every tourist's overstretched digestive tract. 'My most popular sale,' the brown-faced chemist in his gleaming white jacket would confirm with a grin a few days later when I had reason to call on his services. All you had to do was state your needs over the open counter from the street outside.

Our hotel was a colonial-style mansion that owed its façade to the Portuguese influence. Set back from the main road on a small private track, the Valentine Retreat is an oasis of tranquillity amid the non-stop delirium of the outside world. I allowed myself a smile of satisfaction. A large swimming pool and a sheltered green expanse of lawn at the back completed the picture. Perfect!

It had been a long flight, and we were all jet-lagged. I

decided to spend the first day getting my bearings rather than rush into the hunt and start rattling cages like a bull at a gate. If the man who called himself Barry was still in the vicinity after 28 years, he would be around tomorrow as well. No one knew we were here. Like the famous play *An Inspector Calls*, I would be the unexpected arrival ... and, I suspected, just as unwelcome.

First task: to organise transport. 'I strongly advise you not to try driving yourself in Goa,' Don Cleary, the experienced director of Statesman Travel, who organised our trip, had warned me. 'It's not a good idea to hire a car. Taxis are plentiful – and cheap.' The voice of experience was right. After what I'd already witnessed I had no intention of driving in Goa, thank you all the same. But his prediction about the accessibility of taxis was spot on as well. A small fleet waited outside our hotel, while others cruised the streets with the drivers calling out: 'Taxi, mister?' as they passed. For the equivalent of £7 I could hire a cab all day and go anywhere without extra charge. That's about the cost of a London black cab from Victoria Station to Camden Town – on a clear day.

A swim and a shower did wonders for the jet lag. We headed off on the first stage of our quest, alert and refreshed, if a trifle tense.

'In there! That's where my shack was.' Mark jerked a thumb through the left-hand window as our taxi weaved and jolted its way with hair-breadth precision through the mass of would-be suicides clogging the road. We had struck it lucky with the driver we had hired from the hotel. Raju Ashwekar was built like a rugby player and looked the kind of man you would want on your side in a scrap. He had a quiet dominance that he wore like a badge of office. I'd noticed that even the other drivers were careful to be polite to him.

Raju wore the light khaki shirt that had been issued recently to all taxi drivers by the highway authorities in an attempt to keep cowboy cabbies off the roads. He took no prisoners behind the wheel but I felt as safe with him as I would with anyone on this test of nerve and sinew. We hired him for two weeks.

The road had left the tacky pavements and gaudy shop fronts far behind. Now we were passing crumbling mansions, colonnaded monuments to past affluence visible in the trees behind broken stone walls. I counted families of up to a dozen, from the very old to the very young, spilling out on to the front steps or into the overgrown gardens. I had an impression of white paint peeling from wooden balconies, washing strung like rags on clothes lines, dogs and chickens roaming freely, barefoot children with tea-leaf brown limbs playing in the dust. Fishing nets were stretched between trees to catch falling leaves and, presumably, the odd coconut.

This was Ximera. The general air of neglect reminded me of *Gone with the Wind*, colonial houses falling to bits in the Deep South after the Civil War had stripped the landowners of their fortunes and their slaves. Sandy tracks barely wide enough for a car to navigate snaked off into the jungle behind these once-great Portuguese-Goan homes. Beyond, I glimpsed clusters of shacks bunched together like shanty towns under a haze of smoke from smouldering bonfires. Nonetheless, the locals smiled and waved a hospitable welcome. Brilliant white teeth gleamed like toothpaste advertisements against their brown skin and I noticed how clean the children were, and how neatly they were dressed.

I was reminded of something else I had read: 'The people of this region share a common climate, a love of seafood and a natural, unimpeded friendliness resulting from centuries of exposure to alien civilisations from over the seas.' My spirits lifted. At least the natives were friendly.

'Over there, look!' Mark suddenly jabbed a finger across my face at the other side of the road. 'That's the place. Now it's all coming back.'

The sign, in bold black letters on a white board, read: 'BOB'S INN', with the cuisine choices listed below it: Indian, Continental, Chinese, Goan. There was nothing to indicate that behind the lush tropical entrance of palm trees and purple bougainvillaea lay a one-time thieves' den where Lucky Lucan purportedly rubbed shoulders with gangsters and drug dealers.

The possibility that the place had been more like a Fagin's kitchen of villainy than a tavern welcoming passers-by to drop in for a Kingfisher beer and a bowl of tiger prawns was equally indiscernible.

I resisted the temptation to stroll in and order a beer. If Barry was inside, the last thing I wanted was for him to spot me until I had seen and observed him and had a chance to suss out the lie of the land first. Mark seemed unwilling to go in alone and I didn't press him. My one-time dope pusher hadn't elaborated on the 'nasty characters' he'd shared a table with in Bob's place and I hadn't pressed him on this either. I wasn't sure Mark had told me the whole story, and I suspected there might well be some unsavoury characters there that he didn't want to bump into, even after ten long years out of the picture.

I would find out the truth soon enough. Tomorrow was the day we would start with Connie.

Meanwhile, I took a walk on the beach at sunset.

The sun was a glowing bowl on the horizon, sinking into a gunmetal sea at the end of another day. A fishing boat chugged out from the shore on its nightly foray, trailing a bubbling wake at the stern. In the far distance, the silhouettes of huge oil tankers ploughed through the Arabian Sea, cardboard cut-outs against the darkening ocean.

A few last cottonwool clouds scudded across the sky, tinged with pink.

Out there, somewhere beyond the horizon to the south, lay the Maldives. And, after that, nothing until the coast of Africa.

Is this the view that Lord Lucan saw, hour after hour, day after day, year after interminable year, in the open prison he had chosen for himself as he went for his regular evening walks along the deserted beach? If the lone fugitive had turned into a Robinson Crusoe castaway with his wild, unkempt beard and shaggy hair, his watchful eyes would be making sure of one thing: that any Man Friday footprint he came across in the sand would not be a size-11 police boot!

There was little chance of that back in the late seventies and eighties. Today the Tourist Police, the TP, patrol in pairs, eagle-eyed and vigilant, along the wide expanse of beach. More than 200 shacks have sprung up on this particular mile of sand, primitive open structures of wood and bamboo with roofing of dried palm leaves, all of them bedecked with colourful flags. When the season is over the huts are carefully dismantled and stored away before the coming of the monsoons, which would turn them into matchwood.

The huts all have exotic names, like Blue Dolphin, Bob Marley, Kingfisher, Sea Wave and Dreamers. They've sprung up to serve beer and food to the scores of package holidaymakers soaking up the sun under lines of colourful beach umbrellas. No doubt about it, Goa is firmly on the tourist map these days and growing in popularity by the year. It's a very different scene from the one that would have greeted a new arrival in 1975.

After dark, the atmosphere subtly changes. Away from the garish tourist spots along the main road the night falls like a blanket, wrapping itself with a black intensity over the land. The power cuts don't help, with the grid in overload, giving up the ghost for half an hour just after dusk every night as if the engineers have stopped for prayers or popped out for their evening meal. Once I counted four power failures in one evening. You couldn't help but take note when the fans stopped churning and the mosquitoes had their pound of flesh.

I was glad I'd brought a torch. As I had rightly surmised, this is an essential piece of equipment for anyone venturing out after dark, both to see and be seen on the roads and to help pick one's way through the tangled undergrowth, hopefully avoiding the snakes, spiders, scorpions and other local fauna on their nightly forays.

On the beach I had already observed a snake charmer encouraging a sleepy-looking cobra to rear its menacing hooded head from an open basket to entice a few rupees from the sunbathers, and I fervently hoped it had settled back into its basket and stayed there. When a barman at one hotel regaled us with a tale of a guest walking in to find two cobras in the bathroom only the previous week, I made a note of the hotel for future reference of places not to stay.

Back in my own, thankfully cobra-free room, I lay on the bed under the single white cotton sheet, staring unseeingly upwards as the ceiling fan stirred the oppressively humid air, and assessed the situation. A number of things had now become clear.

The tourist explosion had only really happened in the past ten years, though it showed no sign of abating any time soon. Nonetheless, when the man I believed could be Lucan first set foot here, it was long before the first holidaymakers ventured up the coast. The interior had been an even more hostile wilderness of crocodile-infested rivers, paddy fields and mangrove swamps than it was now, virtually impenetrable to anyone ignorant of the trails or mountain passes.

For a man desperately searching for a place to go native

178

where he could bury himself away from the world, it would have looked like the answer to his prayers. The added bonus of discovering how deeply the Portuguese influence, language and ambience had left its mark must have made him feel he'd landed on his feet at last.

Even the beach was less hospitable a quarter of a century ago, when I believed Lord Lucan reinvented himself to defy the world's police. With just a few shacks dotted here and there to provide shelter from the relentless sun, these same sand dunes were a desolate golden prison offering nothing to do and nowhere to go.

We aren't talking 20 weeks or 20 months. We are talking 20 years. With his keen mind and high intelligence, Lucan's enforced exile among the dropouts and druggies would slowly, inevitably, have become a living death.

The social life of Belgravia and Mayfair would have seemed increasingly distant, another world and another lifetime away. In its place rose the daily spectre of a seedy group of gangsters from around the world – hardly the international set to which the earl was accustomed. Drug dealers, flower children and a few bored expats 'living for the moment' – and the next shipment of prime marijuana or hashish – were the main additions to the Goa of that era. The huge clumps of prickly cactus and dense undergrowth beyond the sand dunes that made such a formidable and effective barrier from seeking eyes would have become a claustrophobic prison.

And when the June monsoons broke, whipping the sea into frenzy and lashing the jungle with curtains of rain, Lucan's only recourse would have been to retreat to his bare, cell-like room or to the nearest bar and sit there, brain in neutral, watching the hailstones hammering on the windows and the hours ticking away as he reached for another bottle to blank out the tedium. The monsoons here last at least two months, sometimes longer. Even a backgammon board or a pack of cards could not allay the infinite boredom of his situation. Beer, brandy and the powerful local *feni* were the only avenues of escape he would have had.

It would be enough to send anyone who hadn't been raised in the place to the edge of insanity. Interestingly enough, as I found out later, the local word for coconut is ... *madd*.

The next day I was introduced to Connie.

CHAPTER 20

CONNIE

Mark was understandably nervous about meeting his former landlady. The last time he had set eyes on her she had watched him punch the living daylights out of Gentleman Jim and leave his erstwhile friend in a groaning heap on the ground outside her house. But that was ten years ago. I hoped time would have taken the edge off the memory, thus healing any rift. We needed all the cooperation we could get.

Ten years is a long time to be away and one tree looks very much like another in the jungle. It took Mark an hour to find his old haunt. As we trudged through the scrub and undergrowth, we actually found ourselves going round in a circle. Finally he recognised a building.

'There it is!'

It was a two-storey house with a sloping, red-tiled roof surrounded by tropical shrubbery – and, yes, in an open space at the rear was an old stone well. Two small black pigs suddenly darted out of the undergrowth and vanished just as quickly.

'Are you sure?'

'I'm sure. There's my old room – and there's Connie!'

A flight of stairs at the back led to a kitchen. I heard the chink of crockery and through the open door glimpsed movement inside. In Goa, everyone leaves their doors open. Mark led the way up the stairs, calling out her name. The rest of us, myself, William Hall and Mike Maloney, stayed at a respectful distance behind.

This was classed as a courtesy call, someone looking up an old friend, and we didn't want to frighten anyone.

A middle-aged woman in a simple floral dress came to the door wiping her hands on a towel. Despite Mark's poetic description of her smile, in my mind's eye I had built up Connie as a hatchet-faced Ma Barker, wielding a big stick and an iron will to control her pot-smoking, hard-drinking ménage. This smiling, brown-faced woman with iron-grey hair and dark eyes widening in disbelief was more mother hen than Ma Barker, and right now she was welcoming back the prodigal chick with a huge hug of affection even though he'd only spent a few weeks here all those years ago.

Mark had warned me not to rush things. 'These people move at their own pace. Play it as it comes.' We were introduced as friends from England, and accepted immediately. Connie gestured at some rickety wooden chairs on the porch, produced beer from the fridge and sat down to talk over old times. I liked her immediately and I could see what Mark meant by her smile – it was like the dawn of a new day.

There was a lot of 'remember this?' and 'remember that?' and then it was time to cut to the chase. I switched on the tape recorder.

Constanza 'Connie' Silveira, aged 65. Over the past decade her cluster of stone and bamboo shacks had expanded into a successful guest house, optimistically called Sea View Rooms, despite the fact that the view towards the sea is actually completely obscured by a green wall of foliage, palm trees and thorn bushes. Connie resides here with her own aged mother. We probe, very gently, about the man she and other locals knew as 'Jungly Barry'.

Casually, Mark asks about his old backgammon rival. Connie answers in halting English without query. Her voice is soft, unhurried, and she sits with her hands folded placidly in her lap.

We began with the obvious question.

Where is he?

Her reply changed the investigation in four words.

'Barry? He's dead now.'

'Oh… When did he die?'

'Maybe seven or eight years ago.'

'What was he like?'

'Barry was always polite and friendly, a real gentleman. He arrived in the mid-seventies and stayed in other shacks before coming here. He was never any trouble. He loved to eat fish, especially pomfret [a flat fish like a sole and a local delicacy]. I would also cook him an omelette and my speciality of chicken *xacuti* curry with coconut gravy if he asked for it. He had a very nice voice, very English.

'But he would start drinking early in the day, then fall asleep in the afternoon, often curled up on the porch below my kitchen, where he would pass out on a rug. When he woke up he would go for a walk by himself on the beach, watching the sun go down.'

'How long did he stay with you?'

'All the time until he died. I kept his room for him. But he moved around a lot. He was never in one particular place for long. Once he stayed with me for two years, then went away, then came back again. He would just come and go without explanation. Sometimes he would sleep under the banyan tree in a hammock cut from the hanging roots.'

'Did he ever tell you how he came to be in India?'

'He said he arrived in Bombay on a cargo boat from Africa. He told me he had walked from Bombay and that it took him three weeks. He came *paidal* – by feet.'

'Walked? Are you sure?'

'That's what he said. He told everyone the same story.'

'Did you ask him for any papers or a passport or any identification?'

'In those days we never worried about who people were or what they did. They just turned up. We didn't ask questions. Whatever the foreigners did was not our business. If they had false passports we didn't care. Whatever they showed us we just accepted it.

'I don't remember Barry having a passport. Maybe he did, maybe not. It didn't matter. Today things are different, much stricter laws. Since tourism came to the area everyone must register at hotels, show passports and we must pass on details to the police. There are even special Tourist Police patrolling the beaches.

'In the old days hippies would come walking along the beach with their rucksacks and simply wander up a path until they found a shack to stay. They were well behaved and as long as they didn't cause trouble, they could remain. Everyone trusted me too: they would give me money to keep for them and it would be safe. It was all great fun, everyone sitting around and playing guitars and singing and telling stories.'

'Did he have a surname?'

'No, he was just Barry.'

'How did Barry fit in?'

'He liked the company and he often joined in the groups of hippies, playing a guitar while they sang.'

And then the moment of truth. I produced the black-and-white photograph released in 1974 of the wanted man and after a long perusal Connie agreed that it 'could be' him. Then, after another pause, she added: 'The one thing that upset Barry was the fact that he couldn't wear earrings like the rest of them. He had no ear lobes.'

She had said it so casually. But as I heard the words, my heart skipped a beat. This was a vital piece of the jigsaw. Lord Lucan had no ear lobes. The fact had even been included in the description that went out to Interpol in the days following the murder.

Connie went on: 'Barry's hair was thick and down to his shoulders, so you couldn't really see his ears. It was only when he pulled his hair back and pointed to them that I noticed it. He was quite upset because he wanted to be like everyone else in the camp. "You see?" he said. "I can't wear earrings! It's very annoying."'

'How much did you charge him to stay here?'

'Sometimes 20 rupees a week. Sometimes nothing if he had no money. When Barry first came here the locals would buy him beer or Honey Bee brandy. People would arrive to visit him from overseas, all foreigners. They came from England, from Germany, from Switzerland, and gave him money to support himself. After they left he would have a load of rupees. Then he would buy chocolates and sweets for everyone and hand them round.'

Another bombshell out of the blue. What you might call a double whammy. Who were these 'people' armed with wads of cash? Why would they come from all over Europe to visit an eccentric hobo in an undeveloped wilderness?

'I don't know. Sometimes, early on, they came here. Usually they would see him in Bob's Inn. I never talked to them, and eventually they stopped coming. But to get money to last him through the monsoon months Barry would also take people on jungle safaris.

'That's how we gave him his nickname. He would say to me: "I will bring you back a little lion, Connie!" But there are no lions here, only water buffalo and snakes.'

'Did he ever fall ill?'

'Barry was a very fit man to begin with. Later on I think he had a German lady friend who nursed him if he was unwell.'

'How did Barry die?'

'He died of drink. I was with him shortly before he was gone. It was very sad to see how his condition went down so bad. But, when his friends stopped coming, he drank everything – whisky, brandy, beer, *feni*, all mixed. That's how he lost his head. That's when we started calling him "Mad Barry" or "Crazy Barry". I don't know where he died. I just heard he had passed on and I didn't go to the funeral because I was too upset.'

A hard drinker even in the best of times, and with the bottle providing his only escape route here, it was easy to picture the tale Connie was relating. But, as I listened to her words, I wondered how long Lucky had continued to hope that another group of visitors from his old life, with their cash offering, would turn up.

'Did he leave you anything – a memento or an heirloom of some sort? A letter perhaps?'

'No, nothing. He had no possessions apart from his guitar. I don't know what happened to them. Maybe his friends kept them.'

'Where was the funeral?'

'Barry was cremated in Panjim. Some of his friends scattered his ashes under the big waterfall.'

There was a silence as Connie stopped talking. Then she let out a long sigh and stared down at her hands. When she looked up at me, her dark eyes were clouded over.

'I miss Barry. He was part of our small community, even though he stayed by himself for much of the time. In the monsoon months he would sometimes go to Bombay but I don't know what he did there. All I do know is that he always came back and I was so happy to see him. He always knew his room would be waiting for him.'

That night I went to my own room early armed with a bottle of chilled Kingfisher beer from the hotel bar. I lit the mosquito coil, put it under the window and hoped it would keep the pesky blighters at bay. How on earth had Barry managed to survive in the open night after night? I know that garlic is reputed to keep them away. Maybe they didn't take to coconut *feni*, either. Or perhaps he was just too stewed by bedtime to care. It had proved to be a dramatic opening 24 hours and given me much food for thought.

Barry was dead. It could be a smokescreen but somehow I doubted it. Connie's voice, her face and her manner all carried the ring of truth. In my long career mixing with villains and confidence tricksters I had developed an instinct that told me when someone was lying, and I was seldom wrong. So now the task would be to prove that Barry was indeed Lucan.

The ear lobes were a huge breakthrough and totally unexpected. Mark hadn't mentioned it, because he had never seen Barry's ears under the mane of hair. Back in England in my preliminary research, a statistic had swum out of the Internet: less than five per cent of the world's population have no ear lobes, the normal kind sometimes referred to as 'free' or 'pendulous'. The missing five per cent are defined in two categories: 'attached' and 'soldered'. The figure was cited in the medical report from the autopsy on President John F. Kennedy, who was known to have no ordinary ear lobes.

His lobes in fact were the 'attached' kind, where 'the outside margins of the ears connect more or less directly to the side of the face'. With soldered lobes, the 'union of ear margin and cheek is so direct that there is no discernible lobe at all'.

The report concluded, distinctly unhelpfully for me: 'Since ear lobe type can frequently be determined from photographs, the trait can be useful in identification.' Not with Barry. Not with that hair and beard. I'd have to rely on a personal visual sighting. Another medical report I consulted confirmed: 'It is very rare, a trait that falls under the ear lobe recessive genetic marker, and is not caused by any type of genetic defect.'

It did cross my mind that this rare abnormality has been singled out in crime novels as a feature peculiar to criminals. One of the most celebrated is the super-villain Blofeld, who claimed in the James Bond thriller *On Her Majesty's Secret Service* that proof of his ancestry was tied to a genetic trait – lack of ear lobes, what else?

The fact Connie had recounted about Mark's erstwhile friend Gentleman Jim having regularly called Barry 'Lucky' was quite amazing as well. Especially since she herself had never understood it. Though it took a television documentary ten years later to clue Mark in as to whom he'd met and photographed, it was clear that his old mate had somehow sussed out the truth before Mark ever left Goa.

The final hint of a clue from Connie's account was Barry's remark about 'bringing back a little lion'. There are no lions running wild in India – but there were, of course, lions in the zoo set up by the fugitive peer's mentor John Aspinall, owner of the Clermont Club and one of the Lucan 'inner circle', who was rumoured to have helped spirit his friend Lucky out of the country within hours of the murder. A Freudian slip of the tongue, perhaps, in reference to a wild animal with which he would have been familiar since lions were a favourite of Aspinall's.

Word of the paymasters from abroad was certainly an interesting development. This information definitely warranted further investigation and would perhaps confirm one of the many stories circulating back home – that the earl had been kept in funds by the 'escape committee' of the Lucan Set.

Many, including some of the investigating police officers, believed Sir James Goldsmith was the mastermind behind the escape and certainly he had the buccaneering image to fit the profile. 'LUCKY'S JIM' had been one clever headline I'd noted.

Even the earl's legal agent, the solicitor Michel Egan, who looked after the interests of the Lucan estate in County Mayo, had opined several months after his disappearance: 'Personally I believe Lord Lucan is alive. He had such influential friends he would be able to call on them anywhere in any part of the world.'

Another pundit put it more colourfully: 'The cabal of upper-class friends banded together to protect their friend. The English peer was thus transformed into a legend as potent and global as the Loch Ness Monster!'

I thought about fish. Lucan liked fish. Lady Veronica Lucan would later confirm to me that it was his favourite food. I remembered how in that other life he had left behind for ever he would order fish soup and smoked salmon, with a *premier cru* Sancerre to help it down. Here in this primitive enclave, a fugitive with a taste for the good things of life would find no such luxury apart from fresh fish, which he could pick up for a song. Even today you can dine on grilled pomfret or tiger prawns for less than £2. But the French wine Lucan loved would be non-existent. Even the inferior Indian-bottled wines had yet to find their way into the bars. It was strictly beer and brandy – and fermented coconut juice, the lethal *feni*.

As for his accommodation, Connie had shown me the room

on the end of the porch that Barry had inhabited. I wondered what a life there would have been like. A man could lose himself in the jungle, and lose his mind too. Eventually he would surely have to come to see it, and the other cell-like rooms wherever he moved house, together with the whole 65 by 40-mile area, as an open prison.

But at least here he could come and go as he pleased – and for Lord Lucan anything was better than facing a lifetime's jail sentence back in Britain and the unbearable disgrace it would mean for the family name to know he was there day in and day out.

He had been found guilty of murder in his absence. But as long as the killer's body – unlike the victim's – was never discovered, there would always be a sense of doubt and mystery shrouding the whole sensational case.

CHAPTER 21

'OH, CECILIA...'

Lord Lucan's cold blue gaze takes in the old stone well at the end of the garden. Next to it stands the religious shrine found outside many houses in Goa, thanks to the dominating Catholic influence that existed for centuries before India annexed the country from Portugal in 1961. He nods to himself. This was the place he had journeyed halfway across the world to find, and now at last he was here. He hitches his rucksack higher on to one bare, bronzed shoulder, marches up the path and raps on the open front door. Mama Cecilia appears and eyes the bearded stranger standing in front of her in denim shorts and sandals. 'Do you have a room available?' he enquires in clipped, cultured tones. Mama Cecilia hesitates, then gives him a warm smile of welcome. He would be her first customer.

As I prepared for my interview with her, this was how I imagined Cecilia Pereira's meeting with the hermit-like figure who had materialised out of the jungle on a far-off spring day in 1975. Goans are noted for their hospitality and good nature. If, with the onrush of tourism, the almighty dollar or other currencies are now inevitably making them more commercially minded, in those days there was no such restriction on their attitude or their welcome.

Mark had done his bit for now. I would only need him for one more introduction. That final one would be to a waiter he knew in a bar up the coast who had served both him and Barry in 1992 and appeared to know Barry well. I hoped the guy was still alive. I left Mark to search out the contact and waved him off in a separate taxi to head north in the direction of Calangute.

Despite Connie's welcome, Mark would clearly be happier once he was out of the active investigation and able to return to his young family in England – and so would I. It still wasn't clear whether our travelling companion might have made any enemies, real or imagined, among the dubious set he had mixed with on his first, fateful trip to this jungle backwater. Either way, if he was recognised with me it could well compromise all of us – and, more importantly, jeopardise the entire mission. Every well-honed investigative instinct I had was reverberating with the message that there were people here who knew the truth. However, I was fully aware of the fact that seeing Barry exposed and his real identity exploded into the open might well be the last thing they wanted. Maybe I was getting paranoid but it wasn't worth taking any risks. This place was a small village. Everyone knew everyone else and word would spread like wildfire. The natives might be friendly but I couldn't count on everyone to be so inclined.

Word of my intent might already have reached Mama Cecilia but I would have to chance it. Once again I was going in unannounced and would play it as the cards fell. At least the groundwork with Connie had paid dividends. After sharing her own information about Barry with us, she had pointed us in the direction of Cecilia's house and reminded us that we'd find her restaurant shack down on the beach at the end of the path.

I picked my way along overgrown tracks littered with the dark husks of coconut shells, ducking past spiders' webs that hung like shiny net curtains from the branches of banyan trees. Suddenly I realised just how little had changed in this corner of the globe, an area dubbed by one enterprising travel writer who had looked beyond the beaches as 'the land that time forgot'. At local level, not a lot has moved on.

Barefoot children were heating water in saucepans over a smouldering bonfire. Smoke rose fitfully through the trees to be trapped in the man-sized palm leaves that spread like a green canopy over the jungle. Dogs lazed in pools of sunlight filtering through the branches. The sky above was cobalt-blue. I jumped as a small black pig shot out from beneath my feet to vanish into the undergrowth with a squeal, its small tail waving a brief farewell. Then another followed it, and another. It occurred to me that a large wild boar might be in the vicinity, or at least their mother, searching for her offspring. But as it turned out these were, in fact, not piglets. They were the full-sized specimen of the local sanitation workers.

Then I came upon it in a clearing – the infamous 'pig toilet'. Mark had said, many weeks ago in Britain, that he'd never seen anything like it. Neither had I. Imagine a small stone hut with no door, just a couple of steps inside that lead up to a wooden plank with a hole in it. Below the hole is a chute that takes the excrement away.

This was one of scores of such toilets you can see today in India, particularly where there is a scarcity of water, no drainage system and reliance on the centuries-old method of having wild pigs clean up the sewage. 'Pigs are very clean,' one Goan observed dispassionately. 'They enjoy their work and are extremely adept at it.' Certainly the area at the back was muddy but there were no unpleasant odours. Pigs, eh? I took out my camera and got a snap. This would be one to show round the pub back home.

Fifteen minutes later I located the house I was looking for.

Cecilia Pereira is 62, and a devout Christian, as is her daughter Philomena. When the man who called himself Barry came into their lives, Philo was a bright teenager who would later go on to pursue an academic career after graduating from college in New Delhi. Both mother and daughter have crucifixes tattooed on the backs of their right hands like many religious Goans. Today Mama Cecilia has expanded her guest house. There are bright-red tiles on the roof. Lanterns glow on the open porch and colourful tapestries adorn the walls. There is running water and a toilet in every room now. The proprietor also owns Cecilia's popular bar-restaurant on the beach with its open invitation to the scores of package tourists, most of them from Britain and Germany, soaking up the sun. A dozen rooms have shower facilities, and the charge is 250 rupees a night – £3.50 at the time of writing.

Mama Cecilia was a sturdy woman with high cheekbones and a calm wisdom about her that made me think of a village elder. She sat me down at a table in the porch and brought the first beer of the day. Cautious at first, she finally unbent to talk about the stranger who had settled in their midst. She spoke excellent English.

'Barry just walked out of the jungle one day and asked if I had a room. He said he had come from England and that he had arrived in Bombay by a cargo ship from Africa. He had a very strong personality and seemed a nice person, charming and polite. His voice was unusual – very cultured. So I was happy to have him as my first guest. In those days I only had four rooms. People would come from nowhere, stay a few days and move on. Barry was different. There was something special about him.'

'He stayed many months and called us his "second family". He was very close to us. At first he had no money and I let him stay for free in return for giving my daughter English lessons every day. Goan people are like that, very friendly and hospitable. The fishermen on the beach would let the hippies sleep in their huts or use their boats as shelter.

'Barry paid me when he could afford to, sometimes just a few rupees a week. As I got to know him better, he would sing: "Oh Cecilia, you're breaking my heart!" to me in the kitchen while I cooked his favourite fish meals! He had quite a nice singing voice and would sometimes play a guitar in accompaniment. He also had a flute.

'But in all the months he was with us he told me very little about himself. Barry was here in the district for 20 years but he was quite restless. He never seemed happy to be in one spot too long. He would stay with me for several weeks, then go away and I wouldn't see him for months until suddenly he would be back again. I always found a room for him or else he would simply sleep out in the open on his mat.

'He was a very fit man. He even learned to climb the trees for coconuts. He became one of the *paddeli* [the men who pluck coconuts], though he never went too high!'

True enough. Lucan had never been a Hooray Henry, the kind of chinless wonder who prefers to stay on the sidelines, wafting through the drawing rooms of Belgravia and having his only contact with sport via a TV set. Lucan had been Action Man, throwing himself fully into whatever pursuit provided danger and thrills. So, in an area where the most daring local sport involved shinning up coconut palms, that's what he would have learned to do. The earl had always been accustomed to the limelight and applause that went hand in glove with participation in sports of the sort his set indulged in. Suddenly Mark's story about the public demonstration of

Barry's tree-climbing prowess, and the flourish and bow that capped it off, took on new meaning.

Cecilia continued: 'I did ask him once about his family. He was sitting on this porch having breakfast and I sat down to chat with him. There were no other people around, just the two of us, and he hadn't had his first drink of the day yet. We got talking about our families.

'I asked him: "Barry, have you been married?" He replied: "I do have a wife but I've got a problem with her and I don't want to talk about it." It was the same with his children. He had children, he said, and he loved them very much but he wouldn't say any more. He wouldn't talk about them either. We never spoke about his family again.'

Mama Cecilia's eyes filled with sudden tears as she added: 'I will never forget Barry. I went to his funeral service but not afterwards when they burned him. That would have been too much for me.'

My mind went back to the reports about Lucan's effect on the women he encountered, the debs who'd surrounded him in the years before his marriage. Perhaps there had been more to the attraction than just his title and position.

Mama Cecilia's daughter's memories of Barry are even clearer. Philomena is 40 now, articulate and intelligent, married to a clerk in a local government office. When I showed mother and daughter the notorious black-and-white photograph of the fugitive that had stared out from countless newspapers at the height of the manhunt, Philo recognised him instantly.

'That's Barry! I will never forget his eyes. I looked into them across a table every day for more than a year. He was teaching me English and I was educating him in the local dialect of Konkanese. Looking at this photograph, I see him staring back at me!

'Barry picked up the local dialect surprisingly quickly, because

Konkanese is not an easy language for an outsider to learn so fast. I would translate books into English with him. He was a good teacher, very patient. He would always correct me for my pronunciation and pat me on the head when I got something right!'

I leaned forward. 'And ear lobes? Can you remember if he had any?'

Philomena thought for a moment, frowning. Then she shook her head. 'No, Barry had no ear lobes. He wasn't able to wear earrings like so many of the others who came here. I think that upset him.

'Barry's problem was drinking. He used to drink too much in the mornings and eventually it made him sick. There were some bad times for him and he would stay in his room all day. That *feni* is very strong. Too much of it and people go blind.

'But he seemed a simple person with simple needs. He liked music and always had his flute with him. He would play his backgammon with anyone he could persuade to give him a game, anyone who would pay for his drinks when he won.'

Mama Cecilia simply nodded at the photograph. 'That's him,' was all she said. Her eyes were still moist.

But she went on to tell me more. Over the months, Barry's confidence grew. The man I was now virtually certain was indeed Lucan became bolder as the threat of discovery receded. On Wednesdays, presumably to alleviate his growing boredom, he would explore further afield, going to Anjuna and its famous hippie flea market. The beach there had become a Mecca for the flower-power generation and backpackers arrived from as far away as San Francisco and Sydney to join their brethren by the Arabian Sea.

The market would be heaving with stalls selling all kinds of silverware and jewellery, along with gaudy silks and cottons laid out on rugs on the sand. No one spared more than a passing glance for the suntanned figure in shorts and sandy beard who passed among them. He was just another face in a colourful crowd.

I had obtained all the information I could from this delightful pair. Before I left, though, I had one final litmus test to perform.

'Do you stock any *feni*, Mama?'

'Of course,' Mama Cecilia replied, flashing a smile. It was the kind of smile that said: Are you sure you know what you're doing? 'You want to try some?'

'Yes. I've heard a lot about it.'

She produced a bottle of colourless liquid from behind the bar. It was so clear I could see the rings on her fingers sparkling through it. 'Be careful,' she said. 'This is very strong drink. You want something to water it down?'

'No thanks. I'll take it neat.' I felt I owed it to Barry to drink it his way.

I took a sip – and I thought my throat was on fire! The taste comes close to vodka, but the burning sensation on my tongue and at the back of my throat was all its own. Christ, what was this stuff? You would need a leather palate to survive more than one glass, and Barry had been knocking it back for 20 years!

As for his *alter ego*, in the last three years before his disappearance Lord Lucan had been drinking chilled vodka, neat. *Feni* would be as close as he could get to the real thing – at a much higher alcohol content and a fraction of the price. Even today a bottle of *feni* costs 50 rupees, less than £1, in the numerous liquor stores you can find on Goa's main streets, while Honey Bee brandy will set you back all of 120 rupees for a litre. In Barry's time he would have bought his supplies of home-made *feni* for next to nothing off one of the small road-side stands that can still be found in the interior.

I'm not usually one to walk away from a half-full glass but this was one drink I couldn't finish. Since I had no wish to insult Mama Cecilia, when my eyes finally stopped watering I poured the remnants into a flower pot, hoping the poor plant wouldn't wilt before we had time to make our excuses and leave.

In all we had been there an hour – and what a vital 60 minutes it had proved! I tried not to show my elation as we thanked Mama Cecilia and Philomena and strode off back to the highway, where Raju and his taxi were waiting.

Both mother and daughter had positively identified the black-and-white picture of Lucan as Jungle Barry as he looked when he first materialised from nowhere. I had their confirmation on tape. I had used established police procedure in my questioning, to allow no room for later denial or misunderstanding.

Out of the blue, another tantalising snippet had been added to the growing file of fact and conjecture. In the summer of 2000, celebrated psychic and telekineticist Uri Geller got himself in on the act by declaring: 'Lord Lucan is dead. But despite a High Court ruling that, after bludgeoning his children's nanny to death with a lead pipe, the ruined gambler drowned himself in the English Channel in 1974, I do not believe he died until the early nineties. I did not meet the man. But I use a traditional psychic method called psychometry, placing his picture on my desk and letting my eyes drift out of focus on it. The pictures that flicker on the TV screen behind my eyes, inside my skull, give me clues to the true story.

'Lucan lived for 17 or 18 years after the murder. He planned his "suicide" in a desperate throw of the dice and then, abetted by at least two friends, fled the country. A new life in Australia failed abysmally, with more crimes committed, but his friends held good as nothing in his life ever had. Finally, unrecognisably scarred and dissipated, he died a hopeless alcoholic – in Canada.'

Could you call this bending the truth? But, uncanny as ever, the extraordinary Mr Geller and his psychometry might just have stumbled on something. Wrong country, right man, perhaps. But yet more tantalising theories to keep the pot boiling. I let them stew.

As far as I was concerned, the pieces of the puzzle were all on the table and the frame was complete. Now I was going to start filling in the middle.

CHAPTER 22

Bob's Inn

It was time to pay a visit to Bob's Inn. I waited until after nightfall, around 10.30, when I figured there would be more customers, more conviviality and more of the atmosphere that Lucan would have experienced. By day the place seemed like an innocent watering hole for the retired middle-aged couples who spend their winters in Goa and make sure they leave by June, before the monsoon season strikes.

By night it would be different. There would be business as well as pleasure in the air. Business means talking deals on drug shipments passing through Bombay to Europe and on to the streets of cities and towns throughout the Western world. Heroin from the Golden Triangle of Burma, Laos and Thailand. Raw opium from Afghanistan. Cannabis – 'Paki Black' – from Pakistan. The nocturnal patrons of Bob's Inn were likely to differ from their daytime counterparts in their definition of 'pleasure' as well. Pleasure after dark would mean smoking a spliff of 'grass', passing the cigarette from hand to hand, loosening up, getting high and making new friends.

I went alone that first time, casually dressed in jeans and T-shirt like any other tourist. The gate was half open and I strolled up the stone path to the entrance, past a small terrace on the right where groups of animated diners were having a late supper. Mussels in a large soup bowl seemed to be a popular dish, and a blackboard with the day's specials scrawled in white chalk confirmed it.

The sweet smell of cannabis hit me before I was through the open doorway. Inside, the aroma hung in the air like a curtain of incense. Someone was playing a guitar and the music rippled out into the still night air. As I walked in, the music stopped abruptly and everyone fell silent. Perhaps it was just coincidence, one of those simultaneous silences you sometimes get at a party where, for a brief second, everyone stops talking at the same time. But in that moment I was reminded of the scene in a spaghetti Western where the pianist stops playing and the people stop talking when a stranger walks in through the swing doors of the saloon. All that was missing was my black Stetson, poncho and cigar.

After a moment the buzz started again and so did the guitar.

The interior was just as Mark had described it. A ceiling of thatched bamboo, alcoves with tables for six, a small bar on the left – and, just inside the door, dominating the main room, the famous 'long table' where Barry had held court. The place was busy with almost every seat occupied, but a waiter pointed me to a spare chair at a small corner table near the entrance.

Two hours and several beers later I was one of the gang. Playing it cool, I had smiled and chatted and slowly been accepted for what I appeared to be: a British holidaymaker on his own in Goa, in search of sunshine, sea and sand. And maybe a little fun.

I counted 14 people around the long table, laughing loudly, drinking and smoking. They all seemed to know one another and I had the sense of intruding on a private club. Jeans and singlets seemed to be the dress code for the men, which meant a lot of bare bronzed arms, tattoos and male perspiration. The women mostly wore loose-fitting summer dresses. Even with the windows open to the night and the blades of the ceiling fan spinning, the heat was overpowering. A couple of portable fans had been placed in the alcoves but made hardly any impact.

Studying faces without appearing to, I noted a few interesting profiles in the happy crowd. One or two would have looked at home in a stocking mask and their voices were straight out of London's East End when they shouted for more beer. One shaven-headed character sat stripped to the waist, his entire upper body covered in tattoos from shoulders to waist and down both arms, like the Red Dragon in the first Hannibal Lecter film, *Manhunter*. A sudden thought came to me: Christ, what if someone I've put away recognises me? I was glad to be near the exit.

The guitar music, such as it was, came from a youth sporting a ponytail, a wisp of beard, torn jeans and a T-shirt with the words 'Keep on the Grass!' emblazoned boldly across the back. He couldn't play and when he started singing he couldn't do that either. He was obviously high on pot or booze, or both, but nobody seemed to care. Everyone seemed to embody the attitude of peace, acceptance and general goodwill that had made Goa famous as a destination for the free-love crowd in the sixties.

A noisy poker game was going on in the far corner and at one end of the long table a couple were hunched over a backgammon board, rattling dice vigorously. I wondered if the board they were using was the same one that Lucan had played on. The conversation along this table, the focal point of the room, seemed to be more of an animated shouting match – not aggressive, just loud. That's when I noticed spliffs being passed from hand to hand, openly and without any attempt at concealment, with everyone taking a drag of the soggy stub before passing it on to his or her neighbour.

My own table companion was dark-skinned and I thought he could be Moroccan. His name, he said, was Ahmed. After a few minutes of desultory chat he casually produced a brown lump of marijuana from his pocket and began methodically scraping fragments off the inch-square cube with a penknife on to a square of cigarette paper. He then mixed the flakes into a small mound of tobacco, rolled himself a cigarette, lit it and silently offered me a drag.

Tricky moment. If I declined I would put myself in danger of being branded an outcast by the bar's habitués, who could spot a misfit at 20 paces. But still I shook my head and said: 'Not just now. I've had a bad throat, and I don't want to make it worse. Next time…' The excuse seemed to satisfy him.

Bob himself stood at the bar, a hard-muscled Goan with a bandido moustache and a watchful air, the kind of man who sees everything and says nothing. I made sure I didn't catch his eye because I had already decided to leave it for another time before approaching him.

Separating hard fact from fantasy was going to be my biggest challenge. Somehow I had to penetrate the smokescreen as well as the mist of marijuana clouding Bob's bar. My eye caught a handful of photographs pinned to a pillar in the centre of the main bar area. Through the haze of smoke they looked like snapshots of regulars taken in Bob's Inn, a couple embracing at the bar, other faces laughing at the camera, raising glasses to the photographer. The usual pictures you find pinned up behind holiday bars anywhere in the world. Except that there were two photographs in that portrait gallery that suddenly caused my heart to pound.

One was a 10 x 8 study of a guru-like figure with a tangled beard that was still dark but turning reddish with the sun. No doubt about it. He was a little younger than in Mark's pictures – but it was Barry all right. Mentally I stripped the beard away, visualising the strong, patrician features beneath. His face filled the frame, his blue eyes under the black brows staring to the right with – no doubt about it – that expression I had come to know as the 'Lucan look'. On his white T-shirt the words 'Konkani Safari Tours' confirmed it.

One of the expats at the long table saw me looking at it. 'We call that the Wall of the Dear Departed,' he said. Jack turned out to be a retired car dealer from Essex. 'All of them were old regulars and they're all gone. To get on that wall you had to spend a lot of time in here. And you have to be dead.'

I nodded, impressed with the logic, checking myself from asking: 'Who's that?' because I knew the answer I'd get. Barry had been frequenting this place for years. Advertising his jungle safaris with his own portrait worried me for a brief moment but, since it was only on show in Bob's Inn and by that time he needed the extra income, I imagined he was prepared to take a minimal risk.

I glanced at my watch. Two good hours – it was time to go. I had no intention of outstaying my welcome, not on my first visit. Beneath the bonhomie, something in me detected an aura of menace, an unspoken threat. Don't ask me why, just put it down to the sixth sense of a seasoned cop.

I rose, flapped my hand in a general wave that took in everybody and nobody, and made for the exit. As I passed Bob, I nodded to him. 'Thanks very much. Nice place you've got! Goodnight.'

His smile was friendly enough, though it didn't reach his eyes.

'Come and see us again.'

I will, my friend. You can count on it.

Over the next few days I worked my way into the local scene, moving from bar to bar, shack to shack, careful not to make waves. Mark was still searching upcountry for the waiter he'd known from the bar frequented by Barry. I walked the beach from end to end in the virtual footprints of the fugitive, ploughing through two miles of soft sand that stretched from the Thai Village Resort in the south to the old stone houses of Calangute in the north. I noted how the contours of the beach changed every day, churned by powerful green rollers surging in from half a mile out to burst in an explosion of surf on the sloping sands.

And I came to understand how this man Barry had been able to climb palm trees – a four-mile daily slog through heavy sand, followed by a bracing swim in the surf, does wonders to keep a man's muscles toned, even as the *feni* is playing havoc with his insides.

Shortly afterwards I picked my way through the undergrowth back to the house where he had first stayed, without either Mama Cecilia or her daughter seeing me. The actual shack where Barry lived is boarded up today. The blue wooden bench on which he stretched out on his raffia mat is still there, though splintered and faded now. The porch is littered with palm fronds and pieces of driftwood.

A huge banyan tree stands sentinel close by, the tree in which Barry sometimes slept in his makeshift natural hammock of hanging 'aerial' roots suspended four feet above the ground. It truly is a remarkable example of nature's miracles. I stared up at the majestic contours. What kind of man could sleep in a cradle of branches and vines? It seems Jungle Barry could.

The noble banyan is actually a form of fig tree (*Ficus benghalensis*, to give it the correct nomenclature) that earned its name because it was originally used as a market place by merchants in India. It is an astounding piece of arboreal architecture, because as the branches spread they actually drop down roots into the soil which become stems or fresh trunks. One tree can form scores of these 'props', and the Hindus in particular assist their development by protecting the young roots inside bamboo tubes as they get near the ground. The bark is used as a tonic by Hindu physicians. I didn't actually find any such makeshift hammock on my walkabout, but you didn't need to be Tarzan to see how one could be fashioned from a few pliable roots.

The beach where Barry once roamed is now patrolled by cane-wielding Tourist Police in crisp white shirts, lanyards and blue berets. There has been a very high-profile attempt in recent years to frighten off the dope peddlers and gypsies, snake charmers and silk traders, and keep them from harassing the sun worshippers on their loungers.

Line upon line of colourful umbrellas are spaced out along the vast stretch of sand where the man I was now convinced had been the fugitive earl walked, swam and slept. Using the tricks of the surveillance trade, I watched and listened. I overheard conversations from behind the local English-language newspaper, the *Herald*, published daily in Panjim. And got talking to anyone and everyone who might provide a scrap of information.

I was the grey man, Mr Anonymous. I honestly doubt if anyone I spoke to could give more than a scant description of me a couple of days later.

In the shacks I breakfasted on poached eggs folded into buttered baps with freshly squeezed orange juice, and returned for a lunch of cold beer and fish from the modest menus. I chatted with the owners, gleaning local knowledge and gossip. They had names like Johnny Be Good, Big Alex and Maxie, all of them genial characters who would take orders for fresh king prawns in the morning before sending one of the boys off on a scooter to a small port three miles down the coast to buy them.

The shacks are so fragile that they are taken down in May before the fury of the monsoons erupts, churning the sea into a frenzy as if with some monstrous egg whisk – and fierce enough to drive the huge tanker *River Princess* aground, her massive bulk still there as a giant eyesore after four years left rusting in the shallows.

There has been talk of the ship being turned into a night club, or even a hotel, but both options seem too costly and dangerous to be realistic. At low tide, and if the sea is calm, holidaymakers wade out waist deep across a sandbank to touch her side with their finger tips and stare up in awe like so many pygmies at the empty shell towering above them.

In fact her fate follows an old nautical tradition in these treacherous waters: a recent study from Britain's National Institute of Oceanography estimates that more than 200 wrecks of old Portuguese sailing ships lie embedded in the sands offshore from Goa, 'waiting to be salvaged by those with the necessary courage, funds and will'. The tempting postscript adds: 'The exotic finds by professional salvagers operating along another notorious graveyard of Portuguese ships, the South African coast, are an indication that there is a fortune in diamonds, rubies, emeralds and pearls as big as a bull's eye waiting in Goan waters.'

Next time you come back, Duncan, remember to pack your scuba gear.

At this point, though, the only gear that interested me was the kind you inhale – and that from the perspective of an investigator. Dope is still smoked as a daily recreation on the beaches, only with rather more discretion than in the glory years. A sharp whistle from the thickets behind the sand dunes signals the imminent arrival of the TP. That's when the wedges of cannabis or the smouldering stubs are simply dropped in the sand and buried with a quick sweep of a bare foot, with a pebble to mark the spot so that they can be dug up again minutes later, once the coast is clear.

The day's cabaret is the sight of a policeman racing across the sands in pursuit of a gypsy woman – until she runs sobbing and fully dressed into the sea to get rid of whatever substance she had been carrying. This way she eludes arrest as she is no longer in possession of anything illegal, so she is simply marched off the beach, soaked to the skin, by the officer and his colleague, with a stern caution. More than once I witnessed the TP apply instant justice to a small group who were trying to flog silk sarongs and scarves to gullible tourists, ordering the hawkers off the beach and confiscating their supplies.

Generally I played the part of an amiable tourist, asking around without seeming overly curious. If pressed, I fell back on my other identity: I was researching a book on Goa in the hippie years. The good news for me was that the Goans have two middle names: 'hospitable' and 'friendly'. They address you by your Christian name, with 'Mr' in front of it. Mr Duncan regularly found himself invited into people's homes for a drink, or even a meal.

I met some nice guys and some not so nice guys. One of the former was Remo Fernandes, a singer I bumped into while he was celebrating his fiftieth birthday at a party in his honour in someone's garden. For singer, read legend. Remo is an ebullient, dark-eyed Goan who has earned his fame and fortune composing music for Bollywood movies with titles like *India Beyond* and *Bombay Dream*.

He vividly recalled his own times seeing the flower-power invasion on the beaches when Barry arrived in the mid-seventies. He told me how the centre had been Calangute, which apparently is derived from the word *Koli-gutti*, or 'land of fishermen'. 'Somehow it became a Mecca for hippies from all over the world,' Remo told me, still somewhat bemused by it all. 'They came in their hundreds. Their motto was: "Live for today!" They would make their base around Baga, Candolim and Calangute, where the fishermen would let them stay next to their shacks. These kids would simply knock four poles into the sand and put an old blanket over them for shelter. Then they'd stay for months on end until the monsoons came in the summer and drove them away.

'They would spend their days sitting around a fire playing guitars, singing anti-war songs and smoking dope. We Goans are known for our hospitality and the fishermen would be quite happy to let the hippies live there for nothing and give them food as well. They were wonderful days for anyone who was footloose and carefree and just wanted to escape from the outside world. I saw it at first-hand and it was a time I'll never forget.'

One of the not so nice kind was a burly Goan I got chatting to in a bar up the road and a Bob's Inn regular. His seasoned nostrils detected 'cop' and he would only talk for the record if I promised to guarantee his anonymity. When he did, it was an eye-opener.

'This whole area was known as a transit camp for dealers,' he said. 'It can still be a dangerous place for people asking the wrong questions. Just be careful. People can disappear permanently, and not because they want to. There were some very bad times here when this man Barry arrived. Sometimes gang warfare would break out over drugs. One English gang came from Birmingham. They dealt in heroin, very bad. They came up against an Irish mob and a lot of violence broke out.

'There were corpses found in the jungle. One was washed up on the beach. I myself had a body thrown over my garden wall from the road in the middle of the night. I threw it back again as I didn't want the police questioning me.

'Bob's Inn was the meeting spot for all these people.

There were some big players. We had really heavy people here, drug barons from all over the world, from as far as South America, conducting their business even if the stuff wasn't actually coming through here.

'Barry was with the Irish people, as he told them he came from Ireland. He rubbed shoulders with the big boys, and saw things. But they left him alone. He wasn't regarded as dangerous and he wasn't going to talk to the police. We thought he was probably on the run from something, though he never told us what it was. We just accepted him.'

So Barry became a regular face in the crowd. To my mind his eccentricity became his strength. He was dismissed as a 'character' – and in those days Goa was full of characters who came in all shapes and sizes.

All my instincts now told me that Lord Lucan had found the bolt hole he wanted and that he had stayed there for the next 20 years.

All I had to do now was prove it. Or come up with enough evidence to sway the most biased jury.

CHAPTER 23

THE PLOT THICKENS

The taxi jigged and bounced over the potholes with bone-jarring force, and we bounced with it. Mark had finally tracked down his man and had been welcomed with open arms. In fact, we had both been invited to dinner. Nicholas Tolentino lived somewhere at the end of this rutted road leading into the dark interior, where the moon shone fitfully through the intertwined branches of banyan trees and thick foliage, and smoke hung on the horizon like a grey shroud.

We were somewhere north of Calangute, inland from a scattered coastal village called Baga, an hour's walk along the shore from the hippie commune where Barry had taken refuge. Nicholas had been a young waiter at St Anthony's Bar when the bearded stranger first arrived in the area. The bar is still there fronting the beach. By the time Barry died, Nicholas had been promoted through the ranks to head chef.

Mark had filled me in on all this before Raju's taxi lurched to a halt in the semi-darkness. The pale outlines of stone houses were visible amid the trees, their windows lit by oil lamps and candles. This primitive area is called Arpora. It is little more than a handful of shacks and rest houses carved out of virgin jungle, but several families who have lived there for decades call it home.

Nicholas is patriarch to what is known in modern-day parlance as an extended family. The breadwinner himself is now aged 50. His wife Melina and their four children sleep in one building while four brothers and seven sisters, along with their children and grandchildren, sleep next door. Chickens scratched in the dirt at the rear and I spotted three or four pigs scavenging in the undergrowth over the wall. Most of the brood seemed to be on show as we climbed a flight of worn stone steps to a small area, outside an open kitchen, that had been laid for dinner. Word must have spread. Tiny children with round dark eyes like chocolate drops stared mutely at the visitors as if we had dropped in from outer space.

We could smell the aroma of curry and spices all the way from the taxi and my taste buds were salivating before I even reached the source. Nicholas cut a schoolmasterly figure with his small moustache and spectacles and was living up to his reputation in the kitchen. I was itching to show him the photograph of Lucan that was burning a hole in my briefcase, but again I had been alerted by Mark to apply the softly-softly approach. We mustn't alarm our witness with overeagerness or any show of tension, though it was hard for me to contain both.

We sat under oil lamps with candles flickering in saucers on the window ledge. The chicken curry, served in a huge bowl, was five-star gourmet quality and several bottles of beer helped the party relax. Nicholas started to mellow. He had been courtesy itself to the strangers in his home after an initial wariness in his halting English. This evaporated instantly as we hit common ground with two words: 'Manchester United' – which, when coupled with the name of David Beckham, was a global language. Suddenly the talk round the table had turned into an animated discussion about how this world celebrity practically managed to turn a soccer ball into a boomerang. Nicholas's children and the small grandchildren listened in rapt silence, as polite as any model family, and again I noticed how clean and smart their clothes were, even in surroundings that were at best basic.

After half an hour, Mark judged the moment was right.

'We've got a couple of photos to show you, Nicholas. Is this a good time?'

Apparently it was. I produced the two photographs, one the black-and-white head shot of Lucan, the other of Barry in the rocking chair. Nicholas studied them closely, and finally nodded slowly. 'They are the same person. When I first met him' – a gesture at the clean-shaven 'wanted' picture – 'that was more how he looked, but with a beard which he kept stroking.'

Nicholas tapped the photograph, searching his memory. 'He would appear at the bar from the beach and always sit at the same table. Usually he would try to play backgammon with someone. As the years went on he looked different. He became thinner and his beard grew lighter. But this is still him. There is no doubt of it. In the early days I served him drinks, starting at breakfast time with beer. After a few visits he said: "You can call me Barry!" Sometimes I would serve him lunch, almost always fish curry, and when I finally became chef I was cooking it for him.

'He would go on to brandy, and then *feni*. When he had too much he lay flat out on his back in his chair and went to sleep. We would leave him there. Nobody bothered about it. There were no tourists in those days to get upset, just local people and travellers with backpacks who came mainly from England and Germany.

'I thought maybe Barry was drinking too much because he had problems. I did ask him once but all he would say was that he had had difficulties with the police back home. I never found out what they were. After that he kept quiet. He never spoke of it again and I never asked him.'

One last thing. I wanted to see the bar for myself.

'That's no problem. I'll show you tomorrow. Come before lunch.'

What a charmer! We shook hands affably and fumbled our way by torchlight through the pitch-black night and tangled undergrowth back to the taxi and home.

I was feeling elated. Nicholas didn't have to lie. We hadn't crossed his palm with silver, or with tattered rupee banknotes, to thank him for his help, because there was no need. Mark had become one of the family on his earlier visit and this was simply Goan hospitality at its best.

Another one in the can. How many more to go?

The next day I sat in the seat that Lord Lucan had occupied. Nicholas assured me that St Anthony's Bar hadn't changed in 30 years and probably much longer than that. Red and blue plastic chairs, check tablecloths, the usual garish advertisements for beers and spirits on the walls. A few motorbikes were clustered outside in the sun, their saddles burning hot. The picture windows were flung wide to the sea, along with a spectacular panorama of beach umbrellas fluttering in the breeze like multi-coloured butterflies and bronzed bodies beneath them, some of the girls topless, soaking up the sun.

The bar hasn't changed, but in almost 30 years the view has, and considerably. From his vantage point Lucan would have stared out at a stretch of sand as deserted as the Sahara, wide, desolate and empty. This was yet another prison. An open prison where he could come and go, but a prison just the same.

'Thank you,' I said to Nicholas, finishing my notes. 'That's fine.'

'Come again,' he said. 'You must try the fish curry next time.' In every community, large or small, there is always somebody who knows everything that there is to know about what's going on. And I'm not just talking about gossiping over the garden fence. Here in the boiling pot of Ximera, Bob would be one of those people.

But I planned to leave him until last. If I said or did the wrong thing in Bob's Inn, the portcullis would come clanging down.

Another name had swum out of the shadows, and along with it the place where I could find the man it belonged to. The Spice Garden is a bar-restaurant situated in the very heart of the gaudy Strip on Candolim's main street, where neon-lit bars are linked together as closely as Siamese twins. Naked light bulbs swing from trees in the wind, turning everything into a fantasy funfair, a bobbing fairyland of lights in the pitch black night.

The Spice Garden is long and narrow, its bamboo ceiling overhung with greenery and the walls lined with plants. The tables are on two levels, the more intimate ones hidden behind miniature rockeries. A lone guitarist perched on a stool serenades the diners from a small stage midway down the room.

Vernon Rodriguez is the owner, a handsome Goan of 52 whose features have the weathered look of a man who has lived life to the full. Sharp eyes peer out from beneath the peak of an ever-present baseball cap and his ready laugh is infectious.

His friendly wife Vanessa is Austrian. She does all the cooking and prepares the succulent steaks in the kitchen at the rear of the restaurant. Vanessa remembers how Jungle Barry used to arrive without notice and tuck into a healthy dinner at a rear table – in return for which he would give the customers an impromptu performance on his flute or guitar. 'Barry was a charming man with extremely courteous manners,' she recalls. 'He would converse with me in German. He was also an accomplished musician, mainly classical.'

So Barry spoke German and he was a classical musician. Where else had I heard about a man who hailed from the British Isles and possessed both of these skills? Another two pieces fell into the jigsaw. More coincidences? I didn't think so.

Table for one. I ordered the house speciality, fillet steak grilled traditional Bavarian style with hot sauces and big enough to fill the plate. It was home cooking all right, with Vanessa visible through a serving hatch at the rear, busy in the kitchen. The owner himself sits at 'the boss's table' at the back of the restaurant, where he has a view of the whole place. Right now Vernon was doing the rounds, table hopping to meet the clientele and enquire if the food was to their liking.

When he reached me I shook a hand that had a powerful grip and introduced myself with the story about researching a book. I invited him to sit down, share a beer and answer a few innocent questions. Goa in the sixties, Bob's Inn ... and Jungle Barry? Yes, Vernon knew all three and was happy to talk.

He had been one of the drinking crowd at Bob's Inn, he said, when the man calling himself Barry first appeared in the community.

'What was the atmosphere like around the area at that time?' I asked him.

'Very unsettled. The gangs were here and there was a lot of tension and violence. The Birmingham gang from Britain dealt in heroin. Barry wanted none of it. He would only smoke if someone passed him a spliff and it would be unsociable not to have a drag. But he did very little of it. It was more from politeness than anything else. He did smoke ordinary cigarettes but mainly he was a drinker.

'He was never in trouble. He was with the Irish anyway, because that's where he said he came from. But he was always on the sidelines, and everyone left him alone.

'One thing about Barry that struck me as unusual was how he could read the signs. When there was anything brewing he would just vanish. He seemed to be on the lookout for it. He would disappear before an argument developed into anything. He knew how to avoid it. He could evaporate from trouble in a flash. One minute he was there, the next he had gone.

'I saw it a number of times because these were the bad days. Barry was close to many situations that looked as if they might get ugly – arguments at other tables or a couple of guys with too much drink inside them insulting each other and getting into a serious fight. Or worse, if someone was going to pull a knife or a gun. But Barry never got into trouble himself.'

'How did he strike you?'

'Barry was a very English gentleman even though he told me his family came from Ireland. If Barry was Irish, he didn't sound it. I used to drink with him in Bob's place. He had a beautiful voice, very cultured and educated, with an English accent.'

I produced the black-and-white photograph of the earl. 'Is this him?'

A sharp intake of recognition. 'That's Barry!' Vernon looked hard at me. 'I've seen this picture before, years ago. It was in the papers after the murder in London. He was ill once, months after he first came here and they had to shave him. I saw him lying in bed without the beard. Yes, that's him.'

'If you suspected who he might be, why didn't you report it to the authorities?'

Vernon's shrug said it all.

'And the murder in England? What kind of impact did it make here?'

'Next to nothing. It was a seven-day wonder in the

newspapers. Nobody took much notice of it and by the time Barry appeared here it was long forgotten. No one associated him with it – why should they?'

I could believe it. If it was still another world out here now, it would have been even more so nearly 30 years ago. The local papers probably ran a few paragraphs in the days immediately following the murder before scaling down the story and then forgetting it altogether. The staid *Times of India* almost certainly would have displayed the drama on page one – but for how long? The equally heavy broadsheet *Daily Navhind Times* ('The Newspaper You Can Trust') did likewise. While the brasher *Herald* ('Largest Circulated English Daily in Goa, established 1900') would surely have confined the story to its inside page of foreign news after the first wave of excitement died away.

Yes, it would be a seven-day wonder up there in the lawless patch of border jungle. And these papers never even reached the doors of most members of the immediate populace, many of whom were illiterate in their own language and certainly couldn't read English. Those who could would be more concerned with the issues that dominated their own lives – local politics, crime and sport, the bread and butter of every newspaper in every country on the planet.

As for the hippies who shared Barry's life, the cloying scent of pot in the bars, jungle clearings and their rooms meant more to them than anything that was going on in the outside world.

More significantly for my investigation, Vernon remembers how friends of Barry 'turned up from nowhere' unannounced, to sit drinking and chatting with the bearded hobo in Bob's Inn – before handing over wads of cash in rupees, which at that time were valued at around 40 to the pound.

'Did you see these people yourself?'

'Yes, several times over the years.'

'What were they like?'

'Barry was getting money from England. I saw it with my own eyes. A few months after he first appeared here people began to arrive to visit him, men and women who spoke well and who would sit at the long table in the centre of the bar and pay homage to him. When they were here he held court like a king!

'Barry was an aristocrat, you could see, not a bum. Even in later years, when his friends had all gone and he had very little money, he always retained his dignity and his air of authority. There was something about him that commanded respect, even when he was wearing just his shorts and sandals in that bar.

'These people would laugh and joke with him. Sometimes the table held as many as 20 people, many of them visitors off luxury yachts that were moored in creeks not far away from here. Other times there were just two or three men and women who turned up. The clothes they wore were casual but they were always well dressed.

'More than once, usually close to midnight, I saw one of the men take out a big wad of rupees and hand it across the table. Barry never bothered to count it – he just stuffed it away inside his shirt and went on drinking.

'What made these people stand out from the rest is that this was a time when everyone else was a hobo. Or dealing in drugs. People were turning up here from Vietnam, Thailand, Malaysia, America, England, Germany – from all parts of the world. They would just appear, spend weeks or months living in shacks, and then move on. Barry's visitors were different. From their voices and their manner you would definitely call them high class.'

'What happened when they no longer came?'

Vernon paused while I took a gulp of beer. This time I was making discreet notes. He had voiced no objection but I thought a tape recorder was a bit too obvious in the man's own restaurant. People might get curious.

At last he said: 'What happened to him was so sad. After a few years it was down to nine people. Then less. Then it petered out altogether. The word was that they had all died. Barry became very depressed. There's nothing so awful as to run out of luck and run out of money at the same time. Barry's luck went when his friends stopped coming. His money dried up. He really started hitting the bottle then. Eventually boredom got to him, too. We were all aware of it and helped him as far as we could. We bought him his drinks because he was part of our community. But, I tell you, in the end he was bored to death and that was what killed him.

'It was a tragedy for him but what other choice did he have? Barry was a man going nowhere because there was nowhere for him to go. He was bored to death during the monsoons because he had no new friends to challenge to backgammon. That meant three months or more when he just sat in bars with a backgammon board in front of him, listening to the rain and hitting the bottle.

'What kind of life is that for an intelligent human being, even an inveterate gambler like him? He would challenge people to play with the "gambler's dice" and many times I'd hear him say: "Double or quits!" But very few people would take him on. Barry just wanted some excitement in his life, but in the end all he could do was reach for the bottle to find it.'

'Do you know if Barry had a surname?'

'I only heard a name once and that was one day in Bob's bar when the police came to question some of the people about drugs. We were all taken by surprise. Everyone had to write their names on some kind of form, which the police took away. Barry was next to me at the table and I saw it in his own handwriting: Halpin ... Barry Halpin, that was the name.'

I had two final questions for Vernon.

'How did Barry die? And when?'

'Barry died of cirrhosis of the liver and a few other things, all drink-related. Around January 1996. I was there – in the open-air crematorium in Panjim. We saw him off in style. Let me tell you about it.'

And he told me about it.

I left the Spice Garden and took my time walking back to the hotel. I needed the air to clear my head. The streets were still teeming with traffic and late-night revellers but I hardly noticed them as I threaded my way past the potholes and the bulky shapes of sacred cows clustered in small groups at the road junctions. Now they were just part of the scenery.

Vernon was the most articulate, intelligent and informed witness yet. If everything he said was true, the plot was thickening rapidly. Who were Lucan's benefactors? For me it was further confirmation of the rumours that had spread like wildfire just after he disappeared – of his old friends bankrolling him in his enforced exile from the world as he knew it. And if the Goan police had actually had our man face to face without realising it, it was something else I needed to follow up – and urgently. As for the funeral...

It was time to show my face at the local police station and take them into my confidence. Starting at the top.

CHAPTER 24

CRIME BUSTER

Inspector Gundu Naik sat in his shirtsleeves behind his desk beneath a swirling fan and smiled a smile that, despite the stultifying heat of his office, carried the chill of winter in it. His shrewd eyes studied the two photographs I had laid out side by side on his desk, examining them carefully through his steel-rimmed spectacles. Then he reached into a drawer, produced a magnifying glass and peered more closely. After a full minute in which I sat staring at him intently in total silence, he delivered his verdict.

'If this was a police line-up, I would say these are one and the same person. They are very similar, though of course a man's face changes with the years.'

I had reached the inner sanctum of his office in the Area Police Headquarters by informing his underlings at reception that I was an ex-Scotland Yard detective who wished to discuss an urgent matter with him as part of an ongoing investigation. One cop to another. I had even brought along a copy of my book to prove my identity – it saved the social niceties of a phone call to book an appointment that might take days to set up.

The Calangute police headquarters is located outside the town, past a fork in the main road heading into the interior. A hundred metres up the right-hand branch stands a single-storey white-walled building set back from the road.

The HQ has that solid, slightly forbidding air of police stations the world over. Not exactly hostile, but not spreading out the welcome mat either. It was there to fulfil a function for the state, and the people inside were not here for a holiday. This was the control centre at the hub of three local districts: Madhya, Bradesh and Himachal. I suspected 'control' would have its work cut out to keep law and order over its sprawling field of jurisdiction.

Outside, the heat shrouded the day in a warm, humid blanket. Police cars were stationed in a space at the front while visitors were directed to a car park to the left of the main entrance. Leaving Raju standing guard by his taxi, I strode over to the entrance and up the stairs, feeling the sun burning a hole in my back through my damp T-shirt. This was December. It was already hot and it was going to get hotter.

Inside there was not a great deal of movement. An occasional police officer in short-sleeved blue shirt appeared armed with a batch of papers, cast a casual glance in my direction, then disappeared off again into one of the many rooms on the ground floor. It looked like a quiet day on the precinct.

It may seem odd that I was prepared to walk straight into a police station in another country without so much as a courtesy phone call to alert them that I was coming. But in an investigation like this the fact is that one man on his own can accomplish more and move faster than the best team of police officers 'on official business', or even Interpol. When I was with the Yard on a foreign inquiry, our hands were always tied by formality and bureaucracy. We would find ourselves up against reams of officialdom and diplomatic courtesies that had to be observed. When you're officially representing Scotland Yard, you can't just charge in without warning.

But I could. I found the nearest open door, knocked and went in. Half an hour and two glasses of chilled orange juice later I was sitting in a larger and more imposing office opposite the local chief of police.

Fifty-five-year-old Gundu Naik is the Eliot Ness of northern Goa. He is a crime buster who, with his team of Untouchables, has cleaned up the coastline almost single-handedly to make it safe for the tourists who are now invading his country like the second coming of Vasco da Gama. As well as the popular beaches north of Panjim, Inspector Naik is in charge of 100 square miles of remote jungle with its hidden shanty towns, poverty, crime and squalor.

Deceptively soft-spoken and with scores of officers under his command, he has made a name for himself by his zero-tolerance policy on drugs and by his will to enforce it. The name of Gundu Naik appears virtually every week in the pages of the regional newspapers as he testifies in court to yet another high-profile drug bust on his patch, mainly dramatic seizures of *charas* (grass) or heroin. The language is delightfully quaint at times: 'Inspector Naik had apprehended a miscreant who…'

Behind him on the wall stands a large blackboard showing the department's successes with said miscreants, and those yet to be apprehended. Constantly updated, the list displays the current crime statistics of Naik's 'manor', from murder and mugging all the way down the ladder to unlawful assembly. The letter 'D' in a space alongside each case is prominent. It stands for 'detected'. The thought crossed my mind that the blackboard must be quite a motivation for Inspector Naik and his team when they arrive for duty every morning.

Whether we're talking beach scams by gypsies harassing holidaymakers with cheap silk sarongs and jewellery, or a rip-off in the bustling back alleys of Candolim, Baga and Calangute, his Untouchables are busy cleaning up the town. Naik's long arm is reaching out to reclaim law and order in the jungle where I now knew Lucky Lucan had lived and died, a jungle that was once the exclusive fiefdom of criminals and drug barons.

Now he was saying: 'I only wish I could have met this Barry, but I was not working in this area then. If he *was* the same man as the fugitive, as seems highly probable, then to have arrested Lord Lucan would have been a major feather in our caps. We would have given him a package holiday in our Central Jail in Fort Aguada lasting 20 years! It is situated on the headland and I could have promised him a very good view.' Now here was a man with attitude!

From all reports the 7th Earl had a lucky escape. Aguada Prison, a dark and forbidding place on its headland looking out to the Arabian Sea, has a fearsome reputation that has spread far beyond the borders of Goa. A low, white-walled stone building with sloping grey tiles and small windows, the prison overlooks a line of harsh rocks that would tear an escapee's feet to ribbons. Inside, a network of tunnels links the cells, some of which have no such luxury as windows, and here, in the words of one prison visitor: 'The searing heat makes it impossible to take more than a few steps.' It would have been a bleak world for Lucan if he had fallen foul of the local authorities! I can't see how even *his* resilience could have survived that dank and fetid containment.

Corruption is endemic in India, from politicians to the police, and invades every area of society. It is an accepted part of life. Palms – the human kind – can be greased, and are. In the nineties Aguada Prison featured unfavourably in high-profile drug cases. It became an unhappy home to Britons held on allegedly trumped-up charges in cases where the local police were accused of planting cannabis on them and extorting bribes.

At the time Mark Winch was in the hippie colony raising his

camera to snap an unsuspecting Lord Lucan asleep in his rocking chair, a major scandal was breaking a few miles down the coast. A 28-year-old heating engineer from Oxfordshire named Nick Brown was incarcerated for 16 months in Aguada without trial on charges of possessing 15 grams of *charas*. When his case finally came to court he was given the mandatory ten years in jail.

Only after intense lobbying by his mother and an organisation called Fair Trials Abroad, backed by diplomatic pressure from the Foreign Office, did Nick finally win his appeal against conviction and gain release after serving 23 months. He claimed the drugs had been planted on him. Nick had been arrested at a roadblock while riding a friend's motorcycle and would say later: 'My only crime was not to bribe the police. That's what they were after – money. They pulled me off the bike, handcuffed me, threw me into the back of a jeep, and I knew I'd had it. My mistake was to allow the police to get to my wallet containing my passport and $400 in cash before I did.'

His lawyer, Peter D'Souza, was even more outspoken, a veteran of the Indian legal system who once represented no fewer than 50 foreigners in drugs cases in one year. 'The Goan drug laws have given the police a licence to print money,' he frankly stated in one interview. 'They see foreigners as easy meat. They plant drugs on them and then demand bribes. It's a fact of nature.'

Goa's most notorious case featured Gary Carter and Alexia Stewart, a young couple who were convicted in 1999 for possessing marijuana and jailed for ten years. They spent 18 months in Aguada before being released following unrelenting media pressure on their behalf.

Twenty-nine-year-old Alexia, a language graduate and daughter of an Oxford don, described the conditions in which she was incarcerated. 'There is a cage in my cell where violent prisoners are held. In the other corner is a hole in the ground – a toilet. I got used to the cockroaches, maggots and beetles in the rice early on.' She later revealed how her sea-level cell would flood in the monsoon season as rain poured off the hillside. The low ceilings and tiny windows turned her confinement into a suffocating vault in summer.

Alexia later gave her dramatic account of how police had raided their rented house in northern Goa looking for drugs. 'One of them came in from the garden brandishing a fist-sized plastic bag. He said it was cannabis and they had found it in the house. They would go peacefully, they said, if we paid them the equivalent of £1,500. Foolishly, we refused. We would have paid them ten times over if we had known what lay ahead.'

What lay ahead was the prospect of ten years in Aguada. As it was, 18 months was more than enough. Her sojourn in the crumbling jail that houses Goa's most dangerous prisoners and is notorious for the oven-like temperatures of the cells lit a bush fire in the Western media and finally forced the couple's release.

Once free from the hell-hole and safe from retribution, Gary added his own condemnation: 'My time in jail was much worse than Alexia's. India is notorious for corruption but I never imagined I would be locked up with rapists, murderers and paedophiles. Nothing could have prepared me for life in Aguada. I shared a 30-foot by 12-foot cell with 40 other inmates. It was designed to hold half as many, and we slept on the concrete floor in strict rows. You had to fight over the buckets of water for washing and during shortages we went without washing for days and had to drink green, cloudy water from a well. The heat and humidity were unbearable and malaria was rife. A prison doctor was available once a week for two hours to care for 180 inmates. He handed out sleeping tablets like sweets. The food was inedible – watery lentils, poor-quality rice, dry bread and black tea. The prison was just around the corner from a luxury hotel but it was a world away, out of sight and certainly out of mind.'

Small wonder Barry kept his nose clean. He would have known all about Aguada.

At the time Mark took his chance to spend Christmas on the Goa coast, 30 Westerners were locked up a mile away, many of them on drugs charges. Fair Trials Abroad reinforced warnings about the risks to young Westerners visiting the state, where 'police corruption is alleged'.

It may be located on a beautiful coastline but Aguada is certainly no holiday camp. For decades it has been hailed as Goa's answer to Alcatraz, a frightening and forbidding place that surely served as a deterrent to any would-be drugs smuggler. But now Inspector Naik was telling me: 'Things have changed. In those days in the seventies anyone could vanish here. Today, it is different. The situation has improved considerably.' In 'those days' he had been an administrator pushing a pen in Panjim before getting into the front-line action. 'Districts like Ximera are called wards. Up to five years ago we only had two policemen to control this whole area of 30 square miles around the border. It was an impossible task for them. Today we have a sergeant and four constables for each ward, as well as the special Tourist Police force on the beaches, all of them responsible to me.

'Twenty-five years ago Goa would have been considered a very safe haven for anyone wanting to disappear. Nobody bothered about passports. If an outsider didn't make trouble, he would not come to the attention of the police and could remain undisturbed. No officer would have thought of stopping a stranger on the street and questioning him unless he was behaving suspiciously. It just didn't happen. People would exist on a first name alone. Nobody asked questions or filled in forms. They didn't have to register in a hotel. There would be no police on the beaches, unlike the regular patrols we have today. Nobody bothered.

'Now we keep records, and we question everything. Passports, date of birth, parents, occupation… Even so, we are aware that people slip through the net. I'm quite sure there are still fugitives around this area. Our major problem at present is heroin being brought in by Nigerians. But the penalties are severe, especially for possession of drugs. The minimum punishment is ten years, with no remission. For other crimes, remission is possible – but not for drugs.'

That wintry smile again. 'We have a saying here: "Everyone is escaping from something. Even the tourists are escaping from winter!"'

Good enough. Inspector Naik had spelled it out and confirmed everything I had surmised up to now about the lack of a law-enforcement presence here three decades before – and the ease with which Lucan could have existed without any identifying documents. We shook hands, and his dark eyes gleamed behind the spectacles. 'Let me know what happens,' he said.

'I will,' I promised.

Deputy Inspector Rajesh Kumar saw me to the front steps and out into the heat of the day. DI Kumar is Number Two in the team, only 26 years old but with a high-flying career ahead of him and always in at the sharp end when the going gets tough. A man to watch.

Rajesh explained: 'It is only in the last two years that stringent laws have been brought in to enforce matters. In the old days, the rules were there but they were never implemented. Now all visitors are required to register, whether it's at a five-star hotel or a £1-a-night shack in the jungle. But we know there are still a lot of people out there who shouldn't be doing what they're doing.'

Shaking hands enthusiastically, he paid me the ultimate compliment. 'Yours is the most famous police force in the world. We all look up to you and follow your example.'

Much as we at the Yard may have felt we were the best, there's something eminently more satisfying about hearing such words from a colleague halfway around the world!

In return I'd like to make an offer to Inspector Naik and his Untouchables. Feel free to chalk up another statistic on your blackboard.

Under 'Most Wanted' ... with a 'D'. For 'detected'.

CHAPTER 25

ASHES TO ASHES

Somewhere there had to be a record of Barry Halpin's death. Now I had a surname but I still needed to find an exact date. It seemed the obvious place to start would be Goa's capital. I had no idea of the paper chase I was letting myself in for.

Panjim is an experience in itself, and not for the faint of heart. I wouldn't call it so much a bustling city as a hell of sensory overload in which sheer discordant pandemonium assaults your ears while a churning human sea fills your vision. The air is full of dust and noise. Traffic roars at you from all directions. White-gloved policemen, their helmets eclipsed by dark clouds of exhaust fumes, stand on precarious-looking platforms in the centre of junctions, waving their arms like windmills and blowing whistles to no apparent effect. Yet somehow motorists and pedestrians survive – or, if they go under, they do it quietly enough so that the overall cacophony drowns out whatever sounds they make.

The Municipal Town Hall in Panjim is a large, echoing building in the heart of the city that looks exactly what it is: a colonial leftover. High ceilings and marble floors turn footsteps into a noisy stampede. The wide staircase is like Oxford Circus underground station in the rush hour, filled with people toing and froing between various departments like busy ants. I finally located the man whose name I had been given as the senior registrar: Superintendent Octaviano Dias.

A line of locals sat on hard wooden chairs in the corridor outside his office, craving an audience. Inside, behind a glass window, Mr Dias was clearly a busy man – but he proved to be another charming Goan who was eager to oblige. In this part of the country at least, the face of officialdom wears a genuine smile.

After I explained my mission, Superintendent Dias shook his head in profound sorrow. 'Our files here are inadequate and I would need more detailed information. It will take time. Your friend could be registered locally.' Then his friendly face brightened. 'You think he died of cirrhosis of the liver? If so, that would probably be in hospital, and if he died in hospital you will find the details kept there.' He wrote down directions on a piece of paper. 'Good luck!'

Goa's main hospital was on a road I hoped I'd never have to take again – until it was time to catch the plane home. It was the highway a mile out of town in the direction of the airport where we had already survived *Death Race 2000*. But the faithful Raju was ready, willing and optimistic. I climbed back into his taxi and showed him the directions. He knew the place anyway.

We found the hospital behind a lay-by, a forbidding complex of flaking concrete buildings surrounded by line upon line of vehicles in a car park so confusing that I was reminded of Hampton Court Maze. Cars, taxis and vans jostle to snatch a space and the blare of horns could waken the dead, never mind the living trying to snatch a wink of sleep in their wards.

Without an appointment, I could only brazen it out and hope for the best. I wandered down several blind alleys until I located the registrar's office on the ground floor, picked up speed to march past a dozen patients waiting to be seen, and knocked on the door. A middle-aged woman wearing a blue sari and an air of authority looked up from her desk. I showed her my card.

Mrs Emin Po holds the title of Hospital Administrator and proved to be an island of calm amid the turbulent sea of humanity lapping at her shores, each wave with a problem to be sorted out. Even for a totally unexpected visitor, Mrs Po was a sympathetic listener. I gave her a name: Barry Halpin. And an approximate date of death: the winter of 1995–6. I told her I had come from the UK specially to trace him. The delightful Mrs Po was anxious to give every assistance she could.

'Come back tomorrow. I'll have the ledgers for you,' she promised.

She was as good as her word, even allowing me to use her office to spread the huge bound registers on a desk and thumb through the pages. As I finished one ledger, an assistant took it away and replaced it with another. In all, it took me two hours. Columns of handwritten names scrawled in different-coloured inks listed those who had died in the hospital during the six months between November 1995 and April 1996, along with their age and address and cause of death. Scanning down the pages, I noted how few European names there were – possibly two dozen out of several thousand. And not a Halpin among them.

I bade Mrs Po farewell, thanking her for her time and trouble. She handed me her business card: the Dona Riva

Guest House in Miramar, which she runs with her husband, Roy. So the hospital was her day job. 'Come and stay with us next time you are in Goa,' she said.

I tucked the card away. Why not? I had already formed an attachment to the country and its friendly and hospitable people.

As I was leaving, a thought struck me. 'Where would someone be cremated around here?' I asked. 'Are there many places?'

'The Municipal Crematorium in Panjim,' Mrs Po replied. 'That's where they all go.'

I was in Panjim. I had the afternoon ahead with no one to see and nowhere special to go. She gave me directions: 'Ask for St Inez Church. Everyone knows it. Look for an animal sanctuary beyond it. That's where you'll find the crematorium.'

Goa is full of churches, largely due to the missionary zeal of its Portuguese masters over five centuries, and Panjim has its share, including the massive Cathedral off the main square. It was there that we found a priest who knew St Inez and gave Raju directions. For myself, I was already totally lost in the confusion and congestion of the streets.

On one of the arterial roads leading north out of the city we came upon it at last – an imposing Catholic church that needed a fresh coat of paint. A three-storey office building equally in need of cosmetic surgery faced the main courtyard and housed the registrar's office. I had been informed that this was the 300-year-old church where Lucan's friends had gathered for a brief service before consigning him to the flames. But when I asked if I could examine the records, I was met with a shrug and an apology. No records available. Ah, well.

Two hundred metres beyond, round a bend in the road, and there it was. An animal sanctuary with mules, goats and a small calf grazing contentedly enough in a compound opposite a mosque. In between, a track led up to a huge pair of black steel gates set into high stone walls. The gates were open. Behind them I glimpsed a pall of grey smoke rising into the sky. Christ, someone was being cremated!

My timing could not have been better if I had planned it, even if what I was about to see would be one of the grisliest sights I had ever witnessed. Raju stayed in the taxi trying to conceal his perplexity. I had not taken him into my confidence and he knew better than to ask questions. I had merely informed him that I was conducting some research into the area – though why that involved police stations, hospitals, churches and a crematorium must have given him food for thought, and that didn't even take into account the number of bars I'd visited. But somehow I doubted if anything surprised him any more.

I walked slowly up the track to the gates and peered inside, trying to adopt an air of reverence and discretion. Inside, some 50 men were gathered on the steps of an old stone building, watching in silence as something burned on a glowing pyre of logs in front of them.

My eyes widened in both fascination and repugnance. I had seen Hindu funerals on TV, most notably that of Mrs Gandhi. But witnessing a burning human body in the flesh, or what remained of it, was something else.

Twelve separate pyres stood in two lines under primitive corrugated-iron roofs, wide metal slats waiting for the corpses to be placed on them. The bodies are brought in on curved cradles with two poles slung through front and back so that four mourners can carry them to the blaze. Mass cremations can take place, and do.

Looking more closely, I could make out the shrouded cadaver stretched out on the main pyre, where Lucan's body would have been placed, wrapped in a pale cream-coloured sheet. Burning logs crackled fiercely beneath the human barbecue and grey smoke curled into the sky. Every now and then a small man with a can stepped forward and threw petrol over the body, making the flames leap suddenly into the hot afternoon. A pungent burned-bacon smell of scorched flesh filled the air. Overhead a pair of vulture-like birds of prey circled patiently, waiting to descend on the ashes and pick over any scraps they could find.

So this is the way Lord Lucan ended his days on earth? Vernon's words came back to me from the previous evening.

'They gave him a Viking funeral,' he had told me. The body was wrapped in a sheet, but Barry's bearded face could be seen, its eyes closed, the hands clasped across the bare chest. Less than a dozen mourners, those who counted themselves his close friends, gathered round the pyre, which was piled high with logs, waiting to be lit.

On a warm January day in 1996, they saw Barry off in style.

Someone had the bright idea of dousing the body with *feni*, the 90 per cent (or 180 proof) coconut-juice cocktail that had destroyed his liver as he drank himself to death on it. So instead of the petrol that was customarily used for such purposes, Barry's friends poured bottles of the stuff over the shrouded corpse, then stood back as a mortuary assistant lit the logs with an oil-soaked rag.

A match would have done it.

Vernon recalled the moment as if it had been branded into him. 'I don't know whose idea it was. But a few of us gathered in Bob's Inn after Barry died and someone said: "How about a Viking funeral?"

'We made arrangements with the Municipal Crematorium. They brought him in on a metal litter, wrapped in a sheet but with the face left open so that we could see it. We gathered round him and we soaked him in *feni*. It seemed appropriate since it was Barry's favourite drink and we figured he would have approved. This is high-octane fuel, close to one 100 per cent neat alcohol, so we knew it was going to burn.'

And burn it did. 'Most of the mourners had been drinking,' Vernon went on. 'The flames roared eight feet into the air. We had to stand back because of the heat. One of us wasn't quick enough. He was an Irish guy and the flames shot back up his arm. The bottle of *feni* he was waving went off in his hand. He was burned but not badly. He had been drinking anyway and felt no pain at all.

'But then something terrible happened. There was an almighty bang, as loud as a shotgun blast, and Barry's head exploded in front of us! It made us jump out of our skins. One minute I was looking into his face, the next his whole head had been blown away in a shower of sparks like a firework display.

'The pressure from the heat must have built up inside his skull and it just went off. I'd never seen or heard an explosion like that before. At the time it was very dramatic and one or two of the guys were so upset they had to leave. The flames were really fierce by then. We'd poured so much *feni* on him it was as if he was pickled.

'The next day some of them came back for the ashes and took them upcountry in an urn to scatter under the big waterfall. That was what Barry wanted. He had left strict instructions that there was to be nothing of him left, nothing at all.'

End of Jungle Barry. Thinking back to his old drinking buddy, Vernon sounded almost nostalgic. For me, it meant something else was possible – Lord Lucan had achieved his final wish: to vanish once and for all off the face of the earth.

My enquiries continued. Like a sea angler in search of big marlin, I trawled the area for clues and information. Nothing was too slim to ignore. But I was leaving the biggest fish till last – Bob, founder and owner of Bob's Inn, setting one enigmatic mystery man to shed light on another. Until then, I was content with minnows.

Dental records. Lady Lucan had told me that there were none in London that she knew of, and that her husband's dentist was dead anyway. So any X-rays or a copy of Barry's teeth that I could bring home would be irrelevant. But I was looking for gold fillings, or at least a flash of gold in Barry's smile. All the expats I spoke to who go back to the UK during the monsoon season make sure they have their annual check-up on home ground rather than subject themselves to the ministrations of a local dentist. This would seem grossly unfair to the Goan practitioners, but understandable. If one had to go local, the most likely choice turned out to be Rina Lawande, actually married to one of Bob's cousins. Unfortunately, she proved to be too young to remember the bearded hobo. No records there, and no gold in them thar fillings. Oh well, it was worth a try.

Fresh confirmation of Barry's fiery exit came from an elderly Englishman in nearby Baga who asked to be called 'Julian' and not to be identified 'because I have a criminal record'. I later found out he was a paedophile. Portly and immaculately turned out, he was one of the old school of expats.

Julian told me: 'I first met Barry in 1975, the same year he arrived, when I bumped into him in the street market in Calangute a few months after I myself arrived in Goa. I got talking to this strange guy. He said: "Hello, how are you?" And before I had time to reply, he added: "Would you like a drink?" Then he used a word I hadn't heard before: "*Maddache!*"

'I said: "What's that?" He replied: "Coconut juice. *Feni*. Don't you know it? Come and try it." We went to a bar and I tried it. I didn't like it. It was far too strong. But that was his drink.

'Over the years we used to meet regularly in Bob's place. I watched him consume unbelievable quantities of beer and Honey Bee. Barry loved the stuff. When he was in his cups, he would tell his favourite joke about "the Regiment". He would stand up and call for "A toast to the Regiment. Uniform, yellow. Flag, white. Motto: Beating the Retreat!"

'To humour him we all stood up and raised our glasses with him. Then he would laugh uproariously. More than once he confided to me: "Soldiers run in the family." He liked the double meaning.'

An interesting choice of jest for the descendant of the man who'd ordered the Charge of the Light Brigade... Or perhaps a veiled reference to his own 'retreat'?

Julian likewise remembers the final day that he laid eyes on his old drinking partner. 'I knew Barry was to be cremated and I had a bit of spare time, so I thought I'd go down and see him off. The crematorium was a very unsettling place out there in the open, and rather spooky. There was a corrugated roof and, underneath it, slats. They had laid big logs down and then put the body on it.

'When I got there the face was visible and it was Barry's face I was looking at. He still had his beard. I can see him now, lying there with piles of wood all round him.

'The fire had just been lit. He was wrapped in a sheet, bare-chested. People stood around chatting. There must have been nine or ten of us. It wasn't like a formal British cremation – it was quite a casual affair, really. After all, you couldn't stand and stare at the thing burning all the time.

'Then something pretty dreadful happened, which made me feel sick. There was a horrible bang. It was the most awful sound. And when I looked his head had gone. I was horrified. The pressure must have built up and it just exploded. I felt so bad I had to leave. The head went, and shortly after that I went, too.

'Barry had told us he wanted to be cremated. In fact, he insisted on it. He told me so himself. During one conversation we started chatting about how we would both like to go. I said to him: "I don't really want a hole in the ground where ants can eat me up. I'd like to be cremated." He said: "Me, too!" It was a mutual decision, and we shook hands on it!

'He must have mentioned it to other people because someone else arranged it.'

I showed Julian the two photographs of Barry and Lucan and he nodded his recognition.

'I'm convinced these are the same person. I first met Barry when he looked like that' – indicating the black-and-white portrait – 'though his whole appearance changed over the years. I certainly never saw him with a suit on.

'Barry appeared to me to be a very versatile character. I always felt he could have been an actor. He remained something of a mystery man and I never went too closely into his personal life, just as I didn't want him to pry into mine. That's one of the joys of being out here: people leave you alone and don't ask questions.

'After his death, we were all told he died of cirrhosis of the liver. I'm not surprised. He had been going downhill for some time.'

Julian also remembers what happened after the cremation. 'Barry's ashes were scattered under a waterfall. That's what he wanted, too.'

CHAPTER 26

GOODBYE, OLD COCK!

On any investigation in a strange town, there is always one invaluable source of supply: the local newspaper. Buy it and study it, and a heap of information will spring out if you know where to look. The rule applies from Manchester to Melbourne, London to Los Angeles, Glasgow to Goa.

The paper that most seemed to meet my needs was the *Herald*, published from its offices in Rua San Tome in Panjim. If anyone would have what I was looking for, they would. Sure enough, I struck pay dirt.

Mr Vinayak Pai Bir was a lean, intense man with intelligent dark eyes, a firm handshake and a manner that implied: Let's not waste time. What can I do for you?

As usual I had appeared without an appointment. Perhaps it was my years with the Regional Crime Squad and the drug teams that had given me a thick enough skin to appear on strange doorsteps in what I call the 'full frontal' approach. If you've got nothing to hide, you'll see me. If you start stuttering,

I'll know why. Experience of dealing with the unwashed and the ungodly sharpens your instincts about such things.

Mr Pai Bir's ground-floor office was situated behind a glass window at the end of a panelled room that reeked of good old-fashioned newspaper reporting. A line of desks, men in shirtsleeves crouched over their consoles, the air positively buzzing with energy as the day's events were recorded for posterity.

I thought Mr Pai Bir was the editor as he gestured me to a seat by his desk. It turned out he was the circulation manager. I asked him about death notices and a possible obituary for the month of January 1996, and after a moment's thought he nodded. 'I think we can do that for you.'

'Shall I come back in a couple of days?'

'No. If you'd like to wait we can do it for you now.'

The waiting room was five floors up, with a fine view over the rooftops of the old town and the harbour to keep me occupied while someone dug out the files. Eventually a messenger boy came staggering through the door, hefting a pile of cloth-bound volumes that must have weighed a ton. Dust rose in a cloud as he dropped them on to the desk in front of me, gave me a cheery smile and left.

The *Herald* is a serious broadsheet newspaper and follows a strict formula of national and foreign news with the emphasis on local features, comment, politics, entertainment and sport. I thumbed through the pages. The obituary columns seemed particularly popular, often with half a page devoted to a single person and the same photograph reprinted alongside tributes from a dozen friends and relatives.

It took me the best part of an hour – but I found it. Barry's face stared out at me from the issue of 11 January 1996 in a double-column tribute under the word 'DEATH', squashed between a reference to Mr Guilhermino Pinto, 'who expired on

10 January', and a Requiem Mass for the Soul of Mrs Esmeralda Sequeira, followed by a 'blessing of the grave'.

The notice said: 'Barry Thomas Halpin (Jungly Barry). Born 11–3–38, died 3–1–96. Cremation on Saturday 13–1–96, 12 noon, Panjim Crematorium. Dearly loved and sadly missed by all of us. Good-bye old cock!'

Now there's a fond farewell for you. I photocopied the piece, thanked Mr Pai Bir for his cooperation and left with another trophy to take back home.

Bob's Inn. The moment had come to face the man at the centre of this spider's web of intrigue, a man who over so many years must have seen so much – but who had said so little. The man who, above everyone else I had heard about or met on this extraordinary search for the truth, was the nearest Lucan had to a close friend during the second half of his life.

I chose a quiet time, mid-afternoon, when the last lunch-time visitors had gone and there was a lull in trade, then strode across uneven paving stones to the gates in front of the inn.

Bob greeted me cordially, if a little warily. He cut a colourful figure in a bright sports shirt that somehow seemed incongruous with his powerful physique. He had only set eyes on me once before. Nonetheless, when I told him about my research he invited me to join him in a secluded alcove down a quiet path at the rear, its open façade shielded from the public gaze by a network of greenery. 'The boss's office,' he said with a flashing grin.

The boss brought me a Kingfisher beer, snapped one open for himself, switched on a cooling fan as I switched on the tape, and began his story.

He spoke eloquently, stubby hands gesturing to illustrate a point, his English passable but with surprising exactitude, using words as if he had taken a dictionary to bed with him one night and woken up in the morning with a new vocabulary.

And over the next two hours, the whole incredible story took shape at last. Bob remained tight-lipped about his present clientele but was happy to talk about the past. Now I would have the full picture.

First I tidied up the final details on the funeral.

'The cremation cost 15,000 rupees, which would be around £300 in those days,' Bob told me. 'I paid half out of my own pocket. The rest of Barry's friends clubbed together and paid the other 50 per cent.

'He wanted a cremation. In fact he insisted on it. "I don't want anything left of me," he said to me towards the end, when we all knew he was dying. "Nothing whatsoever!" So, OK, we did as he asked. Someone had suggested a Viking funeral, so we gave him a Hindu-style ceremony which is very similar, sprinkling scented incense on the body and piling sandalwood around it, just like they do for a proper Hindu cremation. There were flowers everywhere.

'Then we poured *feni* all over him, which is certainly not in the Hindu method! And – yes, his head did explode suddenly, just like a gun going off. It was so weird it made us jump out of our skin.

'I closed Bob's Inn for the day. Afterwards all his friends came back and drank and smoked and talked about him for hours. I only allowed his friends through the door that day. It was a great send-off. Barry would have appreciated it.'

Bob raised his glass in a toast to an absent friend and there was a brief silence. To break it and to get him more relaxed, I enquired about his own background. Goans love to talk and Bob didn't disappoint me.

His real name is Pradip Lawande, though he has been 'Bob' to everyone since his schooldays – 'for no reason I can think of'. Aged 52, he is one of four brothers, all successful businessmen. One brother runs the local supermarket a block away and the family are obviously respected in the area. Bob's first job was as a barman at the Holiday Inn in Bahrain, three hours from Goa by plane and today a refuelling stop for the big charter flights from Britain. But, like so many others serving the rich and famous with only a few tips to show for it at the end of the day, he had always wanted his own place.

He came home to Goa to achieve his ambition and Bob's Inn opened on 8 October 1981 with a single small bar and space for 30 customers. By that time Barry would have been in the area for six years. An acre of land including a well at the back ensured Bob could expand, and today his place has seating for more than 100 and a staff of ten waiters to do their bidding.

'In those days Goa was totally different. No apartments, no hotels. It was all jungle or open scrub. There was nothing here except the shacks. Cecilia's was one of the first bars on the beach, but there were no tourists. Today the place has exploded. Everything is more commercial.

'Ninety-nine per cent of my first customers were local people. But the word spread and gradually my place became very popular among foreigners. In the beginning they were all hippies, arriving from nowhere with rucksacks and guitars and very little money. But I was happy to welcome them – I'd been there myself. When I was in my twenties I called myself the first hippie!

'I could understand them. Always I was helpful. They needed a visa – I would get it for them. If people had no money they could drink for free and pay me later … maybe. I was always giving credit – 2,000 rupees, 5,000, sometimes more. That would be over £100 in English money.' His laugh contained a slight edge to it. 'I have to say there are an awful lot of people in the world who still owe me money!'

I had a feeling that Bob's bonhomie could have its limitations, but I kept the thought to myself.

'I created the atmosphere here,' he said. 'Anybody could come in as long as they didn't cause trouble. I gave equal importance to everybody – and I still do. This is my bar and I run it the way I want. I was not strict on rules – I have never been one for regulations. I leave people free to do what they like. They keep laughing, they don't think of trouble, then that's OK.

'The only rule I had was that my bar was a place where you don't ask questions of strangers. That's the way it was then – and the way it still is. Nobody cares about your past. We are first names only. Goa is like that – it's wonderful! I put a condition on my waiters. If ever any strangers come in and start asking questions – don't tell them anything. Just refer them to me. Tell them: contact Bob! Also, another rule: no children. I don't allow them.'

'Why not?'

'It's the wrong atmosphere for kids.'

'How did you first meet Barry?'

'Barry had been in this area for some years before I met him. He was one of my very first customers. He came from nowhere. He was a penniless pauper but great in heart. If he was running away from something, then he had found the right place. If he was wanted for something in Britain, it's not anything you tell the police about here. He told me he had come from Africa and I told him: "Barry, you are just like Vasco da Gama! He discovered Goa too!"' Close enough, if not totally accurate.

'Old hippies always dressed colourfully – or very simply. Barry just wore a pair of shorts and a shirt, or sometimes he took the shirt off and you could see his hairy chest. He sat at the long table playing backgammon and sometimes he would be in the mood to take up his flute or guitar.

'You must remember that there were many others like him

in those days – simple living, always high-thinking, playing music, communing with nature, out there in the open with the sea, the sun and the moon.

'We always used to say about Barry that he was the only person who looked like a hippie, with his hair and long beard, but who could talk brilliantly about history, psychology, any subject under the sun.

'Rarely did Barry talk about himself, though, or his background. To some people he said he had a sister in Australia, to others that she was living in England. I never knew. But over the years I got to know him like a brother. When I love somebody, I love them. And I will protect them.

'People respect me and they respect my place. I know how to run a good bar. All you need is three things: good ambience, cleanness and good food.' And, in this case, a fourth: discretion being nine points of Bob's law.

'That respect includes the police. In those days they came as far as the door, but they never came inside. Twice Barry was questioned. The first time, an inspector arrived without warning to take him away. They got Barry as far as the gate and the policeman said to me: "You know this man? He has no visa."

'I replied: "Of course I know him. He is the best man here. He is like a Goan – why does he need a visa? He gives no trouble. I'll get him a visa. Please release him immediately."' And they did – immediately. 'I never got Barry a visa but they knew I would be responsible for him.

'Another time they arrested him and took him away to the police station. He had been caught outside my bar with two men who were smoking dope. They kept him in the cells for two days. Barry smoked too, mainly hashish, but only when he felt he had to be sociable. He preferred to drink.

'I went to the station and paid a fine. I asked them: "What do you get by arresting him?"

'They said: "What do you get by looking after him?"'

'I said: "Nothing. He is our friend." They let him go because I told them again that I would be responsible for him.'

'Did you ever hear the name Lucan mentioned?'

'Over the years – yes. Friends who came from England would laugh and joke with him and several times I saw them give him money in large wads of rupees. Barry would always stuff them into his shirt. I heard the name Lucan a couple of times, late at night after they had been drinking, but it meant nothing to me then. One of them called him "Lord L" once but he just laughed it off.

'Once one of his visitors produced a cutting from a British newspaper which had an article on Lord Lucan and a photograph. I saw it over his shoulder and remarked: "That looks like you!"'

'And he nodded and said: "That's right. I'm Lord Lucan!" Then he smiled. I never knew whether he was joking or serious and I didn't take much notice anyway. He had a sense of humour and I think it rather appealed to him.

'By then that business had all happened more than seven years before and it was all over and forgotten. No one cared. Maybe a few learned and wise people might have read it and made the connection but they weren't the sort of people who came here. It may have meant a lot in Britain but out here it meant nothing. As for his name, the only time I had seen him write it he was Barry Halpin. But to all of us he was just Jungle Barry.'

'But Lucan was wanted for murder.'

'Yes. But no one ever came out to investigate. Nothing happened. It meant nothing to us out here. Barry was very popular and no one was going to go to the police. Everybody was in favour of him.'

'What happened when the money dried up?'

'That was a bad business. Barry's outlook had always been:

today is today, tomorrow is tomorrow! As soon as he had money, he spent it. When it ran out he would play backgammon for beer and *feni*.

'But then he went totally broke. It was around 1985 and his friends had stopped coming by then. But his mind was still bright and clear and he hit on an idea to make money: jungle safaris. He operated his business from my restaurant, advertising with a few posters like the one I kept for our wall in the bar: Konkani Safaris.

'Barry's idea was that he would take small parties on foot into the jungle and trek through to one of the waterfalls in the interior. He was very fit and used to walk on the beach and swim to keep in shape. He never put on weight and there was no fat on him. And it worked. He would be gone for five or six days to places like the Narve Springs or Arvalem Falls. Or even longer if he went to his favourite spot, the Dudhsagar Falls, deep in the jungle.

'He knew the trails and he knew the places where they could sleep if they didn't want to stay out in the open. That's how he got his nickname of Jungle Barry. And Barry knew all the rest houses where he could get a drink on the way – and made sure they got to those places at the end of the day!

'He could cook food over an open fire for the people he took with him. He only charged 200 rupees a time but that made him 1,000 each trip and out here that could go a long way. He could put something by to see him through the monsoon months. Barry enjoyed those safaris – until his health started suffering with his drinking and he had to give them up.

'The strange thing was that the best-looking girls, the young travellers who would turn up here on their way round the world, would always want to go with him. They loved his company and they seemed attracted to him. What happened in the jungle? I never asked! It was none of my business.'

'Yes, what about women companions? Did he have a love life of any kind?'

'Barry was more interested in gambling and drinking than girls! His good friend was June, a blonde German woman. He would often stay with her in her apartment by the beach and that's where he died. And June died three months afterwards. She went back to Australia and a few weeks later we got a message that she was dead. Nobody ever knew what caused it – maybe she missed him too much. It happens.'

'Did he leave any of his possessions to you, or to anyone you know?'

'Barry had nothing. Only his old guitar and his watch. I don't know what happened to them but if he left anything it would have been to June.'

Bob took a breath, and sat back. 'He was the best man here but he drank such a lot. Poor fellow's dead. But I love him still.'

Bob had spoken simply, and despite some of the dubious company he kept, I believed his words were spoken with complete honesty. Lord Lucan had become so confident of his new persona that he was, in the words of Vernon Rodrigues, 'part of the furniture'. He had grown to like the local people with their unhurried, laid-back attitude to life – and in turn they grew to accept him as one of their own.

Over the long weeks, months and years that he reinvented himself, establishing his new identity until he lived, breathed and believed it, Richard John Bingham, 7th Earl of Lucan, had become Jungle Barry in all but the truth.

CHAPTER 27

WATERFALL

I stood spellbound at the foot of the Dudhsagar Falls, staring up at a sight that was both awe-inspiring and humbling. Deep in the interior of Goa, on the border with Karnataka, the waters come bursting out of the mountainside to cascade 1,600 feet down a sheer rock face, passing under a railway viaduct to tumble into the gorge beneath. The Falls are known as the 'Ocean of Milk', from the creamy surf created by the splashing turbulence on the rocks below, with spray flying 20 feet into the air and a sound like incessant, pulsating thunder.

The railway is a branch line from Vasco da Gama station on the coast, running inland to the junction at Castle Rock, where it links with the main line north to Bombay. Certainly it would have been one route Lucan could have taken when he made his trips to the city to fend off the crippling boredom of the rainy months and lose himself in the teeming masses.

The rail journey would take 11 hours, make a change from

the bus and be marginally more comfortable. The fare in those days, as one expat told me, was 'dirt cheap, especially if you travelled cattle class' and Jungle Barry would have had the funds from his safaris to meet it. Passengers sitting on the westward side are treated to a staggering view of the Falls as the train chugs over the viaduct, stopping moments later at the tiny halt of Dudhsagar itself, which clings like a mosquito to the side of the massive cliff.

The roar of the cataract can be heard half a mile away, above the chatter of the monkeys in the trees and the constant clamour of the birds. It was a sound that would become familiar to Lucan as he led his small bands of backpackers along the trail that he had come to know as an old friend.

The terrain he explored like some modern-day Livingstone is varied and challenging. Few tourists who visit Goa are aware that one-third of the region is a tangled wilderness of jungle and forest. Retracing Lucan's steps on the last leg of his journey to the Falls, I saw for myself how such a vista can burn itself into a man's soul. It was not beyond the bounds of imagination to realise how, over 20 long years, Lord Lucan could take on the persona of Lord Jim – and relish every moment of it.

Making their cautious way through the undergrowth, his loyal followers would have come across glistening spider's webs at ankle height above the trail, pale white fronds of lethal beauty. Nearby, too, would be venomous snakes, wild boar and even the occasional panther, none of them wanting to be disturbed by clumsy human footsteps.

One trekker has vividly described his own encounter with a full-grown panther. 'It crossed from shrub land to our right on to the asphalt road. Then slowly, almost arrogantly, it moved to the green patch on the left and sat at the foot of a tree hardly two feet from the road.

'We were quite shaken. But the beast yawned, giving us the

full measure of his canines, licked his chops and walked slowly away towards the jungle. He had probably eaten a goat for lunch and just wasn't interested in us…' The writing sounds a bit dated, but the animals are still here and so are the hazards. This is the real jungle, treacherous and hostile, an alien place where nature sets her own traps for the unwary.

Barry would have also warned his small team to be on the lookout for signs of the *dole*, wild dogs that hunt in packs and have been known to take on the mighty water buffalo and even a panther, relying on speed and team work. These vicious scavengers run in relays, lunging at their prey and ducking away from horns or teeth until their victim tires, falls to the ground and bleeds to death.

Jungle Barry, owing no allegiance to anyone, carved out his own track to the stupendous Falls. The rocks are worn smooth by centuries of pounding from the waters after they rise to engulf the valley in the summer's ferocious monsoon months. That's when it becomes a no-go area. The gorge is flooded and the warning signs go up for explorers: 'Danger. No Entry.'

But in winter the place becomes an oasis of tranquillity as the rushing water expends itself in shallows and eddies far below. Here, away from the sound and fury of the waterfall, the placid pools are homes for tiny fish no more than an inch long. With luck you can catch sight of a heron standing like a graceful statue perched in the water under the trees, waiting for fish to swim within reach.

Elsewhere among the rocks I saw small clusters of pilgrims sitting cross-legged, meditating and spending hours in rapt silence as part of their spiritual journey. This is the spot where Barry's ashes were scattered. At the end of a long dirt track littered with rocks, broken palm fronds and fallen coconuts was the place where the final leg of Barry's tours culminated. Stepping stones crossing streams led to a form of earthly paradise.

The cynic in me had to admit to an unworthy thought as I stood braced on the slippery rocks and watched the torrent boiling below, where the Falls cascaded into the river. Wasn't another super-villain laid to rest in just such a watery grave? Dr Moriarty! Of course – he plunged to his death in Switzerland's Reichenbach Falls, locked in combat with Sherlock Holmes in a quintessential representation of good triumphing over evil.

Far be it from me to compare myself to literature's greatest sleuth. But at that moment, beside the waters where Jungle Barry's ashes had been scattered, one of the great man's most famous statements came to mind: 'It is an old maxim of mine that when you have eliminated the impossible, whatever remains, however improbable, must be the truth.'

Certainly the unfolding of this investigation had borne out the wisdom of that statement. And parts of Lord Lucan's final truth were unquestionably improbable!

The jungle had become the 7th Earl's second home. He would allow himself up to ten days to get there and back on the trek from Ximera. He could have done it in less but there was no reason to rush – time was one thing he had in abundance. Once he was known to have stayed in the jungle for two weeks. This place of solitude and awe-inspiring natural beauty at the end of the trail where the waters of Dudhsagar Falls tumbled into the gorge was not only his livelihood, it was his literal change of scenery from the endless sea and sand that were Golden Goa.

The rushing waters create a soporific rhythm that would lull Lucan and his faithful followers to sleep on the flat stone slabs. The team leader would lie with just a raffia mat under him, as seemingly impervious to mosquitoes and other insects as he was to the hard stone of his sleeping platform. If they did not reach a rest house, his party would have sleeping bags to protect them from the elements. But not Jungle Barry.

The creature comforts he had enjoyed at home so many years ago were part of a different life and a different persona. Having lost everything in his life and his world, what did it matter to him to do without a few minor comforts?

He even picked up a new camp follower on the way – a half-tame crow which hopped along in his wake or flew from branch to branch ahead of him. 'I saw this great black bird a number of times,' recalled one regular at Bob's Inn, a Scots lass who gave her name only as Carol and who went for several forays with Jungle Barry.

'The thing was amazing – it behaved more like a tame dog, following its master through the jungle! When Barry lay down to sleep on his mat with just a blanket pulled over him, the creature hopped around and pecked at his ankles. Barry would throw it titbits from time to time. Eventually it flew off after a couple of days, back to the coast – but it would return for the next trip.'

Any true birdwatchers in Jungle Barry's party would have had a field day. They could spot the rare wintering spotbill duck, the common bustard and even get a sighting of the wonderfully named masked booby, whose earliest ancestor was believed to have been blown ashore in Goa by the trade winds.

As I trudged back along the track to where patient Raju was waiting with his taxi, I felt a sudden lift of my spirits. There were unanswered questions, of course. There always would be in a case this complicated, this unique. And there were still some loose ends to be tied up. But I was convinced now that the jigsaw was coming together.

Jungle Barry took his last breath in the Whispering Palms apartment block, close to the Taj Village holiday resort on the beach. The Palms are in a prime position, if you're talking property values. Today the view is somewhat marred by the ugly bulk of the *River Princess* stuck firmly aground in the shifting sands, too heavy to move and too dangerously close to the shore for the Indian Navy to shoot out of the water. But ten years ago an apartment would have been a trophy for the rich to fight over. Lucan had died without a penny to his name – but in luxurious surroundings, even if he was beyond knowing or caring.

Inside the ornate marble entrance the foyer is cool and quiet. Too quiet for me, because no one could recall a German blonde named June or a bearded alcoholic eccentric with little time left to live. Two-bedroomed seafront apartments like this are expensive to own, and more expensive to rent. Barry would surely have stood out as he made his way to June's door – either walking tall or staggering. But no one remembered.

Who was this Fräulein June? Despite painstaking enquiries, I never got to the full truth. Conflicting stories had her labelled as a wealthy socialite, bored out of her mind but with nowhere else to go, or a merry widow with the world at her feet.

I had established that she was German. She was musical up to a point – she could play the flute but seemingly not to the level of giving a Mozart recital. She had arrived from Melbourne, where she had a home, and stayed to soak up the sun and the cocktails in Ximera.

I summed June up as a lonely lady with enough money to see her through the rest of her life but, as if to prove the adage, it was not enough to buy true happiness. June – if that was her real name – spent too many hours clinking glasses with the dropouts in Bob's Inn, and at the end the lady vanished just as mysteriously as the enigmatic figure she befriended and cared for in his final days.

I never discovered the names of the two barflies who would have gone back to the Municipal Crematorium the following day to collect the urn with Barry's ashes. Bob couldn't remember them, or wasn't saying. Vernon likewise. Connie, who had been at the funeral service, had been too upset to attend the cremation – which, in view of what happened, was probably just as well. She Had had heard that someone had scattered them 'in the water', but had no idea who or where.

Those unidentified friends must have transported the urn along the main highway from Panjim to the town of Ponda and through the Sahyadri Mountains to Dudhsagar. The journey would have taken them four hours. I could visualise them at the end of their trek, standing on the same smooth stones where Jungle Barry had rested his head so many times, before opening the lid and scattering his ashes into the pool below.

Presumably someone said a few choice words in memory of their old drinking comrade. But perhaps, after all, there wasn't much to say.

Goodbye, old cock!

Had Richard John Bingham, 7th Earl of Lucan, an alcoholic wanted for murder and on the run from the world and from himself, found his last watering hole?

CONCLUSION

The investigation in Goa had lasted five weeks. Mark had gone back after a fortnight. I had stayed until no stone was left unturned. Now I was satisfied there was nothing more that could be done to corroborate the essential facts or locate any more useful evidence. The hunter-gatherer – hunting Lord Lucan, gathering information to buttress the truth – was going home.

In my hotel room that night I packed my case with a mixture of excitement, relief and anticipation. Excitement that I had uncovered so much compelling evidence to convince me that I had actually solved the mystery of Lord Lucan's disappearance. Relief tinged with sadness that I was going home, leaving a country and a people to whom I had grown attached because of their politeness, their warmth and their almost childlike openness. Maybe this was the surface, the one they showed to tourists and visitors 'passing through'. If I lived there I would probably be shown a different face. But in life you take things as you find them. Here in Goa I had found a place I wanted to see again and people with whom I could relax and be myself.

Anticipation? The game wasn't over yet. There were people who should see the photographs for themselves and give an opinion one way or another. The two words I wanted most to hear would echo those I had heard from simple people in primitive dwellings in the Goan jungle: 'That's him!'

In the end it would come down to weight of evidence.

Back home, I consulted my notes. I was convinced I had found our man. For Lucky Lucan, who evaded capture for 21 years by a mixture of skill and cunning, his good fortune was to have a coterie of loyal friends whose wealth and breeding were matched only by their generosity – and their disregard for many of the normal laws that shape human behaviour. But his luck ran out as those friends, whose loyalty had been tested and not found wanting, passed on and left him alone to fend for himself. By then there were new friends who'd taken the man they knew as Barry into their hearts, and though they couldn't assist him financially in the style he might have preferred, the people of Goa had made him part of their family and looked out for him to the end.

By a million-to-one chance, a petty criminal and fellow fugitive had captured him on film. Now I scribbled out the scenario as I saw it from overwhelming evidence and eyewitness affirmation. Lord Lucan…

Arrived in Bombay around February 1975 by tramp steamer or cargo ship from Africa. In fact from Mozambique – in the year it became independent from Portugal – where there had already been numerous 'positive sightings'. Lucan loved all things Portuguese, spent family holidays in Estoril and spoke the language passably.

Made his way on foot or possibly hitched lifts 400 miles down the coast to a lawless enclave of drug smugglers and criminals in the heart of Goa, another former Portuguese colony incongruously situated in the middle of the Arabian Sea coast of western India, a no-man's-land with its own vow of silence that recalls the Mafia's *omertà*.

There he masqueraded as a penniless hippie. But he charmed a local Goan woman, Mama Cecilia, into providing a safe house for him for several months in return for giving her daughter English lessons ... until friends from Britain turned up to hand the stranger 'bundles of rupees'.

Welcomed 'friends', all well-spoken and some with yachts moored in nearby creeks, who called him 'Lord L'. Barry laughed off the reference – but never denied it.

Had a shaggy mane of hair which hid the fact that he had no ear lobes. Lucan had no ear lobes – and less than five per cent of the human race lack them.

Became accepted by the locals as a genial eccentric who could speak knowledgeably on nearly any subject that came up, and was ultimately absorbed into the community.

Played daily games of backgammon – inveterate gambler Lucan's favourite pastime – challenging strangers to take him on for 'beer money', and regularly asking opponents if they had gambling dice – in the style of a dyed-in-the-wool high roller – he said 'it made the game more exciting'.

Led backpackers on safaris to spectacular waterfalls, earning himself the nickname of 'Jungle Barry' and providing himself with enough funds to keep him going through the monsoon months, even spending time in Bombay, in some years, to alleviate the boredom of the jungle.

Spiralled out of control with his drinking when his friends eventually stopped coming and his money ran out. He would down a bottle of Honey Bee brandy for breakfast and go on for the rest of the day to the lethal 180 proof coconut *feni*, which he could purchase for next to nothing. Now the locals called him 'Crazy Barry'.

Died on 3 January 1996 of cirrhosis of the liver, and was given a 'Viking funeral' in the open-air municipal crematorium by a dozen of his barfly buddies, who soaked him in *feni* and set the body alight. Afterwards his ashes were scattered below a 1,600-foot waterfall in the heart of the jungle.

So much for the script.

Now for the scales to weigh the evidence, for and against. The charge reads: Lord Lucan fled to Goa, where he took refuge for 21 years, eight weeks and one day, before being granted his final wish by his friends and literally vanishing off the face of the earth.

Evidence against: There is none, only speculation. Lucan had to be somewhere, either dead or alive. Many people find it hard to believe a man could disappear without trace. OK, he could have jumped off a cross-channel ferry, or driven a speedboat out into the English Channel, scuppering it and deliberately drowning himself as the boat went down. Highly unlikely. He would have had to hope that the fish would take care of his mortal remains and that the sea would break up the boat – regardless of how much of a fluke local experts in sea burials stated that such an outcome would be.

This is what Lady Lucan believes, or has convinced herself happened, in common with some other 'Lucan watchers'. There is no DNA proof from Goa, neither fingerprints, heirlooms, dental records nor samples of his handwriting that might have clinched it. In addition, it would have taken a supreme effort of will for Lucan not to pick up a phone and hear the voices of his children, whom he adored. Then again, doing so would surely have added to the agony of separation.

Evidence for: Lord Lucan had much in common with the mystery man who appeared like an apparition out of the jungle. Too much, for mere coincidence.

They were the same height and build.

Both men lacked ear lobes.

There were other forensically confirmed physical similarities, like the scar on the knuckle, the hairy chest, the set of the eyes, the brows, the upper nose and the hairline.

Jungle Barry was a backgammon addict, Lucan's favourite game. Both men were experts and both played for money.

Barry told enquirers that he came from Ireland, the ancestral home of the Lucans. He arrived within four months of the murder, perfect timing if he had taken the route via Portugal and Mozambique and arrived by ship in Bombay.

The Portuguese connection. Lucan loved all things Portuguese. In happier times he chose the country for family holidays. He spoke enough of the language to get by. He liked the food, especially fish. What better bolt hole than Portuguese Goa?

Barry's manner of speaking. The cultured voice and turn of phrase that comes naturally to someone brought up in a traditional English background. Little things mean a lot.

His own statement to Mark: 'I am part of history.' This is not the kind of remark that someone would invent, even a self-admitted criminal like Winch looking for personal publicity for financial gain.

The actor in Lucan, who would have found it a challenge to immerse himself in such a role – with no cameras to make him freeze. Here was a gambler taking a chance with his future and parading on a stage at the same time.

The image of Lord Lucan climbing a coconut tree is not as absurd as one might think. 'When in Rome…' and, in the jungle, it was a natural act, and quite simple to perform for a man as fit as Lucan would have been before the drink took him over completely.

Barry's ironic reference to 'soldiers running in the family'. Was this deliberately contemptuous, or simply a man having a joke at his own expense?

Playing the flute and guitar. Pianos are conspicuous by their absence in Goa – in all my time there, I never saw a single one. And over many months and with nothing much else to do, a flute and guitar would be quite easy for a man with Lucan's musical ability to learn.

That single line on the Internet about Bob's Inn. Who placed it? Was it someone who knew and felt mischievous?

The 'friends' who turned up with wads of rupees in ready cash, the only form of finance that would be of use to a fugitive. Mama Cecilia mentioned them in the first months when Barry was her house guest, living free. She never saw money change hands, but presumably financial transactions would have gone on behind the closed door of his room. When Bob opened his bar six years later, the action moved there, to be conducted in more sociable surroundings.

Was Lucan being bankrolled by the likes of Goldsmith, Aspinall, Birley and the much-publicised 'escape committee'? If so, it bears out the suspicions of many police officers who were brought into the case. Passing wads of 'readies' across the table in a bar is the kind of cavalier behaviour one might expect from certain types of jet-setters who are convinced they can indulge their in-jokes without fear of retribution. Besides, Lucan, with his gambler's instincts, would probably have enjoyed a little 'close-to-the-wire' excitement from his friends.

Barry's talk of his 'family in England'. So, someone had been left behind...

Finally, the lethal intake of *feni* that took such devastating toll on his liver and his life. Barry was a man without funds, not knowing where the next rupee might come from, apart from the backgammon board. It would be natural for him to choose the cheapest way of drinking himself into a stupor and letting the realities of the world dissipate in a haze of alcohol.

For three years prior to his 'night of madness', Lucan had been addicted to neat vodka, of which the best quality stuff can be 96 proof. Now he found a tipple that had nearly twice the alcoholic content for a fraction of the price. It also tasted the same – or as near as dammit! How could he resist the taste-alike, look-alike *feni?*

His German lady friend – June seems a little too mature to be called a girlfriend. In all my casual questioning of the regulars at Bob's Inn, no one really seemed to know her. If they did, they were keeping very quiet about it for no apparent reason that I could fathom. But June had obviously touched a chord in Lucan. She was attractive and personable. They must have shared an affinity for all things German, possibly down to Lucan's extreme right-wing views and his fluency in the language. The fact that she was at his bedside when he died is significant – and a strong reason why there were none of his possessions, few as they were, left in Goa when she returned to Australia. June died three months later. Of a broken heart, perhaps?

Back home, and facing the reality of a British winter, I found that everything fell into place. For a start, I had avoided the trap of wishful thinking: on the contrary, I had questioned and cross-checked every scrap of information where I could. The game had been played fair and square. No bribery or encouragement for anyone to lie or exaggerate, or to be even slightly economical with the truth.

There remained some loose ends to be tied up. I made phone calls, sent e-mails, knocked at front doors without an appointment. I was a bloodhound scenting the end of the trail, nose down, tail up.

My first call was a personal visit to a detached house on the fringe of the green belt west of London, a neat suburban residence with flowerbeds overflowing with colour and a trim path leading to the brightly painted front door. Obviously, Mr Richard Stephenson was a keen gardener.

Mr Stephenson, now an ebullient sixty-seven and enjoying cricket, rugby and golf in his retirement, served for more than forty years with the family firm of James Locke and Co, and ended up as managing director. Locke's of St James's is the most famous gentlemen's hatters in London, with an international reputation, and has been in existence since 1687. The Stephensons have been associated with them since 1850. A glass case midway inside the carpeted interior of the shop shows small white cards with pinholes depicting the hat sizes of its more celebrated customers, among them Sir Charles Chaplin, the Duke of Windsor, bizarrely Mike Tyson – and Lord Lucan.

'Good Lord! That's him!' Mr Stephenson's opening words were music to my ears as I showed him the photograph of Barry asleep in his rocking chair. And when I showed him the portrait of 'Jungle Barry' and his Konkani Tours: 'That's even more like him!' This was unequivocal confirmation from a man who, when sizing up his client's headgear, must have come as close to Lucan's face as Lucky's own wife.

Mr Stephenson examined both photographs carefully. 'Yes, that's Lord Lucan all right. I fitted him myself on more than one occasion. Size seven-and-a-half. Of course that was a long time ago, but this is definitely him.' Gold dust!

My second call was to an imposing vine-covered grange in the heart of the Thames Valley, where Michael Stoop is spending a leisurely retirement. You remember Mr Stoop? It was his car that was found in Newhaven hours after the murder, with the bloodstains of both Lady Lucan and Sandra Rivett on the foot pedals and a length of lead piping in the boot.

Tall and distinguished, effortlessly courteous, Michael

Stoop, now aged eighty-two, could be a double for the legendary German actor Curt Jurgens with his domed head and thatches of white hair sprouting at the sides. The memories of those 'terrible weeks' are as fresh today as they were thirty years ago, when he received that last dramatic letter from Lucan after he went on the run. 'I had loaned John my car because he hinted that he wanted to take a girl out, and needed something anonymous so that he wouldn't be noticed,' Mr Stoop recalls. 'I never saw him again, and I have never heard from him either.

'My own view, despite what other people have said, is that this was a genuine suicide note to me. I think John threw himself off a cross-Channel ferry to France. If he had been sucked into the screws, he would have been chopped up into little bits. If he had been caught up in a French fishing net, I'm quite sure they would have cut his body loose, weighted it down, and dropped it to the bottom of the sea. Those fishermen simply wouldn't have wanted the hassle of an investigation and all the red tape that goes with it. Also, if they dredge up a body, they lose their entire catch.'

Mr Stoop, known as 'Stoopy' to the gambling fraternity, examined the photographs minutely – and shook his head. No, that wasn't the Lucan he knew. When he heard details of the investigation – the backgammon, the ear lobes and the rest – he shook his head again, this time in astonishment. 'Those,' he said after a pause, 'are the most extraordinary similarities. Truly it is an amazing story.'

He remembered how Lucan at his peak had joined the high rollers in backgammon at the Clermont, when multi-millionaire 'guests' from the Middle East, India and Korea would arrive to take on the house players for as much as five thousand pounds a point, incredible stakes in the sixties and seventies. Lucan himself would be backed by casino money. You needed nerve and verve, and at his peak Lucky had his

271

share of both. Stoop gambled his own funds – sometimes at five hundred pounds a point. 'Those were heady days,' he says now, with a nostalgic smile.

But for a totally positive identification – no luck there.

Helen Shapiro is the widow of world bridge champion Boris Shapiro, who died in December 2002 at the age of 93. A vivacious, attractive woman who knew the Mayfair gaming set as well as anyone and better than most, she now lives in a picturesque cottage in the country near Oxford. 'I met Lucky Lucan many times, usually when he came to gamble at the Ladbroke Club,' she told me. 'I remember organising a charity bridge night when he was one of the stars. He had great charisma, and was extremely witty, with a dry sense of humour and throwaway one-liners that left you speechless!'

I produced the photographs, and she examined them searchingly. At last: 'These pictures are astonishing – and the hands are the giveaway. I remember noticing them whenever I met Lucky. They are just too good for someone trying to disguise himself as a rough-living drop-out – they're quite remarkable, even artistic. You can't alter your hands – they don't grow moustaches or beards!' For me, that was a nine out of ten.

As for Lady Lucan, I must have called at 5, Eaton Row at least twenty times in the weeks after my return, armed with a batch of the Barry photographs. But no one answered my repeated knocks on the cream-painted front door. Not a movement, not a whisper. Could the reticent countess be skulking inside, as has been suggested, refusing to answer the door to strangers? For me, she would remain resolute in that refusal. One visitor described the house as 'a small, exquisite fortress' – not unlike its owner. A heavy drape blocks the front picture window, and the letter box has a cloth over the inside to obscure the interior from prying eyes. People have even been known to poke umbrellas through the slit to try to shift the cloth.

By e-mail, Veronica Lucan insisted that if I wanted her to verify the pictures, it must be done via the Internet. No deal. That way they could all too easily become public property, which was the last thing I wanted.

Our correspondence took a bizarre turn in the summer when I offered to bring the photographs round for her to identify them – suggesting a noon appointment and that I should come armed with a bottle of champagne. The response from the countess was terse: 'I do not see people whom I correspond with over the Internet. And contrary to reports, I detest champagne.' One up to her!

Yes, I had wanted desperately for the man known as Jungle Barry to be Lord Lucan – and in a perfect world, like some bounty hunter of old, to have brought him back alive. But the world isn't perfect, as I know only too well. So I had to play the hand I was dealt.

There would be doubters and 'spoilers' – the old Fleet Street term for a news story intended to rubbish a scoop by a rival paper. That goes with the game too. But the overwhelming evidence must be more than enough to convince an average jury.

But how much certainty does that average member of a jury need to convict? Broadly speaking, the situation falls into two categories, criminal and civil. If there is no 'proof' as such handed to them on a plate, like DNA or CCTV camera footage, a jury can convict on 'balance of probability' (in a civil case) and 'beyond reasonable doubt' (in a criminal case).

Interestingly, relating directly to the issue of probability, Britain's judicial system relies in part on a complex analysis known as Bayes' Theorem. The Reverend Thomas Bayes was an eighteenth-century mathematician whose calculations were published in 1763, two years after his death. The fact that this doughty cleric's theory has lasted a quarter of a millennium says a lot for its author.

His conclusion, which follows a lengthy hypothesis, is relatively simple in summary: 'There is only one kind of uncertainty, and there is only one way of measuring uncertainty. That is called probability. The only logical way to reason in a state of uncertainty is in accordance with the axioms of probability.'

Thus a judge summing up for the jury will tell them: 'What is required by the law is proof of guilt by corroborated evidence. Evidence can only be obtained from witnesses. And so the aim of any trial is to allow the jury to hear witnesses and then to decide if what the witnesses say satisfies them that the charge has been proved.'

In this case the charge is simple: *Lord Lucan took on the identity of Barry Halpin.* I had found independent witnesses and amassed a portfolio of corroborated evidence.

For the vital identification issue, I would refer to a judgement by Lord Denning, the eminent one-time Master of the Rolls, who clarified the meaning of 'beyond reasonable doubt' in the case of *Miller versus Minister of Pensions (1947)* as follows: 'Proof beyond reasonable doubt does not mean proof beyond the shadow of doubt. It need not reach certainty, but it must carry a high degree of probability. The law would fail to protect the community if it admitted fanciful possibilities to deflect the course of justice.'

I went out to India as a sceptic, and returned as a believer. An agnostic finally won over by incontrovertible evidence and the character of the people who provided it on tape, openly and with no reason to invent their stories.

There was one more strand of the case to clear up, a tiny nagging doubt to be resolved. If there was a genuine Barry Halpin, how had Lucan come to choose his name?

The final stop was a personal visit to an address in London EC1. The Family Records Centre in Myddelton Street, Clerkenwell, is a modern red-brick building close to the trendy shopping precinct of Exmouth Market. A flight of stone steps leads up to the double doors, with a sloping walkway for wheelchair access. Inside, beyond the security check, is a world of history collated in a library of bound volumes – indexes of births, marriages and deaths dating back to 1837.

Rows of polished pine shelves stretch out along a vast air-conditioned room curiously shaped like a boomerang. Light floods in from a glass atrium in the centre. The huge studded ledgers are stacked in three sections. Births are bound in burgundy, marriages in optimistic green, deaths in sombre black. The place is a hive of activity and anticipation, mostly buzzing with solicitors and professional researchers gathering vital information for a will, an inheritance or a divorce. Plus, no doubt, the odd private detective.

Anyone registering a birth can work within a month either side of the actual event. I started with the section marked 'Births: June 1937 – March 1947' and narrowed it down to the ledger under March 1938. Nothing. But a month later – there it was: 'Barry T Halpin'. Date of registration: 19 April, 1938.

I exhaled deeply. That was that, then. Now it was possible to construct an amazing scenario. Picture the scene. Lucan, alone and on the run, knowing he had power-brokers who could finance him anywhere in the world that he chose to go, finds himself in Mozambique – courtesy of his good friend Graham Hill who spirited him out of Britain and his own ability to get himself down to Southern Africa – and a Portuguese colony in turmoil.

Remember back to that pub-crawl in Laurenco Marques and the doctor who spoke of a stranger who called himself James, before claiming he was Lucan. Coincidence or what? Accidents happen. So do coincidences. Think about it. Is it beyond the realm of possibility that Lucan met his lookalike across a beer-stained table in a downtown bar in Laurenco Marques and the whole charade began there?

Ever the opportunist, Lucan spotted his man and made him an offer he couldn't refuse. Maybe they went on a drinking spree when Lucky still called himself James. Maybe they struck a deal there and then. Lucan had no need to reveal his true identity to a globe-trotting hobo and could have simply said he wanted to disappear from the world and that he would keep his new-found friend in funds for his assistance.

Strangely, James was the name that would appear on the birth certificate gleefully revealed by the national papers on 9 September, 2003, as part of the synchronised chorus of disapproval when my findings were published. As follows: 'Barry James, son of William Halpin and Eva Ellen Halpin, of Merton Bank Farm, St Helens'. But why James instead of Thomas? What a strange mistake for a registrar to make. Curiouser and curiouser.

One definition of coincidence is: 'An accidental sequence of events that appear to have a causal relationship. To be identical'.

Now if 'James' in Lorenco Marques really was Lucan, doesn't it stand to reason that Lucky would have called himself Barry James Halpin once he took over his newfound friend's identity – if he had never inquired, or knew, about a middle name? And that the name James would have filtered back to his chums in England who were keeping them both on the road and out of trouble?

It's the kind of daring deed that would appeal to Lucan and the actor in him would see it as a wondrous challenge.

So the real Lucan headed for Goa, to take on the mantle of Barry Halpin, while hobo Barry headed off on his travels around the globe. The details of how the deal was struck and the financial arrangements made to keep hobo Barry happy will always remain shrouded in mystery. I can imagine Lucan ordering Barry that the one place he must never set foot on his travels would be Goa. And it would be comparatively easy to set up couriers or even post restantes for the him to pick up funds wherever he chose – once Lucky's paymasters had agreed the score. I would assume Lucan cleared it with them before he even set foot in the docks looking for that cargo ship to Bombay.

My biggest headache when trying to come to terms with this audacious imposture was whether the real Barry Halpin finally decided to call in on Goa. Personally, I remain convinced that he did not.

Despite claims from 'friends' that they had met him, there is no proof to this effect. And some of these alleged sightings simply fail to convince me: one 'close friend' described on a radio interview how Barry had held a wild party on the beach four days before his death, dancing himself into the sand and smoking himself into a stupor with cannabis. But the evidence I gathered indicated that 'Lucan-Barry' only took an occasional puff of the weed to be sociable and for several days before his death was so weak he could hardly stand.

But I have to admit it is true that anyone can be fooled by twins and lookalikes. Funds had obviously run dry. Maybe Barry reckoned it was time to put the screw on Lucan. The prospect of enduring poverty can be bleak indeed, especially if there is a possible way to avoid it.

It is faintly conceivable that at one time there were two Barrys in Goa, meeting briefly before one made a hasty departure – that individual being the impish northerner, to continue bumming his way around the world. The wary Lucan, always alert to the prospect of discovery, could do his own temporary vanishing act for the second time.

In the constant ebb and flow of visitors, ex-pats and passing villainy to that notorious enclave, few would notice or care amid the clouds of cannabis smoke spiralling off the beaches.

On 10 December, 2003, while my findings were still hot, an intriguing item appeared on Amazon.com. It is still there for anyone who cares to look it up. A gentleman named Simon, from Dorset, commenting on the book, stated 'I spent a fair amount of my time in Goa in the 1980s and knew Barry Halpin well. He was a bearded drop-out, who had turned to booze in a big way. He retained his Lancashire accent, but from memory I never once saw him play backgammon.

'However he wasn't the only long-haired, bearded Englishman who had escaped to Goa. I recall an articulate and clearly well-read Englishman who received "out-of-place" visitors from the UK. He did play backgammon and from memory was very reserved.'

'Simon' refers to a photograph of a bearded Barry in the jungle and wrote, 'He is, in my opinion, Halpin.' Then he added: 'The man featured in the rocking chair and elsewhere in the book, is not. He is the articulate, quiet, backgammon playing Englishman I describe. I knew both men. The mystery has in my opinion been solved.'

This is hugely significant and entirely unsolicited.

Remember, 'impossible' is the stuff of illusion and the lynchpin of magic tricks that have delighted old and young alike down the years.

Now, consider one of the most famous conjuring tricks in the business. Aptly entitled 'Escape from Sing Sing', it goes like this: the stage is decked out like the interior of a prison, with two large cages set well back and a few feet apart from one another. These cells stand upright, around six feet high and four feet square, with grey steel bars. They are mounted upon platforms, the barred front doors are hinged and all the sides have roller blinds which can be pulled down.

Once the trick begins, the action is fast and furious. As the magician is about to introduce the act, a convict in striped prison uniform rushes on to the stage brandishing a revolver. The magician grapples with him, flings him into the right-hand cage, clangs the door shut and pulls down the blinds.

Almost instantly a frantic rattling comes from inside the cage, the front blind snaps up – but instead of the convict, the audience find themselves staring at a warder shouting to be released.

Just as he is let out, a loud gunshot from the back of the stalls makes everyone jump – and down the aisle races the escaped convict. He leaps up on to the stage, intent on revenge, but is overpowered by the magician and the warder, then thrown into the left-hand cell. The blinds are pulled down on both cages. The magician, wielding the gun he has wrestled from the convict, fires into the cell. The blinds go up – and again the slippery suspect has vanished. Now the rollers go up on the right-hand cell – and there he is! The warder marches him off the stage while the magician takes his bow.

The noise and speed of the action are deliberately designed to bewilder the audience. And the secret? Two lookalike convicts, identical to all appearances. The cages have loose bars at the back which can be removed and replaced in seconds. These are masked by special curtains in the same grey, so that the audience think they are real bars.

In fact the warden is hidden behind the rear curtain and, as soon as the convict is pushed in and the blinds go down, he swaps places and immediately begins rattling the bars for release. Before the audience can catch their breath, the 'double' comes charging down the aisle.

He too hides behind the rear curtain before the blinds go up, while his 'twin' steps out into the right hand cage to be revealed when they are raised again.

Simple when you know how, as most illusions are. One amusing footnote I unearthed when pursuing this 'impossible' trick was to hear how the second convict – who used to slip around to the front of theatre just as the illusion began – was once spotted by a passing patrolman. He mistook the arrowed figure for a real convict, arrested him and hauled him off to jail. For that one night the 'double' never did make it to the footlights and was not let out until next day. Wonderful stuff!

Back home, I published my findings in September 2003 – and a firestorm struck us! We always knew it would happen and we had our tin hats on as the shells rained down. Any story claiming to solve the Lucan mystery was going to attract its share of spoilers and knockers – even if two of the knockers belonged to a Page 3 girl in *The Sun*.

In a picture caption, Zoe-from-London – bless her – was credited with saying: 'It's hilarious that a well-dressed toff could be confused for someone who looks like Robinson Crusoe.' Others shouted the same strident message. They all missed the point, of course. If Lucan was going to reinvent himself and vanish from high society he would hardly be likely to sport a top hat and monocle.

The Daily Mail's page one lead headline summed it up: 'Lucan's Final Riddle'. That's for sure. *The Mail*'s Mac cartoon had me laughing out loud. A group of genuine toffs are gathered at the bar of the Clermont Club, while at the other end four bearded vagrants swill back glasses of the amber liquid. One member is saying to the barman: 'Don't let them put any more on the tab, Perkins. They can't all be Lord Lucan come to renew his subscription.' Beautiful.

Having been to the Clermont Club myself, I can only say that if 'Jungle Barry' had turned up to renew his subscription, Bob the doorman wouldn't have let him past the threshold.

The speed by which the anti-Lucan lobby tried to destroy our argument was breath-taking. One paper even suggested that I had resigned from the police force amid allegations of corruption. He omitted to mention that corrupt officers are not allowed to resign – if charged, they end up gripping the rails at the Old Bailey.

Within 36 hours *The Sun* was reporting: 'The man said to be missing Lord Lucan was a pot-smoking, big-drinking Northerner who liked his waccy-baccy.' Remember, our Lucan didn't smoke unless he had to. But while the London edition rubbished the claims, an executive from *The Sun's* sister paper, the *Scottish Sun*, appeared on BBC Radio Scotland's *What the Papers Say* to defend the book.

Even folk singer and comedian Mike Harding was vociferous in coming forward to talk about his Barry and wrote a poem which included the words: 'Australia, India, *Africa*, Japan, the bars and streets of most towns in this world had known his sweet wild music. He could get, they said, a tune from a potato.'

So Barry's passport must have been overflowing with visas and stamps. The man could play, says Harding, the concertina, banjo, tin whistle, guitar and mandolin.

Just what is going on here? One e-mail reported Barry's death in Thailand. I stood my ground. And could only go on the record to declare: 'I say to people – please produce photographic evidence that your Barry Halpin is my Barry Halpin.'

At least some of the media had the decency to find fresh witnesses who came down on my side of the fence. *The Daily Mirror* produced communications manager David Jordan, from Cheam in Surrey, who said he spent six months drinking and playing chess with Jungle Barry. His quotes are significant. 'It's the eyes which convince me that Jungle Barry and Lord Lucan were one and the same. Barry was so elusive about his past that someone started calling him Lucan.'

The three of us went out as sceptics and came back converted, as slowly but surely the clues mounted and the pieces of the jigsaw fell into place to create a final convincing picture. And we could say and mean it: *'That's him!'*

Others, of course, have insisted: 'That's not him!' Which is as fair enough as it is inevitable. The only problem that worried me during more than 60 media interviews was that not one of the interviewers appeared to have had read the book. Skimmed through it, yes. Sometimes not even that. They missed the small but vital points that persuaded us as we brought back overwhelming evidence – not proof, because sadly there was no body – that we had found the truth about Lord Lucan.

There is no doubt that there was an actor in Lucan's soul who might well have enjoyed the challenge of assuming another persona in real life. And why would well-dressed, well-spoken English 'friends' arrive from nowhere over the years to hand over cash in bars to a hippie vagrant if they weren't couriers from Lucky's wealthy friends?

In the end, we stand by our guns and by the backgammon gambler without ear lobes who spoke in a cultured voice, said he had left a wife and children back home and, in his cups, declared: 'I am part of history.'

It was Lord Lucan who burned on that pyre.

Now at last the ghost that has haunted the files of Scotland Yard and Interpol for 30 years can be laid to rest.

You, the jury, will make up your own minds.

I know I have.

AFTERMATH

The fallout from the Lucan drama touched many lives. Most of the principal players are dead, although the ripples still appear whenever Lucky's name comes back in the media to haunt those involved and their dependants, however remotely.

Veronica Lucan lives in seclusion in a mews cottage around the corner from the scene of the tragedy that changed her life for ever. A recent interview describes her as 'petite and elegant, with long grey hair, still wearing the gold necklace, bracelet and wedding ring that Lord Lucan gave her'. She has established a website and converses with the outside world through her e-mail address. That, of course, I knew already.

Ian Maxwell-Scott died from a heart attack in November 1993.

46 Lower Belgrave Street was sold in 1977 to wine wholesaler Michael Druitt, 45, a business partner of Michael Caine, who bought the 28-year lease for a bargain £42,000 – and promptly had the place exorcised by the Queen's Chaplain, Canon Edwyn Young. It now has new occupants.

The three Lucan children, brought up as wards of court under the guidance of Bill and Christina Shand Kydd, have pursued their own lives and careers.

Lady Frances qualified as a solicitor specialising in corporate law.

Lord Bingham went to Eton and Trinity College, Cambridge, and then entered the world of City banking.

Lady Camilla read classics at Balliol College, Oxford, and in 1998 she married Michael Block, QC, at St Paul's Church, Eaton Square, almost within sight of the murder house. In 2002 she gave birth to a son, Cameron, whose name was immediately put down for Eton.

Sir James Goldsmith became a Member of the European Parliament in June 1994, backed by the right-wing French party L'Autre Europe. He died in 1997, aged 64, leaving a fortune estimated at £1.2 billion.

His widow, **Lady Annabel**, former wife of Mark Birley, published her memoirs in 2004.

John Aspinall sold the Clermont Club in 1987 but retained his seat on the board up to his death from cancer in the summer of 2000 at the age of 73. In the last interview he gave that same year he said, significantly: 'Lucky reckoned that if he wasn't around any more there would always be a question mark over his guilt, which would be good for his children. The question mark is still there. So he was right about that.'

The stockbroker **Stephen Raphael**, a member of Lucan's social circle, died in the late 1990s.

Lucan's sister, **Lady Sarah,** married a vicar, the Reverend William Gibbs, until recently rector of St Andrew's Church, in the village of West Haddon, Northamptonshire, where he preached until he retired in the summer of 2003. Lady Sarah died on 28 September 2001.

Charles Benson died in 2002, aged 66.

In 1980 the BBC screened a TV documentary called *Into Thin*

Air, with actor Tony Mathews, aged 37 and six feet three inches tall, starring as Lucan.

All the Murder Squad officers involved in the investigation have retired or died.